'*The Emperor's Nightingale* piques the reader's interest by the catholicity of its references, its originality of thought, its felicitous choice of words, and extensive use of interesting anecdotes.'

Dwight Allison, Jr
Former CEO, The Boston Company
Director, Mellon Bank, Avery Dennison

'Astonishing, original, and creatively provocative.'

Tatsuo Arima
Former Japanese Ambassador to Germany

'If humans are to live fully, they must overcome the mental modes of the machine. They must devise institutions that can reflect their nobler impulses of purpose. *The Emperor's Nightingale* suggests important ideas along these lines.'

Charles Berg
Former Dean, Department of Engineering, Northeastern University

'I feel rather like the reviewer whose editor threw *Das Kapital* to him and said "I want 500 words on this by Monday, and, by the way, do you think it will make paperback?" I have no doubt about the book's importance and am sure that it will make paperback, but Bob Monks has struck so much new ground that it is difficult to describe this new book. It is in a category of its own.'

Sir Adrian Cadbury
Former Chairman, Cadbury Schweppes
Founding Chairman, The Cadbury Committee

'Well, I myself prefer to build a new barn and call it "democracy." But if the not-so-idle-rich corporate elite wants to do a little patching and puttying on the old one in order to save it a bit longer, they might as well read Robert's book to get some helpful renovating ideas. But if faceless financiers and their tool, the corporation, aren't completely out of our lobbies, out of all campaigns, and out of our constitution soon, looks like We, the People are going to come in the middle of the night with a can of gasoline in every hand and one fat match!'

Carolyn Chute
Author, *The Beans of Egypt, Maine*
Voice of the white underclass

'The strengths of this book are considerable personal knowledge, experience, and perceptions – which made for credibility – and a very readable writing style. A good story well told.'

William Dean Howells
U.S. Department of State, Retired

'*The Emperor's Nightingale* is fresh, it is original, it is the most interesting thing I have read that falls under the dread rubric of "corporate governance," and most of all, it made me think.'

Richard Koch
Author, *The 80/20 Principle*, and co-author of *Break Up!: When Large Companies Are Worth More Dead Than Alive*

'*The Emperor's Nightingale*, if widely read, could be one of the most significant contributions to reuniting the corporation, our most powerful disembodied force, with the spirit of humankind in nature.'

James McRitchie
Editor, *Corporate Governance*

'This book is a remarkably ambitious undertaking. It is multimodal, intertwining the poetic, the historical, the legal, the economic, and the scientific, with its own emergent language of governance. In formal terms, even *Gödel, Escher, Bach* attempted no less!'

Jesse Norman
Philosopher
Former Executive, BZW

'This is far and away the most thorough and enlightening history of the modern corporation – and the most profound analysis of its current ills – that I have ever read, or expect to read. The range of insights and the depth of knowledge command total respect and admiration.'

Allen Sykes
Corporate Director

'This is a bold and fearless effort, grounded in practical experience and insights, to introduce the disciplines of pure and applied science to the study of corporate governance. It provides a refreshing change from the undisciplined babble of self-serving waffle pontificating about the topic.'

Shann Turnbull
Australian governance expert

'Very stimulating and extremely interesting. The central argument is a tour de force. It is plausible, beautifully revealed, and persuasive for those who are already converted – or are verging on conversion – to the idea that active shareholders can make a positive difference in corporate performance. This book may well bring a few to conversion and it will also win great support from those who for political or ideological reasons have always distrusted "big business." There may be inertia from those who currently run big business and even from those who currently run big pension funds, but in the long run, *The Emperor's Nightingale* could be an incitement to change.'

Sandra Dawson
Director, The Judge Institute of Management Studies, Cambridge University

'Tremendously stimulating. The depth of Bob Monks' scholarship into the new complexity and chaos theories is awesome. The notion that the ownership responsibilities might be separated from the buy and sell responsibilities with respect to institutional money is an intriguing one – and it may very well be that something like this will eventually come about.'

A.A. Sommer, Jr
Former Member U.S. Securities and Exchange Commission
Member, Public Oversight Board

'A most penetrating tale that needs to be told. Restoring the original corporation is so much more attractive than inventing even more complex machinery. This book clearly builds on the previous work that Monks and Nell Minow have published, but takes us beyond the critique of contemporary corporate governance to a viable solution.'

Bob Tricker
Editor, *Corporate Governance: An International Review*

'A very useful review of a lot of the practical issues facing corporate management and the board of directors. Bob Monks uses many good examples to support his arguments.'

Frank V. Cahouet
Chairman, President and CEO, Mellon Bank

'Bob Monks is dealing with a topic of tremendous importance: the future shape of capitalism. He has the makings of a very important and influential book.'

Keith P. Ambachtsheer
President, K.P.A. Advisory Services Ltd, Toronto

'A remarkable union of science and literature: Adam Smith for the next millennium.'

Richard M. Schlefer
Assistant Vice President, College Retirement Equities Fund

The Emperor's Nightingale

Other books by Robert A. G. Monks:

Power and Accountability (with Nell Minow)
Corporate Governance
Watching the Watchers:
Corporate Governance for the Twenty-First Century
(with Nell Minow)

The

Emperor's
Nightingale

Restoring the Integrity
of the Corporation
in the Age of
Shareholder Activism

Robert A. G. Monks

ADDISON-WESLEY
Reading, Massachusetts

Many of the designations used by manufacturers and sellers to distinguish their products are claimed as trademarks. Where those designations appear in this book and Addison-Wesley was aware of a trademark claim, the designations have been printed in initial capital letters.

ISBN 0-201-33996-X

A CIP catalog record for this book is available from the Library of Congress.

Copyright © 1998 by Robert A. G. Monks

Published by arrangement with Capstone Publishing Ltd. Published simultaneously in Great Britain.

Addison-Wesley is an imprint of Addison Wesley Longman, Inc.

Jacket design by Suzanne Heiser
Set in 11-point Bembo by Sparks Computer Solutions, Oxford, U. K.

1 2 3 4 5 6 7 8 9-MA-0201009998
First printing, February 1998

Addison-Wesley books are available at special discounts for bulk purchases in the U.S. by corporations, institutions, and other organizations. For more information, please contact the Corporate, Government, and Special Sales Department at Addison Wesley Longman, Inc., One Jacob Way, Reading, MA 01867, or call 1-800-238-9682.

Find us on the World Wide Web at
http://www.aw.com/gb/

To Barbara Sleasman and Nell Minow: *sine quibus non.*

Contents

Foreword

Dean LeBaron

Like the strands of a helix, Bob Monks' life and mine weave in and out, crossing, separating, then crossing again.

Our first intersection was at Harvard University in 1951. We were both underclassmen, shared many friends, and lived in the same building (attractive to me because it was close to classes, attractive to Bob because it was near the literary societies). His undergraduate studies were more classical than mine (he majored in history, and I in psychology), but he went on to Harvard Law School and I later to Harvard Business School. These years are often called formative, but I would argue that Bob has never stopped forming himself – and, I might add, those around him.

The strands of our helix intertwined again 26 years later when Bob assumed the post of chairman of The Boston Company. His aim was to turn this old-line trust company into a new-line money-management firm, and he often called on me for informal advice. The company I had founded, Batterymarch Financial Management, was dedicated to using technology and quantitative techniques to lower investment costs and boost investment returns. Bob used the example of Batterymarch to demonstrate to his colleagues the viability of these approaches. He adopted many of our techniques, and his efforts led to the successful sale of the bank to American Express in 1981.

Our next intersection was in the early 1980s, when Bob was heading up the US Department of Labor's pension division and I, in addition to my work at Batterymarch, chaired a Securities and Exchange Commission committee on tender offers. I believed that the best way to prevent hostile takeovers was through good performance – not mechanistic defences. Takeovers, I argued (somewhat paradoxically), would *diminish* if corporations remained *open* to them. With exposure to the possibility of takeovers, companies and their directors would act in the best interests of those who elected them, the shareholders. Takeovers, then, would not occur because companies would continuously renew themselves. I also took the then-radical position that professional investment managers should recognise the economic value of the proxy votes in their hands.

The message I sounded at the SEC was nothing short of a clarion call for shareholder activism. What I didn't know was that Bob had independently reached the same conclusions.

Bob was, and is, best known as a vigorous investor advocate, a pioneer in corporate governance. He was the first, to my knowledge, to identify corporate directors as the pivotal balance for the interests of managers and shareholders. And he developed a firm, Institutional Shareholder Services, to advise institutions of voting opportunities and responsibilities, and an investment company, LENS, to invest money in companies where shareholder activism could bring about performance improvement.

Most recently, and momentously, we connected when I invited Bob and his wife, Milly, to join me at the Santa Fe Institute for a weekend conference on complex adaptive systems. Bob took to the topic right away. When he heard scientists explain how a small event could be amplified through a system, Bob saw his own shareholder activism in a new way. When he learned that systems that strive for stability decay, and that those living at the edge of chaos thrive, Bob found an explanation for what he had been doing all along – a theoretical foundation for his own work in governance. It was like watching the apple fall on Newton's head.

Complexity has given Bob a new language with which to express his ideas. This same language is becoming part of the lexicon of leading management consulting firms. Most are actively researching complexity and incorporating it into their day-to-day practices. I expect that 1998 will be the year complexity dominates business conversation, and this book will lead the way. My own field, investment management, may delay adoption of these principles until another market cycle demands new answers. On Wall Street, it seems, innovation waits for a bear market.

In this book, Bob, combining his firm grasp of corporate governance and his intense study of complexity, describes how corporations behave through the stages of their life cycles. From angry shareholders to concerned chief executives, almost everyone knows at a gut level that the present system is not working. This book attempts to explain why. Better yet, it proposes a path for positive change. Bob's analysis is coherent and venturesome – and likely to offend most readers. I predict that everyone will disagree with some part of it, but readers will surely find Bob's book a valuable stimulus for their own thinking. It prescribes adaptation, not destruction, using the charming folk tale of 'The Nightingale' to make its point. Bob shows that synergy really does exist – not as a single burst of energy but as a continuous, healthy adaptation to business conditions.

To the surprise of many friends, Bob takes a moderate course. He does not condemn corporate managers for their ironclad budgets, rigid forecasts, and attempts to control the uncontrollable. Rather, he provides informed support for the view that business must consist of smaller independent units (called 'agents' in the complexity world) who pursue their own aims but who collectively achieve what is beyond their individual capability (swarms).

Although Bob has adopted Santa Fe as his new intellectual home, we must not forget that his ideas of flexibility, openness, and integrity are rooted not in the American south-west but deep in his personality. He embodied them long before he set foot in Santa Fe.

This book sets a standard. Bob's ability to bring complexity and governance together for the first time – another helix of sorts – should encourage the development of different corporate structures, different shareholder entitlements, and different participant interests. This intersection, like that of two friends meeting again, will produce new insights for years to come.

Dean LeBaron
deanlebaron@compuserve.com
Lake Sunapee, New Hampshire
11 September 1997

The Emperor's Nightingale:
A Reader's Guide

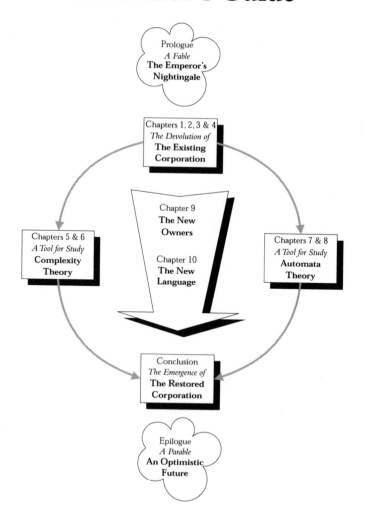

Prologue
A Fable
The Emperor's Nightingale

Chapters 1, 2, 3 & 4
The Devolution of
The Existing Corporation

Chapter 9
The New Owners

Chapter 10
The New Language

Chapters 5 & 6
A Tool for Study
Complexity Theory

Chapters 7 & 8
A Tool for Study
Automata Theory

Conclusion
The Emergence of
The Restored Corporation

Epilogue
A Parable
An Optimistic Future

Executive Summary

The modern corporation is poised for change through increased activism from shareholders. This book explores the origins, dynamics, and significance of this change using the languages of poetry, science, and governance. Prepare for an adventure!

Prologue

A fable: The Emperor's Nightingale.

1   *The Emperor's Nightingale: Harbinger of Corporate Restoration*

Humankind and all its creations struggle to reconcile the predictable and the dynamic. This is the moral of the timeless story of 'The Nightingale' by Hans Christian Andersen. It is also the nature of the corporation, a human creation of special importance.

2   *The Disconsolate Dawn of the Modern Corporation*

Two hundred years ago, Adam Smith sounded an alarm. The corporations of his day posed a threat to society because by their very nature they sought unlimited life, size, power, and license, externalising risk as they pursued these aims.

3   Four Corporate Dangers

Smith's insights give us our way in to see corporations for what they really are. Corporations are not human, although they are formed by humans and should serve human purposes. Nor are they machines, although they have some internal laws that operate mechanistically. Instead, they are artificial life forms – or, to use a current scientific term, complex adaptive systems.

4   The Limits of Conventional Corporate Wisdom – and How to Surpass Them

We are in denial about the corporate problem. Seven panaceas prevent us from finding the solution to the problems inherent in the modern corporation: the CEO 'philosopher-king', corporate chartering, independent directors, well-structured boards, independent experts, the free press, and multiple external constraints. Taken separately, each of these can lull us into dangerous complacency. Taken together – along with the actions of independent, informed, motivated, and empowered shareholders – these elements are transformed from panaceas to solutions.

5   The Corporation and the Economy as Complex Adaptive Systems

Like all complex adaptive systems, corporations have both regularities (predictable, mechanistic laws) and dynamics (forces for change). Corporate regularities, which are shared by other manmade institutions, are the drives for unlimited life, size, power, and license. Corporate dynamics, which are shared by all CASs, are multiplicity, spontaneity, accommodation, adaptation, transcendence, and metamorphosis. These dynamics can counterbalance the four corporate dangers of unlimited life, size, power, and license – bringing instead long-term life, appropriate size, balanced power, and greater accountability to long-term owners.

6   Modelling Corporate Accountability

Agent-based computer modelling can advance our inquiry. Our 'Brightline' model represents, among other factors, the dynamics of externalisation in interactions among four key agents in the large publicly held corporations: customers, corporations, government, and shareholders. Companies compete for customers by reducing their liabilities through externalisation. An aggressive management that is compelled by its shareholders to function within government-determined limits on externalisation will generate superior values over the long term.

7   Intermezzo: The 'Four Phases' of Corporate Life

Analogising to 'cellular automata', we see that there may be 'classes' of corporate life: doomsday (Class I), stagnation (Class II), chaos (Class III), and true orderliness (Class IV). In many runs of an automata model, only the first three classes emerge. From time to time, however, true order imposes itself at the brink of chaos. Is the corporate world poised for positive change in this sense? Will our 'Class II' stagnation be followed by 'Class III' conditions, or by true order, the desired 'Class IV?' To make such a shift, active shareholders may be the agent needed.

8   Stone & Webster: A Journey to the Edge of Chaos

The Stone & Webster story shows how apt the cellular automata analogy can be in a single company. In this case, stagnation (Class II) could have been followed by chaos (Class III). Fortunately, active shareholders moved the company toward orderliness (Class IV).

9   The New Owners

Institutional shareholders, the key agents in fiduciary capitalism, are not monoliths. Institutions elect, pay, and work their trustees in different ways. Conflicts of interest and investment horizons also vary. Of all institutional shareholders, private pension funds show the most promise. They and other funds need to find their 'voice' as New Owners.

10   The New Language

The New Owners are universal, long-term, global, and humane fiduciaries. They can use their unique status to follow three important imperatives, identified 20 years ago by David Engel: (1) obey the law, (2) inform the public about the corporation's impact on society, (3) minimise corporate involvement in politics. Laws are not perfect, but they are the corporation's best proxy for justice. The New Language of ownership takes this justice into account, even as new idiom continues to evolve in dialogue with management's more traditional language of profit optimisation.

Conclusion: The Restored Corporation in the New Millennium

Listening to the beautiful truth of the nightingale, we are 'tolled back' to our true selves. We can wind up the golden bird of short-term profit maximisation, or welcome back the nightingale of long-term economic value rooted in the social good. Which will it be?

Epilogue: The Nightingale Sings – 2010

A parable: an optimistic future.

Preface: The Shape of the Future

> *'Every one of these complex, self-organizing, adaptive systems possesses a kind of dynamism that makes them qualitatively different from static objects such as computer chips or snowflakes, which are merely complicated ... Instead, all these complex systems have somehow acquired the ability to bring order and chaos into a special kind of balance. This balance point – often called the edge of chaos – is where the components of a system never quite lock into place, and yet never quite dissolve into turbulence, either.'*
> **M. Mitchell Waldrop, *Complexity: The Emerging Science at the Edge of Order and Chaos*, pp. 12–13**

One day while reading a best-seller about an emerging new science – Mitchell Waldrop's *Complexity* – something caught my attention: it was the image of a butterfly whose flight sets in motion an entire weather system on the other side of the globe. 'Small events', noted the author, 'have great consequences'.

Could it be, I wondered, that my field – the field of corporate governance – is approaching some 'great consequence'? Could it be that what appears to be at times static, at times chaotic, will become – at least for a time – dynamic, yet orderly?

In my view, the answer is yes. Based on all the evidence I see, the modern corporation is on the verge of a profound restoration: a return to its original, highly adaptive and accountable form. Which 'butterfly' will bring about this potential, pending, ready-to-happen 'weather system' remains to be seen. But this new system will come, I believe.

I have come to this belief through experience. For the past three decades – first as an executive, then as a public servant, and finally as an investor – I have tried to work as an agent of change in corporations large and small around the world. As a part of this effort, I have tried to understand the way corporations balance powers, a process commonly referred to as 'corporate governance'.

My study of corporate governance has sent me into the worlds of accounting, economics, ethics, finance, law, and politics – to name just a few of the many academic disciplines that have loaned their talents to this increasingly important field. Along with others – notably my partner Nell Minow – I have written histories, proposed models, and issued warnings.

In *Power and Accountability* (New York: HarperCollins, 1992), Nell and I protested the lack of balance between these two elements in today's modern corporation. We traced power through the rise of management hegemony in large public companies, and we saw the possibility of effective accountability in the emergence of the institutional investor as trustee and majority shareholder. In *Corporate Governance* (Oxford: Blackwell, 1995), we argued that institutional investors, as permanent, universal owners, can and should exercise a crucial decision-making role in corporations. In *Watching the Watchers* (Oxford: Blackwell, 1996), we called this emerging role 'pension fund capitalism'.

Since the publication of *Watching the Watchers*, I have been privileged to discuss this idea with some of the finest minds in the country – including some affiliated with the Santa Fe Institute, an organisation devoted to the emerging new science of 'complexity'.

Using a blend of science, intuition, and experience, we are attempting to identify the 'agents' within corporations and describing how they interact. We are also studying how corporations act within the larger economy.

As a result of these recent inquiries, I have come to believe that we watchers of corporate governance have been missing something. We can see the agents, we can see their interrelations, we can see how these interrelations change, but we all somehow seem to be at the mercy of that change – always chronicling it seconds *after* it occurs, forever using language from the past.

How very different it would be to see the corporation as – in the words of the complexity community – *a complex, self-organising, adaptive* system that has *the ability to bring order and chaos into a special kind of balance.*

Frankly, until recently, I saw no signs of such a system. Instead, I saw a machinelike system increasingly based on non-dynamic, non-living, *non-human* principles: a profit-seeking missile of unlimited life, size, and power operating under the stealth of human guise. And I saw that this system was delivering increasingly unacceptable results to the human beings who created it.

But my readings in the science of complexity have given me new hope. If the true nature of the corporation is to be adaptive, and if the forces for a return to this true nature have been building over time, then it will take only the tiniest catalyst to trigger them.

My focus here is the *once and future potential* innate within modern capitalism, and its chief agent, the large publicly held corporation. I bring good tidings. Despite all appearances, the modern corporation is not a juggernaut moving inevitably away from its original integrity and crushing souls on its way to a destiny that will be more of the same. Nor is it an exercise in riding the entropies of chaos, as some have suggested. Rather, the modern corporation is a complex, dynamic system undergoing a 'phase transition' into a new expression of its intrinsic nature – a system for creating wealth for its owners and for society in general. I call this transitional process *corporate restoration*.

This is not just wishful thinking – something we all 'ought' to try because it's the 'right' thing. Instead, it is a real process that is likely to occur soon, given the nature and history of corporate governance to date – that or stagnation moving directly into utter chaos. Which will it be?

I for one am betting on corporate restoration. As I hope to explain in this book, the *restored corporation*, operating through greater accountability to long-term owners, is the most efficient, beneficial, and, I dare say, *natural* way to order the elements of our current corporate governance system.

So come with me on what I hope will be a fascinating journey. First we will look at the history of the modern corporation, starting with Adam Smith's day. Then we will visit the exciting new science of complexity – one very different from the science most of us learned, a science that limits our ability to see trends outside the pendulum. We will ask how this science might help us see corporations as complex systems, and as agents within the larger complex system of the world economy. In conclusion, we will define our vision of the 'restored corporation' as the long-awaited return of true corporate integrity.

Only the passage of time will provide definition and confidence as to the scope of complexity and its applicability to very large corporations. What is clear today is that complexity – with its dynamic interactive languages – provides a unique lens through which to understand corporate functioning. In the same way, agent-based modelling and the models known as 'cellular automata' give insights into the vital role active shareholders can play in restoring integrity to the corporate system. Recalling and anticipating our ongoing economic life in this way explains many seeming anomalies, resolves many perpetual debates, and offers immense hope for the future of free enterprise.

Robert A.G. Monks
Cape Elizabeth, Maine
December 1997

Acknowledgements

I owe the greatest thanks to those to whom this book is dedicated and to my other colleagues at LENS: John Higgins, Charles Woodworth, and Bob Holmes for their persistence and loyalty in creating the category of fiduciary capitalism. Dean LeBaron's energy and courage, both commercial and intellectual, have both led and heartened our paths through the last half century.

Indispensable to this book, particularly to Chapter 6 and the graphic illustrations, is the creative genius of Ric Marshall, my son-in-law and friend. Richard Burton from Capstone has given this project a sure and avuncular touch of critical help. My editor Alexandra Lajoux must be one of the greatest talents I have ever encountered. Her ability to explore new areas and to connect the languages of traditional and emerging intellectual categories has helped bring this book from hope to reality.

Many thanks to those who reviewed this manuscript: Dwight L. Allison, Jr, Keith Ambachtsheer, Tatsuo Arima, Charles Berg, Sir Adrian Cadbury, Frank Cahouet, Andrew Campbell, Jonathan Charkham, Deepak Chopra, Carolyn Chute, Shannon Clyne, Jeff Coolidge, Laura Cousins, Sandra Dawson, Arthur Dubow, Jeff Gates, Charles Hampden-Turner, James E. Heard, Dr. John Hendry, George Herrick, William Dean Howells, Arthur Kleiner, Richard Koch, David C. Korten, Minoru (Ben) Makihara, James McRitchie, Peter Murray, Ralph Nader, Jesse Norman, Hugh Parker, Dick Schlefer, A.A. Sommer, Jr, Allen Sykes, Bob Tricker and Shann Turnbull.

Given the kind of book I have tried to write, it is certain that the treatment I have accorded various subjects will not be pleasing to all. I trust you will agree, though, that these topics are worthy of attention. I will be very grateful for your reactions.

Robert A.G. Monks
Cape Elizabeth, Maine
December 1997

Prologue

A fable: The Emperor's Nightingale.

Prologue:
The Emperor's Nightingale

By Hans Christian Andersen
Retold by Robert A.G. Monks

This retelling is based on the original Danish text and my own sense of the story, with help from all of the translations and retellings cited throughout this book. Many thanks to Solveig B. Madsen of the Hans Christian Andersen Museum in Odense, Denmark (H.C. Andersens Hus, Odense Bys Museer) for sending me this story in the original Danish.

Once upon a time in China there lived a Chinese emperor surrounded by Chinese people. This was long ago and far away, but this story is very important to all of us, which is why I am telling it to you now.

The emperor's palace was magnificence itself. Everything in it and around it was made entirely of porcelain – a substance so fragile, so valuable, and so expensive that everyone had to be very careful walking around. The gardens there were vast – even the gardener couldn't tell you where they ended. But those who ventured beyond the gardens found even greater wonders: a deep sea by a dark forest, and within the forest, a nightingale – one that sang so beautifully that even the hardest working fisherman, one who had to cast his nets constantly just to survive, would stop to listen.

'Good Lord, what a song!' he would cry, and then forget all about it as he went back to work. But the next night he would say the same thing.

People came from around the world to see the emperor's city, with its beautiful palace and gardens. But it was the nightingale they remembered and talked about when they got home. Some even wrote books about it – and one day the emperor was given one. Sitting on his gold throne, he read on and on about the beauty of his city, its exquisite porcelain palace, re-markable gardens, etc., etc., and the emperor smiled and nodded.

Then he saw something that made him stop reading: 'Yet of all these things, the nightingale is the best of all.'

'The nightingale?' the emperor cried. 'What's that? Never heard of it. Not in my empire! Why didn't anybody tell me about this?'

He rang for his chamberlain, a man of such eminence that if anyone of lower rank ever spoke to him he would only say 'P!' which is totally mean-ingless.

'You see these books?' sputtered the emperor. 'They say that there is a highly remarkable bird in the Empire ... the "best of all." Why am I the last to know about this?'

'I haven't heard a thing about it, Sire,' said the chamberlain. 'It has never been presented at the court.'

'The bird must come to sing for me! Everybody knows what I own but me!'

The chamberlain looked high and low for the bird, and in his panic he even spoke to people of lesser rank. Finally he came upon a scullery maid who knew where the creature lived. He promised her a permanent position in the kitchen and even a chance to watch the emperor eat if she would only lead him there. So she led the chamberlain and several ladies-in-waiting to the forest to find it. They searched and searched ...

'Listen,' the maid whispered suddenly, pointing to a small grey bird perched on a branch. 'Look! There it is! Up there!'

'That's the nightingale?' the ladies-in-waiting all cried. 'Why, she's the plainest little thing we've ever seen!'

'Little nightingale,' the kitchen maid cried. 'Our great emperor wishes you to sing for him.'

'With pleasure,' the nightingale said. And it began to sing its heart out.

Everyone loved it, and the chamberlain invited the nightingale to come and sing at the Court. 'You will thrill his High Imperial Majesty with your *charmante* song.'

'I sound better outdoors,' the nightingale demurred, but it flew along with them anyway out of respect for the emperor's wishes.

How the palace sparkled that night – polished on every surface, reflecting the light of thousands of gold lanterns! And the people were sparkling, too, dressed in their finest silks and satins, their shining eyes fixed on the little grey bird perched on a gold bar next to the emperor's throne.

The bird's song was so beautiful that it made the emperor cry tears of joy; its music went straight to the hearts of all who heard it. When the nightingale finished, the emperor was so pleased that he insisted on putting his gold slipper around the nightingale's neck as a token of respect. 'No thank you,' the nightingale said. 'I have seen tears in your eyes. What else could I ask for?'

The emperor was so delighted with the nightingale he commanded it to remain at the palace. The bird lived in a gold cage, which it left only twice a day for its regular walks. Twelve servants accompanied it, each one holding on to a different part of the long, royal ribbon tied around the bird's legs. That was no fun at all for the poor bird!

A month passed, and then one night, a large package marked NIGHTINGALE arrived for the emperor. 'Why, this must be another book about our marvellous bird,' said the emperor, but it was much better than that. It was a bird to end all birds – an artificial nightingale made of gold and adorned with diamonds, rubies, and sapphires! Around its neck was a ribbon that bore a modest message from no less than the emperor of Japan! It said: 'My nightingale is nothing compared to yours.'

But the emperor of China had his doubts about that. This new bird was wonderful! When it was wound up, it sang like the real nightingale and even bobbed its tail up and down in time to the music. The minute the courtiers saw the gold nightingale, they got very excited. 'How beautiful it is!' they cried, and they insisted that the two nightingales sing together.

But the duet was a disaster. The gold bird sang the same song over and over again in the exact same way, while the real nightingale sang her notes in her own natural way. Then the artificial nightingale was wound up and made to sing alone. Its singing was so perfectly regular. And it was certainly much prettier to look at than the real nightingale! Thirty-three times the courtiers listened to the gold nightingale sing its song. And if the emperor hadn't stopped them, they gladly would have listened to it a dozen times more! The emperor explained that the real nightingale must be allowed to sing.

But where was it? No one had seen the bird fly out the window back to its home in the green forest. 'What an ingrate!' the courtiers cried. They quickly consoled themselves with the artificial bird, hearing it for the 34th time that very day. How much better it was than that little grey one – not only on the outside but on the inside.

The music master made a little speech:

'My Lords and Ladies, and above all Your Imperial Majesty, the bird we retained is superior to the one we lost. The real bird was too unpredictable – you never knew what was coming next! But with the artificial bird everything is perfectly planned and determined. Things are as they should be and not otherwise. We can make an accounting of the real bird. We can open it up to see the human logic that has gone into making it – every turn of every little cog and wheel.'

'My thoughts exactly!' whispered the courtiers to each other.

The following Sunday, the music master went to show the bird to the people. They, too, were delighted, except for a fisherman who had heard the real nightingale. 'It sounds pretty, and similar to the real bird,' he thought, 'but something is missing.'

The real nightingale was banished from the land.

The artificial nightingale wore the imperial gold slipper around its neck, and perched in the gold cage to the left of the emperor's bed. (The emperor considered the left side to be the most important, for that is where the heart is, even in an emperor.) The music master wrote 25 volumes of analytical commentary on the artificial bird. All the courtiers claimed to have read and understood it, because they didn't want to look stupid.

Things went on like this for a year. Every night the court gathered to hear the gold nightingale sing, and sometimes the people got to listen. As time went on, eventually everyone in the empire knew every note of its song by heart, and that made them enjoy listening to it even more. Even the boys on street corners were singing the song: 'Zizizi! Klukklukkluk!'

One evening as the emperor lay in bed listening to the artificial nightingale, he heard a terrible sound: Pop! Whizzz! Whirrrrrrrr ... The gears inside the bird had snapped and the wheels had ground to a dead halt.

The emperor sprang out of bed and immediately summoned his personal physician, but he was no help. Then he called for his watchmaker, who slowly patched the bird together through trial and error – but warned that his repairs might not last long. The cogs were very worn down, and replacement parts might not produce any music at all. What a catastrophe!

Now the bird was wound up only once a year, and people could barely enjoy listening to it, worrying that it might break again. Every year the music master proclaimed that the bird sounded as good as new, and everyone nodded, but they all knew it wasn't so.

Five years passed in this way, and then a great grief came upon the land. The people's beloved emperor got so sick the doctor said he might not live much longer. A new emperor was named. People milled about in the streets waiting to ask the chamberlain for news. But all the chamberlain said when he came out was 'P!' as he shook his head.

The emperor lay so cold and pale in his bed that he seemed dead. The courtiers who saw him ran out to make the announcement, their sounds muffled by all the cloth that they had set down to deaden the clatter of footsteps. It was quiet. So quiet.

But the emperor was not dead yet. He could feel the silvery moon shining on him through the open window, past the velvet curtains and heavy gold tassels surrounding his bed. He could sense the gold nightingale motionless beside him, so silent in its gold cage.

The emperor could hardly breathe! A weight was sitting on his chest. Death was staring right at him, wearing the imperial crown and holding the imperial banner and sword! And behind Death, in the folds of the velvet curtains and in the strings of the heavy gold tassels, he saw spirits, and heard them whispering of his good and bad deeds.

'Music!' he cried. 'Music! Chamberlain!! Bang the big drum!' He wanted to drown out the voices – but they continued, and the faces kept nodding at everything he said, the way people do.

The emperor turned to the gold nightingale sitting in its cage. 'Please, I beg of you, sing! Sing! I have given you a cage of gold and I placed my very own gold slipper to wear around your neck. You must sing to me.' But of course the mechanical bird stayed silent. There was no one to wind it up.

Suddenly, a torrent of beautiful notes burst through the window. The real nightingale was perched on the branch outside. It had heard about the emperor's illness and had come to bring him comfort and hope.

'Sing on,' said Death.

The little bird sang of Death's home, the quiet churchyard, with its white roses and old trees and tear-soaked grounds, and Death himself began to feel homesick. Abandoning the emperor's regalia piece by piece, he floated out the window like a morning mist.

'Thank you, thank you, nightingale!' the emperor cried. 'I banished you from my kingdom once. Yet you came and sang to me and saved my life with your song. How can I ever repay you?'

'You have already rewarded me,' said the nightingale, 'when I saw the tears in your eyes the first time I sang for you.'

'You must stay with me always now,' the emperor then said. 'I will smash the gold nightingale into a thousand pieces. I will give you a new golden cage and my gold slipper, and you shall sing only when it pleases you.'

'No,' the nightingale replied. 'The gold bird did the best it could. Keep it here with you, as before. I cannot live here. My home is the forest. But I will not forsake you. I will come every night at sundown and sing outside your window. I will sing about people who are happy and people who suffer. I will sing of good, and of the evil that is hidden from you. The little songbird flies far away – above the nets of the tiredest fishermen, above the thatched roof of the poorest peasant – far away from you and your court. And I will do this because you are a good ruler, and most of all because you have a good heart.'

And then the little nightingale flew away.

The next morning his servants crept back in to take a look at their dead emperor. Imagine their surprise when they heard him say 'Good morning!'

The End

1

Humankind and all its creations struggle to reconcile the predictable and the dynamic. This is the moral of the timeless story of 'The Nightingale' by Hans Christian Andersen. It is also the nature of the corporation, a human creation of special importance.

1

The Emperor's Nightingale: Harbinger of Corporate Restoration

> *The story that I am about to tell you happened long, long ago. It's for that very reason I want you to hear it now – so it won't be forgotten.*[1]

We humans have told stories since the dawn of time. In every hour of every day of every generation, new narratives emerge and old ones re-emerge, transformed. Yet within this seeming chaos, there is order. The number of our stories, though large, is finite. And when we group stories together, we can almost begin to count them.

Some stories are myths, explaining the origins of humankind and their gods. Others are legends or sagas, recounting the acts of historical figures. Still others are complex tales ('fairy tales' in English, *Märchen* in German, *contes* in French – every language has its term) aiming to entertain and enlighten. These tales show variety, yet as a group they have certain recurrent motifs, such as animal helpers. One scholar has counted exactly 2400 recurring motifs – no more, no less!

It is not surprising that fairy tales repeat themselves. Marie-Louise von Franz, a scholar who has devoted her entire career to the study of these narratives, has concluded that they are the *single most universal type* of story. More than myths or legends, says von Franz, they provide a unique 'bridge to the human' through their interconnected themes. This is true whether a tale is in its infancy or whether it is being told (and embroidered) for the thousandth time.

'To me the fairy tale is like the sea, and the sagas and myths are like waves upon it', writes von Franz. 'Unlike myths and sagas, a tale rises to be a myth and then sinks down again into being a fairy tale. Here again we come to the same conclusion: fairy tales mirror … the human psyche.' Fairy tales do not try to explain life, but to explore its paradoxes: alive/dead, true/false, dynamic/predictable, genuine/artificial – at times opposed, at times reconciled. These are the timeless tensions resolved in 'The Nightingale' by Hans Christian Andersen.

THE EMPEROR'S NIGHTINGALE

This splendid narrative begins by describing a continuum from structure to spontaneity. We meet the emperor, ruler of China, renowned for his vast gardens and many possessions, all maintained with great control and artifice. And we learn that beyond his mannered gardens, near toiling peasants, in the middle of a forest, a nightingale sings. Even at these first notes, we begin to wonder when and how these two realms will meet – and soon this comes to pass.

For many years, it seems, the common people have drawn strength and consolation from the nightingale's song, but word of its charm does not reach the emperor until visiting dignitaries write books about it. Overtaken by jealousy and curiosity, the emperor seeks out the nightingale and commands it to live and sing in his court. The nightingale attracts a noble following, and all seems well. But we readers, knowing that no real bird loves a cage, wait for the complication – and soon it comes.

One day, the emperor receives a mechanical nightingale from a rival emperor. This new bird, made of gold and singing the same song again and again, becomes the new darling of the court. By the time the emperor pleads with his subjects to pay attention to the real bird, it is long gone. Only when the golden bird breaks down and the emperor approaches death does the real nightingale return to sing, healing the ruler.

The revived emperor says he will 'smash the golden nightingale into a thousand pieces', but the true nightingale urges him to keep it in a place of honour. He begs the nightingale to stay, but the nightingale declines. Instead, the bird will live in the forest, returning every evening to sing to the emperor the entire truth of his empire.

And so the dynamic and the predicable are reconciled. Both are part of the human experience and always will be.

★★★

A happy ending, yes, but with a moral imperative: to value the real over and above the artificial. The real nightingale is truly alive. Its song is adaptive, touching and touched by a full range of human experience. It has healing properties. Though mortal, it endures. The artificial bird has simulated life. Its song is repetitious, capturing and releasing only one part of the human score. Its breakdown sickens its owner. Though programmed to be immortal, it dies. In short, we see the bad things that can happen when an artificial life form takes the place of a truly living one. Instead, the two can and should coexist.

LEGACY

Andersen dashed off this story in two days, inspired no doubt by his love of the 'Swedish nightingale', Jenny Lind. But the tale has clearly transcended its historical genesis to take on a far broader meaning. Since its first appearance in 1843, 'The Nightingale' has been translated, retold, danced, painted, and enacted hundreds of thousands of times in thousands of places. As I write this text, the Internet holds 54,076 web sites containing both the word 'nightingale' and 'emperor', most of them retelling or mentioning Andersen's simple tale. This compares to only 12,473 sites mentioning 'Cinderella'.

Why the tremendous popularity of this particular story? What is it about it that grips the popular imagination? What major forms of artificial life emerged in Andersen's day and persist until today? One comes to my mind and may come to yours: the modern corporation.

Andersen never took direct aim at the 'heartless' corporation, as his mentor and friend Charles Dickens did in *The Old Curiosity Shop* (1840) and *Dombey and Son* (1846–1848). But this concern – and related concerns about industrialisation – may help explain why he wrote 'The Nightingale', and why readers have found it intriguing ever since.

The word 'corporation' originally meant something closer to 'embodiment'. As suggested by its root word (*corpus*, from the Latin word for body), a corporation unites its elements so completely that they become one. Thus 16th-century historians wrote (before standardised spelling) of the 'corporacyon mystical of Christ', or the 'corporation of all who are in the booke of life'. This sense of unity carried over to the term's original applications in trade in the 16th century, when travelling traders first formed 'corporations' to share their risk.

In the early 17th century, during colonisation of the New World, the risk of business ventures grew – along with the desire not only to share but *to avoid* risk. In this era, a new form of business enterprise arose: an artificial entity created as a means of transferring risk. Within a few centuries, this new structure had become the dominant form of enterprise. The golden bird of the corporation was out of its box, wound up, and going strong.

DEEP BLUE

Today the corporation seems invincible – very much like the steam drill that laid ties faster than the legendary railroader John Henry, or IBM's Deep Blue computer that defeated chess champion Garry Kasparov 3½ to 2½ in the sixth game of their rematch after only 19 moves. IBM declared victory. 'One hundred years from now, people will say this day was the beginning of the Information Age', exulted IBM's C.J. Tan. 'Historically for mankind, this is like landing on the moon or being the first human to climb Mount Everest.'

Yet to paraphrase poet Robert Frost, something there is that doesn't love a juggernaut. Something there is that wishes for the victory of the older, the smaller, the plainer things of life – things that have neither price tag nor predictability, and yet form the foundation of all value and meaning. Kasparov's spontaneous words – in a broken English that had more eloquence than a Shakespearean sonnet – said it all.

'It was nothing to do about science ... It was one zeal to beat Garry Kasparov. And when a big corporation with unlimited resources would like to do so, there are many ways to achieve the result. And the result was achieved. [But] I feel confident that the machine hasn't proved anything. It's not yet ready, in my opinion, to win a big contest.'

What does Kasparov mean, '... to win a big contest'? Doesn't he mean that 'real' chess is ultimately human versus human? Machine versus human will never be a truly big contest. The world of the artificial nightingale is the world of the machine. It is a world we will inherit if we fail to encourage the dynamic in our corporations. The only way to save something sacred – the 'real game of chess' – is by restoring the integrity of the human scale.

We find ourselves rooting not just for Garry Kasparov, but for his cause, the game of chess – a cherished symbol of adaptive human intelligence. Will chess come to an end as a game because a computer figures it out? 'It's possible', said Grandmaster Ilya Gurevich on the day of Kasparov's defeat. By the same token, it is also possible that giant corporations, by gaining limitless life, size, power, and license, could take the challenge and vitality out of business. Possible, but not likely.

CONFIDENCE

Thanks in part to stories like 'The Nightingale', we have confidence that there will always be something ultimately mysterious and alive about our collective world, and by extension, our corporations. Despite their mechanistic traits – traits that lock in their worst qualities while crowding out their best ones – corporations continue to be adaptable and dynamic. We must encourage this quality.

Andersen's story tells us that in their best incarnations, our companies are living, breathing systems that we may not always understand or appreciate. As managers in the court of life, we find it easier to understand simple, mechanical structures, such as the plans, laws, rules, and 'numbers' we make to bring predictability to our corporate results. We tend to apply these solutions – rather than holistic intuitive ones – especially as our organisations become larger, and as ownership separates from management. But there is a better way.

There is nothing wrong with our impulse towards order. We humans are good at detecting and enhancing it. The rote machines and short-term plans we make work well, and they are useful. But we should not let our success in that realm blind us to superior alternatives.

The emperor may not completely 'own' the real nightingale, no more than a shareholder can truly 'own' a corporation. But he has a special responsibility toward this dynamic creature. Rather than letting the corporate 'machine' work for itself under rigid rules that stop short of true growth and vitality, owners must value the corporation as a dynamic, living creature, and they must participate as owners in that life. Managers, too, have an important role in this scheme: to heed owners when they say, 'Let the real nightingale sing'.

2

Two hundred years ago, Adam Smith sounded an alarm. The corporations of his day posed a threat to society because by their very nature they sought unlimited life, size, power, and license, externalising risk as they pursued these aims.

2

The Disconsolate Dawn of the Modern Corporation

> *One day a package arrived for the emperor; on it was written:*
> **Nightingale**. *'It is probably another book about our famous bird,'*
> *said the emperor. But he was wrong; it was a mechanical nightin-*
> *gale.*[1]

The history of the modern corporation properly begins with a voice crying in the wilderness. The voice belonged to Adam Smith, a 'professor of moral philosophy', and the wilderness he surveyed was the newly global economy of 18th-century Europe. Something was wrong, he thought, with the way the economic leaders of humankind were conducting their economic affairs …

Smith trained his prophetic sights on the dominant form of corporate business in his day: the so-called 'joint stock company'. Less than two centuries old in concept, this risk-sharing system had evolved during Smith's lifetime into a dynamic driver of an expanding global economy. It brought into being the famed 'East India' companies backed by the Dutch, French, and British governments. And it gave rise to Britain's own 'Hudson's Bay' and 'Massachusetts Bay' companies, which in turn helped build a new nation. In further corners of the globe, there were the 'Royal African' companies and the once-powerful 'South Sea' company.

Created under royal charter or Parliament, often with special privileges that gave them strong advantages over other entities, these ocean-spanning enterprises commanded great respect – even awe – in Smith's era. Despite many failures long forgotten, these companies were still doing the impossible: achieving returns without (it seemed) commensurate risk. Who would dare question the alchemy of this golden bargain?

SMITH'S VISION

Enter Smith. As a political economist, he understood the appeal of the joint stock company, but he found it more dangerous than the two other common business forms of the era – the 'regulated company' and the 'copartnery'. He explained why in his unabashed *Inquiry Into the Nature and Causes of the Wealth of Nations*.

The *regulated company*, said Smith, was no more than a large professional guild (then called a 'corporation of the trades'), operating under the protections of monopoly. Without those protections, regulated companies were doomed to failure, both individually and collectively.

The *copartnery,* Smith declared, was a worthy, but limited form – ideal only for the investment of small amounts of capital. The copartnery, he noted, spreads risk among a fixed number of copartners, each of whom puts his entire wealth at risk.[2]

The *joint stock company*, however, was another creature entirely. It had greater economic merits than the regulated company, and higher utility than the copartnery. It appeared to thrive under any and all conditions, despite adversity and all manner of failure.

Smith correctly sensed that the intrinsic merits of this form would thrive well after his death. Therefore, he critiqued its flaws with special zeal. Like the regulated business, said Smith, the joint stock company often operated with special privileges that limited its risk. Yet in addition to monopoly protections, the joint stock company had an intrinsic fail-safe: *the amount of risk each individual investor took on in such a company was limited to the amount of the investor's original investment.*

Smith grudgingly admitted that for larger endeavours such as banking, insurance, and transportation (canals and waterworks), this form was inevitable. But he expressed his doubts about its applicability elsewhere. There was too much about this risk transfer that bothered him. The sensible Scotsman sensed that the wealth of the joint stock company was all too often fool's gold. In *The Wealth of Nations,* he reminded readers of past failures of joint stock companies – some 55 since the year 1600, including the spectacular crash of the South Sea Company, which led to the Bubbles Act of 1720, an early corporate reform.[3]

More significantly, however, Smith exposed four underlying dangers in the joint stock company, predecessor to the modern corporation. He observed that these entities tended to seek:

- unlimited life
- unlimited size
- unlimited power
- unlimited license.

Corporate danger number one: the quest for unlimited life

It bothered Smith first and foremost that joint stock companies, like regulated companies, could *outlive their original purpose* – in most cases, the advancement of national trade through colonisation. Speaking in general of companies that enjoy government protections (as did both the joint stock company and the regulated companies of his era), Smith observed: 'These companies … have in the long-run proved, universally, either burdensome or useless, or have either mismanaged or confined the trade.'[4] He also argued in favour of a limited life for corporations. A period of protection through a special charter has its purpose, 'But *upon the expiration of the term, the monopoly ought certainly to [terminate]* and the trade … laid open to all the subjects of the state.'[5]

Corporate danger number two: the quest for unlimited size

It also disturbed Smith that joint stock companies, granted indefinite life, *continued to grow in size of capital.* 'Such companies … commonly draw to themselves *much greater stocks than any private copartnery can boast.* The trading stock of the South Sea Company, at one time, amounted to upwards of thirty-three million eight hundred thousand pounds. The dividend capital of the Bank of England amounts at present, to ten millions [*sic*] seven hundred and eighty thousand pounds.'[6]

Corporate danger number three: the quest for unlimited power

Smith also fretted about the *unlimited powers* of these companies to *misman-age their unfairly excessive profits*. The once-famous failure of the South Sea Company, which ceased to do business as a trading company in 1748,[7] left barely a ripple in England's economic seas, as did the reforms it inspired. As recently as 1773, new corporate reforms had failed to restrain the misman-agement of the country's famed East India Company. The company was operating at a profit, but continued to contract debt. '*The great increase of their fortune had, it seems, only served to furnish their servants with a pretext for greater profusion*, and a concern for greater malversation, than in proportion even to that increase of fortune.'[8]

Corporate danger number four: the quest for unlimited license

But most of all, Smith worried about the *lack of accountability* in the joint stock company. Large capitalisation does not ensure vigilance, claimed Smith. 'The directors of such companies … being the *manager rather of other people's money than of their own* [will not] watch over it with the same anxious vigi-lance with which the partners in a private copartnery frequently watch over their own. *Negligence and profusion therefore must always prevail in such a company.*'[9]

Other people's money … It's a theme we hear again and again in *The Wealth of Nations*. Even more than the perils of monopoly, 'malversation', and the assorted other ills he lambasted in his economic treatise, Smith was wary of the separation of ownership and management, and all of the conflicts of interest this could breed.

In one of the longest passages in *The Wealth of Nations* (six pages without a paragraph break), Smith railed against the perpetuity, size, and ultimately power of Britain's East India Company. Toward the end of his diatribe, he made his central point: 'No other sovereigns ever were, or, from the nature of things, ever could be, so *perfectly indifferent* about the happiness or misery of their subjects [as] the proprietors of such a mercantile company are, and necessarily must be.'[10]

THE MODERN ERA: CAVEATS UNHEEDED

Could these fulminations have come from the same *Wealth of Nations* acclaimed for its defence of free markets? Did this bible of capitalism really contain an attack on the limited liability corporation – the very engine of enterprise for the next three centuries? Given the impact of this book, why were these words unheeded?

One reason may be prematurity. Smith was simply ahead of his time with respect to corporate dangers. In the late 18th century, the chartering of 'joint stock companies' was still extremely rare and tightly controlled, curbing the life, size, power, and license of nascent corporations in both Europe and the New World. In America, even after the Revolution, when the mitre of royal control passed to the states, there lingered the sense that corporate status was 'privileged' and ought to be restricted to categories having an element of public interest. And so well into the next century, the four potentially negative dynamics of corporations were kept in check.

The corporate life span, for example, was intentionally brief in Smith's day. As Supreme Court Justice Louis D. Brandeis noted in his famed 1932 dissent in *Liggett*, early Americans recognised the utility of the corporate form, but they also mistrusted it. Incorporation for business, said Brandeis, 'was commonly denied longer after it had been freely granted for religious, educational, and charitable purposes. It was denied because of fear. Fear of encroachment upon the liberties and opportunities of the individual. Fear of the subjugation of labor to capital. Fear of monopoly. Fear that the absorption of capital by corporations and their *perpetual life* might bring evils similar to those which attended *mortmain*.'[11]

Size, too, was closely watched in America's early years, Brandeis noted. 'There was a sense of some insidious menace inherent in large aggregations of capital; particularly when held by corporations. So at first the corporate privilege was granted sparingly; and only when the grant seemed necessary in order to procure for the community some specific benefit otherwise unobtainable. The later enactment of general corporation laws does not signify that the apprehension of corporate domination had been overcome.'[12]

By the early 20th century, however, the dangers of the corporation had *grown* even while public concern had – ironically – *diminished*. This irony was not lost on Justice Brandeis. 'The prevalence of the corporation in America has led men of this generation to act, at times, as if the privileges of doing business in corporate form were inherent in the citizen, and has led them to accept the evils attendant upon the free and unrestricted use of the corporate mechanism as if these evils were the inescapable price of civilized life, and hence, to be borne with resignation.'[13]

The Old Testament style of Brandeis compels response, but none has emerged. Why not? The reason for our increasing indifference in the face of increasing dangers is not that we have no problem. Rather, it is that *we cannot see the problem* because we ourselves have decked it out in pleasant camouflage. It is very hard to hate something that appears to give us something (profits) for little or nothing (limited liability) – *especially if that something seems to be an extension, or, worse yet, a clone of ourselves.*

FOUR HUMAN DELUSIONS

Yes, it is our own vision that has prevented us all from seeing the dangers of the modern corporation even as it has evolved from the tiny straw dog fought by a once obscure Scottish philosopher into an economic Goliath the size of a nation. And to understand that problem of vision, we need only to look in the mirror. For as the corporation has grown, we have come to see it in all too human terms – the present author included.

Human delusion number one: the corporation as 'person'

Perhaps the greatest obstacle in our quest for corporate accountability is the problem of human camouflage – our perception of the corporation as a person – an extension of our own human nature. This we will call the 'big person' delusion. At times, we describe the corporation as nothing more or less than a large human being – sometimes good, sometimes bad, but always family. This false belief makes all the corporate dangers invisible to us. The corporation is not a person, it is a *system*.

Humans, too, are systems, but of a different nature. What is the difference between the human 'system' and the corporate 'system'? How can we link the two? The recent work of Ralph D. Stacey is instructive in this regard. In *Complexity and Creativity in Organizations*, Stacey describes organisations and human beings as complex systems.

Despite parallels at the external level (which we will comment on and expand in the next chapter) there are radical differences at the *internal* level.

Although Stacey does not discuss the corporate form *per se* in his book, his points apply perfectly to this type of organisation, which perhaps more than any other human organisation has been made in the image of humankind.

According to Stacey, human systems, unlike other systems such as organisations (read corporations), have the following 'internal structures':

- Human agents and groups of human agents get caught up in sequences of responses driven by emotion and aspiration, inspiration and anxiety, compassion and avarice, honesty and deception, imagination and curiosity.
- Human agents share a common purpose but also develop their own individual mental purposes, leading to tension between conformity and individualism.
- Some human agents are, or become, more able and/or more powerful than others and apply force and persuasion, whereas others follow.
- Human agents are conscious and self-aware – that is, they can adopt the role of observer and think systematically.

Not so with corporate systems! Corporate systems *cannot* exercise emotion, inspiration, compassion, honesty, or imagination – or their opposites. Corporate systems *cannot* have a sensitivity to the collective. Corporate systems *cannot* be persuaded. Corporations *cannot* be conscious of themselves: they 'do not know what they do'. So says Stacey.

While agreeing with Stacey's overall point, I would like to raise one important difference. In my view, corporations *can* have a measure of these human traits when they are still 'owned and operated' by an individual or a small group of individuals. They lose these traits when they become corporations in the modern sense identified by Adam Smith – that is, entities that separate ownership and management. They take on a life of their own as systems in their own right, and as agents in the world economy, a larger system. We will return to this point – one of the driving themes of this book – in the following chapters.

Human delusion number two: the corporation as 'machine'

Another hindrance in our quest for corporate accountability is our perception of the corporation as a machine – a tool pliable to our needs.

A machine, according to one definition (advanced over a decade ago by

Donald N. Zweip of the Worcester Polytechnic Institute, in Worcester, Massachusetts), is a 'device for producing useful work, composed of combinations of *rigid* or resistant links formed and connected in order to alter, transmit, and direct the application of force in a *predetermined* way'.

We often see corporations as 'machines' in this sense. We speak of the 'engine' of growth, 'gears' of productivity, 'brakes' to progress – all terms from the highly contained world of mechanical physics. Candidly, even in writing this book, it was very hard to avoid this imagery in speaking of the corporate form. This is the legacy of Isaac Newton, which Adam Smith shared with us. It is a great legacy – yet one not great enough for the task before us: understanding corporations as what they really are, where they really are – as complex systems within the larger complex system of the economy. This leads to two more delusions.

Human delusion number three: the economy as 'person'

Just as we tend to think of our corporations as big people, so we tend to think of the economy itself as having a human personality. Like Adam Smith, we tend to believe that the economy is guided not by the dynamics of its own structure and interactions, but by a benign outside force. Symbolising the human consciousness of the economy, we borrow Smith's notion of an 'invisible hand'.

It is hard to tell exactly what Smith meant by this image, which has so enchanted subsequent generations. He appears to attach no particular importance to it, using it only once in all of *The Wealth of Nations*. Moreover, these two key words are buried like needles in a haystack-sized defence of free trade. Here is the key text, narrowly quoted:

> '*By preferring the support of domestic to that of foreign industry, [an individual] intends only his own security; and by directing that industry in such a manner as its produce may be of the greatest value, he intends only his own gain, and he is in this, as in many other cases,* led by an invisible hand to promote an end which was not part of his intention.'

In this particular passage, Smith does not stress the rationality of the economy, but rather the *unconsciousness* of its agents – a very modern concept indeed (to which we will return in Chapter 5). But we heirs to Adam Smith – quite significantly – have made something quite different out of Smith's point. We have comforted ourselves by connecting that hand to a body, and that body to a mind. We have believed with him and a bevy of followers up to the present time that the economy acts in a rational way – much like a large, ideal human being. Wrong again.

As we shall see in the following chapter, the economy does not always act sensibly, neither in its parts nor as a whole. Rather, it is a complex system with peculiar traits of its own – traits that do not always add up to the neatly balanced charts, graphs, and curves we humans have wished on our world.

Human delusion number four: the economy as 'machine'

Our idealized notion of the economy as a large sensible person is only slightly less foolish than our notion of the economy as a rational machine. In *The Future of Leadership*, Randall White and his co-authors note succinctly that 'Linear models of the world based on Newton's idea that action leads to reaction are insufficient to handle some kinds of circumstances – namely complexity and uncertainty.'[14] How true this is.

In his *Philosophiae Naturalis Principia Mathematica*, Newton went as far as a human being could go in analysing and understanding the mechanical aspects of our world. Many of his discoveries endure today. Yet his vision was in the end limited – as is all science apart from the question of meaning. John Archibald Wheeler spoke forcefully to this point over a decade ago at the Herman Weil Centenary Congress at the University of Kiel in Germany. In a brilliant speech, he outlined the limitations of classical physics:

> *'Those laws, so beautiful, so necessary for an understandable, meaningful world, and on first inspection so full of structure, turn out every one of them on closer look to be built in large measure on tautology, mathematical identity, the most elementary statement of algebraic geometry: the principle that the boundary of a boundary is zero. How strange, we say at first. And then we ask ourselves, how could it have been otherwise?*
>
> *'At the beginning there were no gears and pinions, no corps of Swiss watchmakers to put things together, not even a pre-existing plan. If this assessment is correct, every law of physics must be at bottom like the*

second law of thermodynamics, higgledy-piggledy in character, based on blind chance. Physics must in the end be law without law.'[15]

As heirs to Newton and to Smith, we must take these wise words to heart. Too often, like Smith, we see the essential traits of the economy as 'mechanics' rather than as genetic properties susceptible to evolution.

Chart 2.1

A Human Truth

~~FOUR HUMAN DELUSIONS~~

The corporation is a complex system

~~THE CORPORATION~~   ~~THE CORPORATION~~
~~IS A PERSON~~   ~~IS A MACHINE~~

and so is the economy

~~THE ECONOMY~~   ~~THE ECONOMY~~
~~IS A PERSON~~   ~~IS A MACHINE~~

SUMMARY AND CONCLUSION

In summary:
   The corporation is

- not a person
- not a machine.

   The economy is

- not a person
- not a machine.

To replace these four delusions (shown in Chart 2.1), we offer one complex truth: the corporation and the economy are both complex systems.

These systems seek

- unlimited life
- unlimited size
- unlimited power
- unlimited license.

In the following chapter, we will explore the dangerous dynamics of this corporate 'programming' in greater detail.

3

Smith's insights give us our way in to see corporations for what they really are. Corporations are not human, although they are formed by humans and should serve human purposes. Nor are they machines, although they have some internal laws that operate mechanistically. Instead, they are artificial life forms — or, to use a current scientific term, complex adaptive systems.

3

Four Corporate Dangers

> *'It is not to blame', said the music master. 'It keeps time perfectly and according to the rules of my own system.' Then the artificial bird had to sing alone ... Thirty-three times it sang the same melody and still it wasn't tired. People were only too willing to hear it from the beginning again, but the emperor thought that now the living nightingale should also sing a little. But where was it?*[1]

In the earliest days of free enterprise there was little distinction to be drawn between ownership and management of business entities. In most cases these roles were played by the same individuals, who brought to the economic system their own personal goals and aspirations and, in turn, their own sense of accountability.

For better or worse, this direct personal involvement provided the essential driving force of our economic growth and development. Like the real nightingale in Andersen's story, owner-managers sang songs filled with the sounds of their own individual and very human personalities.

As these private enterprises grew and evolved, however, new forms of ownership emerged, beginning with the various forms of partnership and proceeding to the development of the modern corporation. In this form an immediate gap appeared, and then widened, between the functions of ownership and management. As a result, the direct human involvement of individual owners grew increasingly removed from management.

The need to bridge this gap has in turn provided the foundation for much of our contemporary system of contract law and our standards of accounting practice, all formal mechanisms devised to codify and monitor the various relationships between and within business entities.

The development of the modern publicly held corporation accelerated this process tremendously, as represented by the rise of major US federal regulatory organisations ranging from the Securities and Exchange Commission (SEC) to the recently created Independent Standards Board,[2] both powerful sources of standards for corporate life.

The key advantages of the corporate form – limited liability and a vastly expanded capacity for raising capital – have led in turn to the development of a corporate culture far removed from the greater concerns of individual owners, with a resultant focus on near-term growth and profitability. This tendency of large corporations to organise themselves around short-term interests is increasingly a matter of public concern. Despite the continued existence of other business forms, large publicly held corporations dominate the developed world's economic landscape.

The problem of 'short-termism' is far more pervasive than critics have acknowledged to date. In the usual commercial parlance this is a term managers and others use to blame shareholders for their preoccupation with quarterly – even daily – results. This preoccupation, critics say (and rightly so) has generated a culture antithetical to good management. The implication here is that if only shareholders would let managers manage, decisions would be made for the 'long term'. My question is, how long is long enough, and who is most likely to stay for the watch? Management and directors are likely to be limited to their own tenure, which is very rarely longer than 10 years. We will need a longer-term perspective, and we are more likely to find it in long-term owners.

In the absence of clear owner-driven values, the managers of many publicly held corporations have become increasingly powerful, filling boards to suit their own agendas and commanding enormous personal compensation and severance packages. Like the mechanical nightingale, corporate boards, in the name of representing owner interests, increasingly sing the same song over and over, a song that management has been all too pleased to hear.

These boards and managers hire corporate counsel on the basis of their ability to externalise accountability, ethically as well as economically. All too often, corporations use their powers of self-transformation to play a shell game. Instead of transforming themselves to enhance long-term value, many corporations use acquisitions, divestitures, and restructurings for lesser purposes – to control disbursement of profits to shareholders, to manipulate competition in the marketplace, or to avoid the payment of public taxes.

With their tremendous power to influence public policy and the public economy, these boards and managers have become increasingly account-able only to themselves. Instead of embracing the challenges of adaptation to and effective engagement in a dynamic, living economy, these short-term driven companies seek to bend the rest of the economic system to their own needs.

Historians may well look back on the 1990s as a time when corporations trampled the public interest in the pursuit of their own ends. Few in our time would share that view. We all have discomfort, but we are very much like the frog described on the cover of Charles Handy's inspired account of *The Age of Unreason*. 'If you put a frog in water and slowly heat it, the frog will eventually let itself be boiled to death. We, too, will not survive if we don't respond to the radical way in which the world is changing.'[3]

★★★

This brief history of the corporate form represents my best attempt to ex-plain in plain English what can happen when ownership and management separate. In facing this problem, we have to stop looking for a familiar an-swer based on human experience.

Corporations are neither people with hearts nor machines with perfect logic, but rather systems with their own dynamics, driven entities that seek unlimited life, size, power, and license, eventually to the point of threatening the entire economic system with the loss of credibility – and, perhaps exist-ence. This is the fear George Soros expressed when describing 'The Capitalist Threat' in the February 1997 *Atlantic Monthly*. The extreme doctrine of com-munism leads to state domination, but extreme laissez faire capitalism is no better, since it can lead to 'great instability and eventual breakdown'.[4]

Is this an extreme possibility? Does the modern corporation pose dangers to the public? Read on and decide for yourself as we revisit the 'four dan-gers' Adam Smith first warned us about over two centuries ago – namely the corporation's voracious quest for unlimited life, size, power, and license.

CORPORATE DANGER NUMBER ONE: THE QUEST FOR UNLIMITED LIFE

Just as the image of an 'invisible hand' can symbolize the rational intelli-gence that wishful thinking would project onto the economy at large, so the image of the 'dead hand' is a powerful symbol of the death grip corporations can have on what they own. Indeed, the legal term for this phenomenon, *mortmain* (from the Old French for dead hand), has passed into European and American law around the world as a distinct condition to be avoided. *Mortmain* laws, which exist to this day, restrict the rights of individuals and corporations to own certain resources, such as land, forever.

What then of the ultimate *mortmain*, the corporation's attempt to own itself forever – to seek, as it were, eternal life? This is contrary to the very idea of life, which implies mortality. That is, if the corporation is to be a 'living' structure, it must also risk 'death' in some form.

Yet some corporations go on and on simply because they get a grip or 'lock-in' on a market (a concept we will revisit in the next chapter). Are these truly living corporations, or is this the night of the living dead? Consider the fact that virtually all of the large corporations that provided war materials for Axis countries in World War II are still powerful today: Krupp, Mitsubishi, Mitsui, Solvay, and Citroën–Peugot come to mind. Does their longevity prove their vitality? Not in all cases.

Inconveniences of immortality

Corporations collectively may have perpetual life as a species as long as they remain harmonious with the principles of nature – principles to be explored in later chapters. Individually, however, corporations should risk mortality. Yet they avoid this risk, impelled by the fundamental law of bureaucracy, and helped by current systems for ownership, taxation, and pay.

- *Ownership.* As it is currently conceived, ownership is forever. There is no limit under the current business system to how long an owner can reap returns from an investment. But this need not be so. What would the corporate world be like if owners, as Australian shareholder activist Shann Turnbull has suggested, had a finite claim?
- *Taxation.* Companies do not pay federal taxes on account of growth in value, until a taxable event occurs. The death of a corporation through liquidation can be a taxable event. Companies would rather live an unhealthy life than die and pay taxes.
- *Bureaucracy's 'Law'.* It is in the nature of bureaucracies to get bigger. A bureaucracy (or a bureaucratic company) cannot get bigger if it dies. So it continues living at all costs.

- *Pay*. Executive pay is based on sales and profits, and no incumbent wants to take a hit. Managers would rather save the bad news for the next guy or gal. Lucky for them, many significant costs – for example, the cost of decommissioning a nuclear power plant – can be deferred indefinitely. (For a cartoon showing this, see Fig. 3.1.) By not reporting these future costs, and by externalizing other costs (as discussed below under Danger Number Two), the corporation can live forever, and always put off into the sunset the payment of expenses.

This last point is worthy of special attention, because it has caused an Orwellian change in the theory of executive pay. Once upon a time, only owners reaped huge rewards from the growth of a company. Now it is *any* current manager!

Fig. 3.1

Instant founders

For as long as there have been businesses owned by one group and managed by another, the question of excessive compensation has loomed large. President Franklin Delano Roosevelt cursed the executives who reported earnings in excess of $100,000 per year in the middle of his nation's Great Depression.

Philosophers have speculated as to whether an ideal ratio exists between what is paid to the entry level worker and to the principal executive. These range from Plato's five times, to the ten to 12 multiple common in Japanese trading companies, to the 40 times traditionally characteristic of American companies.

About a dozen years ago, the salaries of American executives began growing so far so fast – out of comparison with the past, with other countries, with any comparative norms – that it went literally out of human sight. Many executives have reached the levels of *hundreds of millions*. In 1996 Roberto Goizueta of Coca-Cola, before his untimely death from lung cancer in 1997, reached the level of *$1 billion* in total compensation for his services as an executive. This represents a fundamental change in kind. Outstanding executives are *now going to be treated retroactively as if they were the founding owners of the companies they manage*. Their frame of reference is no longer the high-school-graduate office boy they once were. It is rather the Bill Gates story of basement-to-billions (27 at last count).

Gates deserves his fortune and Goizueta deserved his. Like the ideal entrepreneur in the economics of Alfred Marshall, Gates has given back (through innovation and low pricing) more than he has received. The same can be said for Goizueta, considering the returns he generated for shareholders of Coca-Cola. But in too many cases, the wealth at the top signals an undesirable insulation from employees and owners.[5]

CORPORATE DANGER NUMBER TWO: THE QUEST FOR UNLIMITED SIZE

At a workshop on 'Evolutionary Paths of the Global Economy', held at the Santa Fe Institute on 8–18 September 1987, economist Brian Arthur surprised other economists when he said that the dynamics of 'growth' would become the 'dominant' feature of economics for the next 25 years.

Growth – in the vision of Arthur and others – is not always pretty. It can come from positive feedback – a kind of geometric pattern that can 'lock in' inferior technologies. The result is growth of a product (and its makers) that comes not from merit but from a chain reaction. A common example of lock-in is VHS versus Beta for videos. The latter was better but came too late to succeed.[6]

Now, 10 years later, Arthur's comments seem prophetic. Here's a report from Philip W. Anderson, a Princeton physicist who was at the workshop.

'Brian pointed out to us the many regimes in which the standard assumptions of equilibrium theory, such as diminishing returns, concave utility functions, etc., *manifestly break down and drive positive feedback behavior and exponential explosions.* These include economies of scale and large start-up costs … Web-like effects involving the intricate interlocking of technologies are also of this type.'

Just as organisms within a lineage tend to increase in size (Cope's Rule)[7] so corporations tend to increase in size. Like long corporate life, big corporate size can evolve irrespective of merit. In the 1970s, Chrysler achieved the dubious distinction of becoming too big to let die. The Carter Administration bailed out the auto-making giant. During their 'bubble' economy of the 1980s, Japanese companies achieved gigantic size. For example, the market value of publicly held golf clubs (that is, the price of their shares multiplied by the number of shares outstanding) was equal to the entire Australia stock exchange! And in the 1980s and early 1990s, Credit Lyonnais reigned as the largest bank in Europe – and went on to become the largest bank failure in the world's financial history.

As a corporation increases in size, it also increases in complexity. What are the implications of this dual growth? To increase in size requires funding, which comes from profits. How does a corporation's quest for profits affect its behaviour?

The search for profits

The corporation's search for profits is 'relentless', as political scientist Oliver Williamson says in his book, aptly titled *The Mechanisms of Governance*.[8] I will not pause here overlong to support this general proposition, but will pass to the several areas where corporations have pressed the limits and definition of rules in order to extend their profitability.

A company is held to account in the marketplace. One of the principal elements of a company's marketplace appraisal is its performance as recorded by certified public accountants. Bolstered by the professional education and prestige of accountants, the efforts of the SEC and of self-regulatory standard-setting organisations such as the Financial Accounting Standards Board and the New York Stock Exchange, 'the numbers' – constrained by generally accepted accounting principles (GAAP) – provide a preponderantly honest and consistent picture which is susceptible of sophisticated interpretation.[9]

But no one should be under any illusions that GAAP numbers provide a reliable basis for determining the value of a company. They are what they say they are – no more, no less – a statement of financial condition based on principles consistently applied. This is the essence of the corporation's mechanistic nature: something we must live with but something that we cannot assume has human interests at heart.

For example, in recent years, the integrity of GAAP numbers has squarely been strained by the continuing proliferation of 'restructuring' charges. The pattern of taking a special charge to account for unusual and non-recurring circumstances is doubtless a useful convention. The pattern of taking charges every year in amounts that often dwarf the reported 'earnings' is to make a mockery of the whole process. Former SEC Commissioner Steven Wallman states flatly: 'It is troubling then that financial accounting and disclosure are no longer keeping pace with changes in the business world. Competitive challenges and novel corporate opportunities appear more quickly now than ever before.'[10]

With the dramatic changes in corporate condition reflected by massive charge-offs, anomalies emerge that illumine the limitations of the process. For example, Westinghouse, one of the Dow Jones 30 companies in America with a seemingly sustainable capacity to generate a billion dollars a year of cash flow, has only a nominal net worth according to GAAP. 'From 1991 to 1995, 26 of the companies that constitute the Dow Jones Industrials took 69 restructuring actions, including asset write-downs. In the process, they charged away more than $49 billion of stockholders' equity.'[11]

A further problem with GAAP is that it places emphasis on traditional assets that have increasingly little to do with the generation of income in a world dominated by new invention and informed by the communications revolution. A report prepared by Arthur Andersen for 11 large British companies states: 'In successful companies, the value of such [those not reported on the financial statements] assets is growing as a proportion of total shareholder value. Indeed, Margaret Blair, a Brookings Institution economist, has calculated the relationship between tangible assets (property, plant and equipment) and total market value for US manufacturing companies in the

Compustat database. In 1982, she found, hard assets accounted for 62% of the companies' market value; ten years later they made up only 38%. And these were industrials.'[12]

Corrective calculations

It is instructive to follow the 'corrective' calculations that one analyst uses to convert reported accounting data into a meaningful foundation for public value of a well-known company. Here's Merck. (Even I can do this math, so fear not and read on.)

- Step one: calculate average pre-tax earnings for the past three years. For Merck that's $3.694 billion.
- Step two: go to the balance sheet and get the average year-end tangible assets for the same three years: $12.953 billion.
- Step three: divide earnings by assets to get the return on assets: 29% (a nice business, pills!).
- Step Four: for the same three years, find the industry's average ROA.
- Step Five: calculate the 'excess return'. For Merck, the excess is $2.41 billion. That's how much more Merck earns from its assets than the average drug maker would.
- Step six: pay taxes. For Merck (average tax rate: 31%), that's $1.66 billion.
- Step seven: calculate the net present value of the premium. That yields, for Merck, $11.1 billion.

And there you have it: the calculated intangible value (CIV) of Merck's intangible assets, the ones that don't appear on its balance sheet.

Externalities – the power to place costs elsewhere

An important corollary to the corporation's search for unlimited size is the aforementioned notion of externalities. In a previous book, co-author Nell Minow and I described the corporation as 'an entity ... so powerful that it quickly outstripped the limitations of accountability and became something of an externalizing machine, in the same way that a shark is a killing machine

– no malevolence, no intentional harm, just something designed with sublime efficiency for self-preservation, which it accomplishes without any capacity to factor in the consequences to others.'[13]

In using the term 'externalizing' here, we were referring to the externalisation of costs – making others (taxpayers, customers, and so forth) pay for costs that should rightly be assumed by the corporation. The notion of externalities, which goes back two centuries, has received renewed attention thanks to the work of Brian Arthur and others at the Santa Fe Institute.[14]

Corporations are driven by the imperative of short-term value maximisation. They want to have an immediate profit, and they do not care (remember, they are not human) if this profit is achieved at the expense of others, including future generations. (See Fig. 3.1 again.)

Corporations have wide and long-term social impact that extends well beyond those items that are generally included within GAAP. These externalities range from the costs of training, medical and disability expenses arising from work, unemployment, and impact on the environment. The fundamental question is, should the general public continue to bear these costs, or should they be borne by the private sector – the corporation and its shareholders? This is a political question and it has been answered in dramatically different ways in different countries. We will return to this point in Chapter 7, 'Intermezzo: The "Four Phases" of Corporate Life'.

CORPORATE DANGER NUMBER THREE: THE QUEST FOR UNLIMITED POWER

What is 'power' in the scientific sense? In physics, it is 'the rate at which work is done or energy is transferred'.[15] The higher the rate, the greater the power. In politics, power implies control, authority, or influence over others. How does the corporation attempt to increase its hegemony systematically? Is there a 'survival of the fittest' here, as in the old Darwinian system, or will fitness decrease over time, as suggested by some complexity research?[16]

The rules under which corporations are chartered are created by the political government of their domicile. The 'externalising machine' inevitably inclines to attempt to dominate the sovereign. The most dramatic example of attempted dominion is the ability of the corporate community over the decades to dominate the quality of the legal professions and, thus, over time the interpretation of the law. This is the only explanation for the phenomena culminating in the 1976 decision of the Supreme Court of the United States in *Bellotti* versus *First National Bank of Boston*. In this famous (or infamous) decision, business corporations were confirmed in their constitutionally protected right to participate as 'persons' in the political process. Just think of it! The creature, with its unlimited resources, could now rule its creator! If only Mary Shelley were alive today to tell this tale. For now, the following must suffice.

The roots of corporate power – Bellotti *and corporate 'personhood'*

It is testament to the persuasiveness of generations of corporate lawyers that the Fourteenth Amendment to the US Constitution has been interpreted for well over a century to safeguard First Amendment rights for corporations. Justice (now Chief Justice) William H. Rehnquist, writing alone in dissent, appears to appreciate the essential problem of a creature taking over its own parent:

> *'There can be little doubt that when a State creates a corporation with the power to acquire and utilize property, it necessarily and implicitly guarantees that the corporations will not be deprived of that property absent due process of law … A State grants to a business corporation the blessings of potentially perpetual life and limited liability to enhance its efficiency as an economic entity. It might reasonably be concluded that those properties, so beneficial in the economic sphere, pose special dangers in the political sphere. Furthermore, it might be argued that liberties of political expression are not at all necessary to effectuate the purposes for which States permit commercial corporations to exist. So long as the Judicial branches of the State and Federal Governments remain open to protect the corporation's interest, in its property, it has no need, though it may have the desire, to petition the political branches for similar protection. Indeed, the States might reasonably fear the corporation would use its economic power to obtain further benefits beyond those already bestowed.'*
> Bellotti *versus* First National Bank of Boston, *435 U.S.*
> *765,826,827 (1977).*

Power over elections – non-partisanship and the purchase of the entire political process

Since *Bellotti* the extent of corporate involvement in elections has increased dramatically. One new pattern has evolved. To the consternation of Republicans, big business has persisted in contributing substantial amounts to both political parties. Republican congressional leaders threaten reprisals on those who support the enemy. A stronger imperative is involved for business. The political parties are, in effect, subsidiaries of big business. What is important is that the whole process become dependent on business' financial support. This, rather than the success of either political party, is the essence of corporate strategy. I have earlier referred to my personal experience with this phenomenon in the insurance industry (*Power and Accountability*, p. 207).

The nature of political fundraising has changed the face of federal elections. We have been accustomed for a century or more to the spectacle of one special interest group or another 'buying' access and influence. But that strategy now seems too modest. The Business Roundtable provides a new level of sophistication in political power and communication that business lacked in past times. It hedges its bets! Now large corporations give money to *both* political parties. What is at stake is not partisan favour, but *domination of the entire political process by the business sector*. Business money has become virtually intrinsic to the political process.

An indispensable part of the lobbying effort is the financing of political campaigns. The post-Watergate 'reforms' allowed corporations to establish and pay the operating expenses for political action committees (PACs) that can solicit as much as $5000 each per election from their employees or members.

PACs, virtually all of which are physically located in Washington, DC, provide the easiest and the largest source of funding not only for incumbents but for all candidates for federal office. In 1996, a record $2.7 billion was contributed to the US presidential and congressional campaigns.[17] There is no way that grassroots campaign money can be raised so quickly and in such quantity.

This amount includes only direct contributions to campaigns, a restricted area under US campaign finance laws. It does not include unrestricted 'soft money' – which may be given without limit for 'party building'. In the 1996 elections, the two major parties raised more than $250 million in soft-money donations. Based on trends through mid-1997, says a spokesperson from Common Cause, a public interest group, soft–money donations could be triple that amount in the 1998 elections.[18]

> '[W]hile special interests have been lavishing soft money on both parties for more than a decade, some experts believe that it's now being used more blatantly to influence the parties and policy makers.
> 'Consider the beleaguered tobacco industry, which has long been a big soft-money donor to both parties. The Food and Drug Administration moved this year to regulate nicotine as a drug ... Not surprisingly, perhaps, the tobacco industry has been channeling record amounts of soft money to the Republicans. In fact, the three leading soft-money contributors to the Republican party in the first half of 1995 were Philip Morris Cos. Inc. ($729,749), RJR Nabisco Washington Inc. ($286,450) and Brown & Williamson Tobacco Corp. ($260,000). Philip Morris's contributions to both parties represent more than a sevenfold increase over its soft-money gifts of $99,000 to them during the same period in 1994.'[19]

Power over lawmaking – lobbying

From power over elections flows power over lawmaking, another key threat within the danger of corporate power-seeking. Perhaps nowhere does the raw power of corporate energy reveal itself more obviously than in this infamous industry – ongoing in every capital city in every major country in the world, bar none. In Washington, DC, the lobbying economy exceeds the government itself, and is growing geometrically. In the first half of 1996 alone, lobbyists spent $400 million to influence government.[20]

House Majority Leader Dick Armey (R-TX) recently released a study showing that the number of lobbyists per congressman has risen from 31 in 1964 to 125 in 1993. According to this study, the lobbying industry has grown significantly during the past few decades, from 16,271 individuals in 1964 to 67,062 today. According to the Armey report, the lobbying industry is the single largest private sector employer in Washington, DC, accounting for one-sixth of the private sector workforce and generating more than $8.4 billion in revenue every year. 'If the District of Columbia's lobbying industry were its own economy, it would be larger than the entire economies of 57 countries.' In addition, the report notes that 'Washington, DC has three times as many lawyers as the entire nation of Japan and twice as many law firms as churches.[21]

The problem of excessive business influence threatens to challenge the legitimacy of the entire democratic system. A good symbol of this is the success of the gambling industry, which spent $2 million in the 1993–1994 election cycle in influencing laws. 'In only five years, the gambling industry has bought its way into the ranks of the most formidable interest groups in American politics, spending huge sums to gain the kind of influence long wielded by big business, big labor, and organizations of doctors and lawyers.'[22] An even better symbol is the tobacco industry, which spent more than $20 million to lobby Congress in 1996 and has lobbyists registered under the Lobbying Disclosure Act.[23]

The very existence of a huge lobbying industry in a free market economy bears testimony of its effectiveness: given such a huge investment in manpower, there must be some return from it. Those who seek such proof need go no further than corporate welfare.

Power over government resources – 'corporate welfare'

Another mode of power sought by corporations is power over government resources – a form of entitlement otherwise known as corporate welfare. Wealth redistribution by government is increasingly important in contemporary society. It takes many forms: government franchises, contracts, subsidies, and the use of public resources. Corporations have effectively organised themselves to share in the 'government created' wealth. The most recent example is GazProm in Russia – a corporation that controls foreign exchange resources and thus exerts considerable power over the government. Certainly the *chaebol* in Korea have had that same character.

At the instigation of former Labor Secretary Robert Reich, both parties and think tanks representing the entire spectrum of Washington, DC, political thought (The Progressive Policy Institute on the left and The Cato Institute beyond the right in the libertarian sphere) discovered the extent of federal resources that go every year to large corporations without satisfying rudimentary tests of 'public interest'. The numbers are enormous, so large that it is clear beyond debate that meaningful reduction of the seemingly endemic 'deficit' can be achieved by eliminating a significant portion of 'corporate welfare'.

'The fact that major corporations don't have to pay their own way ...

deforms the entire political system. It is the availability of hundreds of billions of dollars in taxpayers' loot that has encouraged the creation of PACs and consequent flow of special interest money into politics. Companies such as Archer Daniels Midland simply buy access to politicians in both parties, access lacked by the people who pay the bill. As a result, the only way to "clean up" politics is to eliminate the benefits up for auction, not to rerig the political game.'[24]

An entire industry exists in Washington, DC, in order to participate in government business. Business effectively and persistently tries to persuade the legislative and administrative elements of government to create new rules, or to amend existing ones, so as to protect existing advantage or to create new ones. Both political parties have spoken disparagingly about 'corporate welfare' (predictably, neither has done very much about it). The Progressive Policy Institute, which was given pre-1992 election credit for defining the 'New Democratic' party, proposes reforms that would save $131.2 billion over five years[25] while The Cato Institute, a leading libertarian think tank, recommends 'getting businesses off the $80 billion annual dole'.[26]

In summary, more PACs means more lobbyists means more corporate welfare and further skewing away from the public interest in the allocation of public resources. This vicious circle is self-reinforcing. Because representatives in the United States and other countries receive funds from industries represented by the lobbyists, there is virtually no political libido for taking on corporate welfare, notwithstanding that it has been identified and publicised by all shades of political sentiment.

Power over 'independent' agencies and professions

Corporations are able to pay the highest prices for goods and services. The most prestigious professions depend on securing their share of corporate business in order to prosper. This leverage has been compounded in recent times by increasing percentages of the 'best talent' entering business related professions. As George Soros lamented in his aforementioned manifesto, 'What used to be professions have turned into businesses'.[27]

Harvard President Derek Bok bemoans this shift. 'Money also seems to have contributed to the most important set of career changes that took place in the past twenty-five years: the movement of tens of thousands of highly educated students away from teaching and government service into more highly paid jobs in private business and law practice. As we have observed, not only did the numbers of young people entering schools of law and business double and treble; their intellectual level also rose significantly. In 1950, law and MBA students were only of average ability; their test scores were far below those of classmates in medical schools, engineering or graduate (PhD) studies. By 1990, the situation had changed; business now rivalled that of applicants to any other graduate or professional school.'[28]

The movement away from the professions and toward businesses is driven in part by the simple fact that businesses yield more power than the professions. Proof of this fact can be seen in the stunning defeat of a sensible proposal for stock option accounting in the United States.

There has been great concern lately over the extraordinary increase in the level of compensation for the top executives of US corporations. The current levels of pay would have been unimaginable in earlier times in the United States – and they are utterly out of sync with the pay levels abroad today. Management pays itself without effective overview by anyone. In recent times, management has even managed to dominate the national accounting system with respect to a key aspect of its compensation: stock options. Thanks to the efforts of The Business Roundtable, the US Congress voted down a sensible measure that would have required corporations to record stock options as an expense. This particular situation – described at length in Chapter 4 – gives a rare insight into corporate power gone amok.

Power over the judicial process

The sheer talent available to business has had vast impact in its relationship with government. Consider those situations where the stakes are high enough to warrant litigation. The antitrust suit that the United States government began in the waning minutes of the Johnson Administration and waged against International Business Machine Company for almost 20 years until the presidency of Ronald Reagan demonstrated the capacity of a private company with unlimited resources to create a legal competency that ultimately triumphed over the government.

Turning to a more recent example, General Electric (GE) overwhelmed the government and secured a rare direction of acquittal in a case involving alleged price fixing in the diamond markets. GE has many redeeming characteristics (see box, 'General Electric Company', in Chapter 5). Nonetheless, it has engaged in enough allegedly criminal activity to warrant concern.

GE's general counsel, Benjamin W. Heineman, Jr., is generally considered to be one of the most talented and resourceful individuals to hold such a job in a private corporation. Thus in the diamond-fixing matter, 'The government prosecutors were outspent, they were outnumbered, and in the end … they were outlawyered. A de facto 25-lawyer powerhouse firm – composed of top litigators from 475-lawyer Winston & Strawn, 380-lawyer Arnold & Porter, and Columbus' 256-lawyer Porter, Wright, Morris & Arthur [the trial was located in Columbus], in addition to GE's Kindler – opened its doors for two months in Columbus [1994] and simply blew away the smaller, less cohesive, seemingly less prepared, and less experienced government team.[29]

There is perhaps no better example of the tired advice 'get yourself a good lawyer' than GE's success in this case. William W. Horne, writing in *The American Lawyer*, put it bluntly when he said 'the government's case may have been there, but [GE] took it away'. According to Horne, 'GE mustered an army, sparing no expense. While a guilty verdict probably would have resulted in a verdict of up to $10 million, the company spent "approximately $20 million" on outside costs, according to one knowledgeable source, and several million more on internal costs, to defend itself against the price-fixing charges and related civil claims.'[30]

The economics – spending $30 million to avoid paying $10 million – make no sense unless we consider the corporation's drive to exert power in every direction. With such dynamics at play, one might ask if the US government will ever have a chance of winning a legal proceeding against a major corporation on an issue that the company deems essential.

Another facet of the corporate power drive in the judicial arena can be seen in the art of settlement, epitomised by the recent effort of tobacco corporations to pay a fixed amount – $368.5 billion – for both past and prospective individual claims for tobacco-related damage. If there are greater costs (and there will be), society must bear them, wrongly or rightly. This is the epitome of the aforementioned 'externalisation', a problem this book will explore later in depth. For now, let it be sufficient to note that business will always push for a dollar limit in payment for its wrongs, while society will always incline towards separate consideration of each situation in its context.[31]

Early in the election year 1996, both houses of the 105th Congress passed over the veto of President Clinton The Private Securities Litigation Reform Act, a bill that limited the liability of accountants and others with respect to 'tort' liabilities that have plagued corporate America. While the bill did not set the absolute ceiling on liabilities desired by industry, it was, nonetheless, yet another important step in the ominous process in 'externalising' the liabilities of corporate functioning.

Now, midway through the 106th Congress, another step is underway: a new Product Liability Reform Act. This bill, 20 years in the making, would cut loose one of the few remaining ties holding corporations steadfastly to human values like a string to a kite. If this bill passes, as it probably will, who knows who will be damaged and how much by what corporate malfeasance? I shudder to think.

Granted, the abuses targeted by these two bills require attention. The United States has developed the special litigation techniques of 'derivative' and 'class' suits pursuant to which claims can be prosecuted – oftentimes on 'spec' by the attorneys – on behalf of a whole class of persons similarly affected. This has resulted in very large recoveries in many cases, and very large attorneys' fees, causing substantial grief to the corporate community. But in this case the cure is worse than the disease. Class–action suits provide the individual with his or her only effective means of redress against large and powerful interests that would otherwise be overwhelming.

CORPORATE DANGER NUMBER FOUR: THE QUEST FOR UNLIMITED LICENSE

What happens when basic ties of accountability are broken in a system? Jeffrey Johnson urges scientists to develop a 'language of structure' that will contain new vocabulary to describe constraints in complex systems. 'The central idea is that *relational structure constrains* the behavior of systems.'[32] Also, Jim Crutchfield notes that commonality between systems arises not only from similarity of shapes and behaviour but also from 'constraints in those shapes and in how behaviour can change as you vary a control parameter'. And so we must ask, what relational structure should 'constrain' or 'control' the behaviour of our corporations?

Just as the corporation externalises costs in its quest for unlimited power, so it externalises accountability in its quest for unlimited license. For example, the multinationals doing business in apartheid South Africa said they were not to blame for the country's tragic history, just as today the big oil companies like Royal Dutch Shell and Mobil defend their presence in Nigeria. They all say that they are part of the solution, not the problem. This assertion is highly questionable – as are the common sayings that corporations satisfy their 'debt to society' when they pay fines for criminal activity, and that the fines they pay can 'deter' future crime. If so, why is there so much corporate crime? (See Appendix to Chapter 3, 'The Line-Up: Corporate Crime'.)

License to break the law without paying (much)

We take comfort in the existence of corporate criminal laws, but this very term is a misnomer. If a corporation commits a crime, how can it be punished beyond the payment of a fee?

Instead, corporations have treasuries to be fined. Thus from the perspective of the corporation, the decision whether to obey the law is one of many that involve a cost/benefit calculation. Will the costs of disobedience discounted by the probability of being discovered, prosecuted, and fined equal the costs of compliance?

Because we see corporations as people or machines, and not for what they are, we tend to minimise the effects of corporate crime. If we think of corporations as people, we might think they will somehow feel guilty. And if we think of them as machines, we might think they will break down, as crime does not pay. We fail to recognise that *corporations do not respond to incentives and penalties applicable to human beings.*

Research by Melissa S. Baucus and David A. Baucus of Utah State University shows that 'penalties for illegality, including lower financial performance, do not prevent subsequent violations in part because managers do not receive clear, direct feedback on the magnitude of penalties for wrongdoing. Illegality has a prolonged or delayed impact … on firms' financial performance, so managers may not experience immediate feedback comparable to feeling the burn of a hot stove.'[33]

Obeying the law is the duty of every citizen, but corporations are not like other citizens. Indeed, one might say they are not 'citizens' at all – despite attempts to act like good ones. As Thomas Jefferson once observed, 'Merchants have no country. The mere spot they stand on does not constitute so strong an attachment as that from which they draw their gains.' How true this is of today's large multinational corporations!

When the market place overwhelmingly approves and supports companies whose activities have been repeatedly branded as 'criminal', it seems clear that government does not have any effective means of inhibiting what it characterises as unacceptable corporate conduct.[34] This is the clearest expression of the inability of a human-based modality – criminalisation of unacceptable conduct – to have a real impact on the corporate system.

This was brought home to me personally in 1981 in hearings before the late Senator 'Scoop' Jackson for Senate confirmation of my nomination as Director of the United States Synthetic Fuels Corporation (Synfuels). One of the provisions of the enabling law made it a crime for the corporation to enter into any field of business other than as specifically prescribed by the statute (*ultra vires* in its common law nomenclature). I asked Senator Jackson what Congress would do if Synfuels inadvertently did enter into a forbidden area. Was I, as a director, going to go to jail? Jackson didn't even pause. 'No', he said. 'We just want to get your attention.'

To date, the problem of corporate crime has been played out as a kind of grand hide and seek, with management as the hiders and government as the seekers. Where have the owners been?

One of the competitive attractions of conducting business through corporate form is that liability for the venture's costs is limited to the amount of the investment. This 'limited liability' notion appears to excuse shareholders from further responsibility respecting corporate property. At this juncture, it might be useful to cite Adolf A. Berle's well-known maxim: 'When an individual owns a horse, you have to feed it, clean up after it, and when it dies, you have to bury it … A corporation has none of those responsibilities.'

Yet even the most devout free market proponent would agree that there are activities that corporations should undertake notwithstanding their irrelevance to profit maximisation. For example, most would agree that corporations should obey the law. The public demands and deserves no less. Much damage has been caused consumers – whether from silicone or tobacco – by the failure of companies to disclose publicly what they themselves know about the impact of their products on society. After the defective product has been used by a generation of consumers, the problems of legal liability make it impossible to impose retroactive disclosure requirements. Why shouldn't the directors of a company take a personal responsibility for ensuring that the public learn promptly all that is known about the risks of a product? This full and prompt disclosure might not help marketing in the short run, which is why it isn't presently the practice; but it is essential to mitigate damages to consumers.

Plainly, corporations must exist in a civil society where the rules are made by governments. A decent relationship with government is essential for the operation of business. Yes, as they say, rules are made to be broken, and every law has a loophole. But the corporation itself will need to exercise restraint in this regard, refraining from undue interference in lawmaking. Such restraint can help restore accountability to the corporation – an important accomplishment, as we shall see in later chapters.

SUMMARY AND CONCLUSION

Corporations that attempt to lock in immortality through *mortmain* techniques for perpetual life may succeed for a time. In the long run, however, like the mechanical bird, they come to an ungracious end. Because corporate change has been gradual and its consequences largely unanticipated and unintended, no one seems to have noticed the absence of owner accountability. As with the nightingale in Andersen's tale, one must ask, 'Where is it?' Missing also is a measurement of the toll exacted by enjoyment of property without responsibility.

The problems of the modern corporation will not solve themselves through an efficient market, a bell curve, or a matrix. These tools, to cite physicist John Wheeler again, are 'beautiful and necessary to understand our world'. They are not, however, the whole story – no more than the mechanical bird that sang so enchantingly for the emperor.

Yes, it is true that the problems we have described are mechanistic and repetitious. Yet they are being perpetuated by obviously dynamic creatures – creatures we cannot ever 'fix' and with which we must learn to live – but how?

First and foremost, we must expand our language, and hence our vision. In the following chapter, we will press at the limits of corporate wisdom, examining common beliefs in the harsh light of reality.

In later chapters, we will begin our study of corporations as complex adaptive systems, and explore how the involved owner can help 'restore' the corporation to a more living paradigm by reconciling the corporation's two natures – its superimposed mechanistic nature, born of its own instinct for self-perpetuation, and its underlying dynamic nature, born of an innate responsiveness to human needs.

4

We are in denial about the corporate problem. Seven panaceas prevent us from finding the solution to the problems inherent in the modern corporation: the CEO 'philosopher-king', corporate chartering, independent directors, well-structured boards, independent experts, the free press, and multiple external constraints. Taken separately, each of these can lull us into dangerous complacency. Taken together — along with the actions of independent, informed, motivated, and empowered shareholders — these elements are transformed from panaceas to solutions.

4

The Limits of Conventional Corporate Wisdom – and How to Surpass Them

> *And he summoned his chamberlain, who was so grand that if any-*
> *one of lower rank dared speak to him or ask about something, he*
> *would only say, 'P!' And that doesn't mean anything at all.*[1]

What is healthy corporate governance? Expanding on the opening lines of *Corporate Governance*, I would define it as 'the relationship among various participants in determining the direction and performance of corporations consistent with the public good'.

This last phrase makes a point that seems lost on many of us in the waning years of the 20th century: The key participants in corporations – directors, managements (and other employees), and shareholders – are answerable not only to each other, but to all other participants, such as customers, suppliers, and communities. Moreover, they are ultimately answerable to the public in general. After all, in any free economy, it is the people who give corporations the right to exist, and it is ultimately the people whom corporations must serve.

A certain mayor of New York City, Ed Koch by name, became legendary in his walks about the city, asking the men and women in the street 'How'm I doin'?' This question echoes – and is echoed by – democratic leaders in every major city from Abidjan to Zurich today. In modern political life – even in countries not considered to be pure democracies –

government with the consent of the governed has become a given. Not so in modern corporate life.

Can you imagine the CEOs of a typical large publicly held corporation doing what Mayor Koch did? If such an unlikely inquiry ever did take place, conventional wisdom would answer as follows:

> 'Keep up the good work. You have increased sales and profitability of the corporation, keeping the government from interfering. And you have stayed out of trouble (except for a few run-ins with the federal government – but you paid the fines, so who's remembering?). As for accountability, you get high marks. Your stockholders have elected an independent board of directors to monitor your performance, and under the board's watchful eye, you have done well. Your salary is in the hundreds of millions, but you deserve every penny. The corporation's stock price went up during your tenure, and you benefited – but so did shareholders. All is well.'

Unconventional wisdom, however, would say something else entirely.

> 'The question is not how you are doing, but how the corporate system that employs you is doing. And that system needs an overhaul. Yes, the company you serve has grown bigger, but this is due more to the unconscious workings of the corporate system than to any human genius. As for profits, you need not gloat. You have made them at the expense of the general public, by externalizing your costs. (No wonder our taxes are so high!) You also made some of them through illegal acts that made a lot of money and cost very little. What malfeasance will be next? If crime pays, you can bet it will persist. Your corporate elections are a sham, and your salary a scandal. High stock prices are well and good, but how long will they last? We need a new means to build long-term wealth through greater accountability.'

THE LANGUAGE OF DENIAL

Those who belong to the school of conventional wisdom are suffering from denial – defined by *The New Shorter Oxford Dictionary* (1993) as 'a refusal to acknowledge the existence or reality of a thing'. This refusal is understandable. Modern corporate reality is difficult and painful to accept.

The hard reality is that the corporation is something we citizens and our government cannot easily control. As discussed in Chapters 2 and 3, the corporation is a system for transferring risk from owners to others. Left to its own devices, this system will seek unlimited life, size, power, and license for itself. This is in a sense the corporation's 'basic program'. That is the bad news.

The good news is that corporations are not merely systems. As we will see in Chapter 5, they are complex adaptive systems. This means that they do not operate in linear fashion, but are subject to dynamic change. They possess various traits, including multiplicity, spontaneity, accommodation, adaptation, transcendence, and metamorphosis. These traits can mitigate and even nullify the dangers inherent in the corporate system, given the right conditions. In Chapter 6, we will attempt to identify these 'right conditions' and see how they work using the science of computer modelling.

In the present chapter, we will clear a path for this scientific effort by dispensing with its nemesis – conventional wisdom and the language of denial. This task will not make us many friends. None of the major participants in corporate life – not directors, not managements or employees, not shareholders – wants to see the corporation as a system. Behind this denial there is fear – justifiable fear of the growing lack of accountability in our corporations.

The split between ownership and management that troubled Adam Smith over two centuries ago has become a gulf in our century. This was the central thesis of *The Modern Corporation and Private Property*, by Adolf Berle and Gardiner Means, published in 1932.

Ever since Berle and Means proclaimed the end of ownership control (and responsibility), the various participants in corporations have been scrambling to articulate a credible theory of governance while at the same time turning a blind eye to the way corporations actually behave. We all agree that large corporations should be accountable to the general public, and we proffer all manner of ingenious formulations for protecting the public interest. Ultimately, however, these protections have failed us.

Ralph Nader and Mark Green have waved the 'red flag' in this regard: 'We must redesign the law to keep up with the economic and politic evolution of giant corporations, which are tantamount to private governments. One definition of "government" would be "an entity that can tax, coerce, or even take life"... [Corporations] spend decisive amount in elections, determine which towns thrive and which gather cobwebs, corrupt or help overthrow foreign governments, develop technology that takes lives or saves

lives … The economic government is largely unaccountable to its constituencies – shareholders, workers, consumers, local communities, taxpayers,
small businesses, and future generations.'[2]

   Although this language is confrontational – even belligerent – it is one of
the most realistic descriptions I have ever seen of the problems we face.
Unfortunately, however, Nader and Green were not quite as adept in forming a solution. Their answer to the corporation's lack of accountability was
more government intervention. As most business executives know, the big
government approach rarely works and can be counterproductive.

THE SEVEN PANACEAS

The present chapter will describe the seven most prominent theories of corporate accountability that have been advanced in the past two centuries,
arguing that each of them, *taken alone*, is more panacea than true cure. That
is, each of these notions has merit if taken as part of a greater whole. And
prominent defenders of these ideas do see them in this light. But too often
the mere presence of *one* of these deterrents to bad behaviour brings a false –
and dangerous – sense of comfort.

Panacea one: the CEO philosopher-king

This is perhaps humankind's oldest and most deeply ingrained notion of
corporate accountability. Historian James Willard Hurst describes it elo-
quently in his magisterial study of American corporations from Colonial
days to the year 1970. 'The notion seemed to be that big-company management should play a legislative role, seeking a fair apportionment of benefits
and burden among all sectors of the community affected by the corporation's activity … How corporate management would provide a comparable
arena was left undefined, though there was considerable implication that no
competition of interests was necessary where the detached good will of
managerial philosopher kings would put all relevant values in proper array.'[3]

   Hurst describes this theory in the past tense, speaking only of America.
He might well have put it in the future tense and spoken of the world at
large, as the notion of the corporate *philosopher-king* persists to this day around
the globe. CEOs today exercise near-monarchic powers. With our acquies-

cence, they are free to advance their own personal interest in compensation – even to the point of harming the interests of the general public, not to mention corporate shareholders. We will return to this point at the end of this chapter when we look at the story of the incredible disappearing stock options.

Panacea two: chartering

Another panacea says that if a state and/or federal *charter* sets proper limits, then the corporation can serve the common good. The facts prove otherwise. Hurst shows that every generation of Americans has tried to use these methods without success. As I have explored extensively in my other writings (for example, in *Corporate Governance*), chartering jurisdictions merely 'race to the bottom' as they lower standards of public accountability to attract corporations. Running this race has weakened the power of charters to curb corporate behaviour.

Further enfeebling the effectiveness of charters has been the growth of the multinational corporation, which by definition has divisions or subsidiaries operating in multiple jurisdictions. If a multinational corporation wants to engage in a behaviour that is not legally permitted in one jurisdiction, it can simply shift it to a division incorporated in a jurisdiction where the behaviour is allowed.

Panacea three: independent directors

Yet another common theory – one that has come into prominence only in the past three decades – is the notion that controls can come from *independent directors* nominated by independent committees and elected by shareholders. Certainly directors without business ties to a company are more independent than those with such ties.[4] Yet true independence – as well as true nominations and elections – remains elusive. How can an individual selected for a well-paying and prestigious job, notwithstanding his or her compliance with the most exhaustive legal criteria of 'independence', be expected to stand in judgment of those who accorded him this favour in the interest of an amorphous group of owners? Only men and women of the highest character can do this, but the best solutions cannot depend on character alone.

The available guides to the essential role of 'independent' directors – whether it be The Cadbury Report in the United Kingdom, its close derivatives in Australia, Canada, New Zealand, and South Africa, or the current iterations of the Council of Institutional Investors in Washington, DC – contribute much to corporate governance, but their key terms gloss over the impertinence of reality. Directors are not 'nominated', they are selected by the incumbent directors (however independent) and the chief executive officer. Shareholders do not 'vote', whether or not they mark a slate card; only those named on the company proxy will be elected.

Ultimately, independence is a matter of personal character; it is not susceptible to formulaic prescription. I have worked with at least one individual – Dwight Allison in the US – whose integrity is so intense as to be luminous. In many other cases, the search for such a director requires that we be modern-day Diogenes, lamp in hand. This is not acceptable. We cannot have a system that depends on the luck of stumbling across an occasional honest man.

Panacea four: well-structured boards

One level of abstraction up from directors, *well-structured boards* also rank high as a favoured solution to governance problems. This is the 'party line' of The Business Roundtable's *Corporate Governance and American Competitiveness* (March 1980): 'The American system of corporate governance works well, it has excellent and proven self-corrective mechanisms. It is hoped this document has demonstrated the ways in which boards of directors work and are accountable. We also hope that this statement may provide directors with additional ideas for improving the structure, operations, and accountability of the boards on which they serve.'

All is for the best in this best of all possible worlds; trust us. Alas, this notion too proves questionable. If we cannot count on all our independent directors to be truly independent, then no amount or quality of structure can change this fact.

This statement may seem dire to readers in countries such as the UK, where the role of the chairman and the CEO are split, or in Germany, where a two-tier board widens the scope of oversight. These practices can greatly increase the independence of boards and improve their structure. Yet *even corporations with perfectly independent directors and perfectly structured boards* can remain insensitive to the needs of the public. To ensure such sensitivity, as we shall see, an additional agent is needed: the active shareholder.

Panacea five: independent experts

Another popular view holds that corporations need only the proper *'independent experts'* to review and bless the balancing of public and private interests. This solution has been proffered by such respected (you guessed it) experts as guru Peter Drucker, lawyer Marty Lipton of Wachtell Lipton in New York, and former sole trustee of the New York State Fund, Ned Regan. The experience with 'experts', however is disheartening. The tendency to generate opinions satisfactory to present and prospective customers is strong. 'Fairness' opinions – whether of the prospective value of Time Warner stock, or in the leveraged buyouts that were the source of the Kluge, Heyman, and many other fortunes – have turned out to be wrong, not by percentages but by orders of magnitude.

Panacea six: the free press

Yet another view, also widely held, sees the *free press* as the ultimate check on corporate actions. The basic story goes as follows: the truth shall set you free; journalists tell the truth and publishers publish it; therefore, a free press means freedom from oppression. Yet we must ask ourselves just exactly how free publishers are to publish all the news that is fit to print, when such a large percentage of their revenues derive from advertising.

This is a serious problem. As Morton Mintz and Jerry Cohen observed in their great American critique, *Power, Inc.*: 'If the press won't oversee the overseers, who will?'[5] (See box.)

THE PHONEY FREEDOM OF THE PRESS

An effective system of governance in the US depends on the continued existence of a free and energetic press. But we must recognise that the continued effectiveness of the press rests on slender supports. There is always the problem of the power of advertisers and the potential for censorship. The principal national television net-

---

works are owned by major conglomerates: Westinghouse has recently acquired CBS, Disney owns ABC, and GE owns NBC. Major business magazines (with the exception of *Forbes,* which has never published an article offensive to advertisers) are also part of publicly owned companies – Time Warner owns *Fortune* and McGraw-Hill owns *Business Week.*

For a long time, the traditional family owners of several of the nation's leading newspapers have perpetuated their control (and presumably, thereby, editorial integrity) of the publicly owned enterprise through two classes of stock – the one owned by the family having multiple votes and effective control. By and large, the families have kept faith with the public. This includes the Taylor family and the *Boston Globe,* the Grahams and the *Washington Post,* the Sulzbergers and the *New York Times,* and the Chandlers and the *Los Angeles Times.* All of these families have shown a strong and admirable independent streak. Yet families are mortal, and no one has yet devised a foolproof scheme for generational succession.

Unlike many European countries, the US has never had a tradition of substantial public involvement in communications. We have no BBC with an express charter to define and broadcast the 'public interest'. Our public television and public radio are much admired, but they operate on the fringes of American communication – fringes that have been getting shorter with each new round of congressional budget-cutting. Irrespective of ownership, the fundamental concern is simply this: How can one serve two conflicting masters – profit maximisation and news integrity – when they are so often incompatible?

Frank Rich, writing in the *New York Times,* observes, 'The press isn't perfect, but if anyone doubts that its freedom is essential to democracy, the cowering of ABC and CBS before Big Tobacco is a perfect illustration. If bottomless corporate coffers can … scare off news organisations as huge as CBS, who will defend the public interest?'[6]

The press clearly enjoys First Amendment protection against encroachment by government in its freedoms. No comparable protection is extended to the general public against abridgement of the 'freedom of the press' by corporate owners. This is not an indictment of the corporate owners of US communications companies; it is rather a reflection that a 'free press' and long-term profit maximisation appear to be inconsistent imperatives to inform management. It is difficult to imagine that NBC would initiate 'investigative reporting' of its corporate parent, GE; nor does it seem likely that CBS will sic '60 Minutes' on to the all-too-prevalent vicissitudes of Westinghouse.

Time, Inc. attempted to ensure editorial independence by maintaining a specific 'freedom of the press' governance structure that appears to have survived its merger with Warner. This is certainly a step in the right direction.

Ultimately, there is conundrum. Shareholders expect Disney, GE, McGraw-Hill, Time Warner, and Westinghouse to maximise long-term profits. This is the imperative to which American management has so successfully addressed itself in recent years. On the other hand, the continued viability of a society in which business influence is so strong depends on the functioning of a free press.

Panacea seven: multiple external constraints

Finally, there is the view that corporations are subject to *multiple constraints*. This idea was advanced (but only tentatively) by noted corporate governance attorney and scholar Ira M. Millstein over 15 years ago. He described not only state and federal chartering, but also the *economic* constraints of competition and law, the impact of the *tax and regulatory schemes*, and the constraining influence of *social values* on corporate decision making.[7] He expressed hope – but by no means certainty – that this ensemble could prevent 'unlimited and unconstrained' corporate power.[8] This is certainly the best general model advanced to date, but it still falls short of a full solution.

I see a similar limitation in the views of Carl Kaysen, editor of *The American Corporation Today: Examining the Questions of Power and Efficiency at the Century's End*.[9] He says that to ensure competitiveness and fairness, we cannot rely on the workings of the marketplace, but must involve government – notwithstanding its current unfashionableness: 'Both the efficiency and the equity questions call for some response beyond reliance on the market. How much the political process will produce appropriate response, how much managerial initiatives will try to anticipate such responses and successfully shape them in ways more acceptable to business is impossible to predict ... I project into the future a history in which pressures from the side of political institutions as well as the market have been an indispensable element in shaping the evolution of corporate structure and behaviour and moving it in a more socially desirable direction.'[10] A true statement, but far from complete.

Taken *together*, these seven concepts can go a long way in improving the governance of corporations. Each can be a valuable palliative – if not an ultimate cure. Taken individually, however, each is subject to generating blind faith – and a blindness to the real impact of events. The following example should illustrate this point.

THE BUSINESS ROUNDTABLE, STEALTH COMPENSATION, AND THE POWER OF THE 'GOVERNANCE' MYTH

Perhaps no phenomenon illustrates the tenacity of the first and foremost panacea – the CEO philosopher-king – better than the meteoric rise of The Business Roundtable (BRT), an organisation representing the 200 or so largest US companies.

Until the arrival of the BRT, large US corporations tried but failed to exert power over their rulemakers. Big business – despite the public fears of 'trusts' or 'monopolies' – was a relatively clumsy, uncomfortable, and ineffective element in American politics during the pre-BRT years. Whether it was General Motors' getting caught in the 1960s hiring a private detective to deal with the nuisance of Ralph Nader, or a Big-Business-backed 'real Republican' President Richard Nixon going off the gold standard, calling himself a 'Keynesian', and invoking wage and price controls in his first term, evidence of *faux pas* and frustrations abounded.

In the mid-1970s, however, this maladroitness changed to machination – and power, with the birth of the BRT as a new kind of organisation. Only CEOs could participate; deputies were not acceptable at meetings or in committee work. The organisation would have small presence in Washington. Key staff would be provided by the CEO, who would chair approved projects.

It was the perfect platform for the philosopher-king panacea – and for touting the effectiveness of charters, directors, boards, experts, the press, and the magic mix of economic, legal, and social constraints. This was image-making at its best, with tremendous political consequences. Kim McQuaid said it well in *Big Business and Presidential Power: From FDR to Reagan:* 'With the birth of the Roundtable, big business in America may at last be said to have come of political age.'[11]

The BRT's early years

One of the first major issues tackled by the BRT was the hostile takeover phenomenon of the 1980s. It was the era of the so-called 'raiders' like T. Boone Pickens and 'arbs' (*arbitrageurs*) like Ivan Boesky. No company was immune – not even mega-oil companies like Gulf Oil or Phillips Petroleum, Pickens' ambitious targets – not to mention Koito Manufacturing Company, an auto parts supplier to Toyota in Japan. Unable to persuade Congress to curb hostile takeovers, the BRT devised an ambitious program to protect its members through 'control over the processes of corporate governance'.[12]

Throughout its brief history, BRT has enjoyed the involvement of some of the ablest leaders in the country. Bruce Atwater, former CEO of General Mills, chaired the group's task force on corporate governance and helped shape the nation's definition of this term. When one takes into account the true 'cost' of the time of CEOs, general counsels, and other top staffing the emergence of the BRT represents a huge commitment of resources by Corporate America to the political arena. It also means that some of the best talent in the country has been directly committed to achieving 'big business' government agenda.

This involvement has been largely successful – for the corporations of America and the people who head them that is, not for the general public. There is a fine line between the interests of the corporation and those of its top executives. By contrast, the public interest and a corporation's interest often diverge, despite Charles Wilson's famous words about the good of GM and the country.[13]

Stealth compensation

The divergence of public and corporate interests can been seen clearly when we consider how easily the CEOs of America's largest companies were able to continue paying themselves with a type of wealth that has zero impact on the income statement.

A very large part of the pay of top executives derives from the grant and exercise of stock options – the preponderance of the hundreds of millions of dollars paid to CEOs like American Surgical's Leon Hirsch, Coca-Cola's late, great Roberto Goizueta and Disney's Michael Eisner came from option profits. Reflecting a wave of public concern over CEO compensation, the Financial Accounting Standards Board (FASB) revived its dormant recommendation that corporations record the 'fair value' of the option and charge them against earnings (like other compensation expenses) at the time of grant. By not making such a charge, said FASB and other critics, CEOs were in effect paying themselves 'stealth compensation'.

Managements opposed the FASB's suggestion with a ferocity never before unleashed with regard to any public proposal. The Roundtable developed a comprehensive and successful strategy to deal with this threat to its members' wallets. In early 1992, John Reed, chairman of Citicorp, serving as chairman of the BRT's accounting principles task force, learned about the stock option accounting plan in a meeting with FASB executives. Then, joined by Atwater and several other BRT members, he rallied BRT members to take suitable steps to deal with the problem. In a letter to all BRT members dated 23 June 1992, written on the organisation's letterhead, Reed wrote:

> 'We need help from BRT CEOs in the following areas:
> 1 Communication with and education of your public accountants.
> 2 Communication with and education of your compensation consultants.
> 3 Communication with FASB now, before their views become solidified.
>   We believe these contacts would be most effective if made by CEOs.'[14]

Behind this seemingly innocuous plea for 'education' lay a campaign of suppression. Reed was asking his fellow CEOs to prevent key advisors from expressing their honest views of the appropriate accounting treatment for stock options. As journalist Alison Leigh Cowan reported in the *New York Times*: 'Corporate America is quietly seeking to muzzle the compensation consultants who routinely provide information about executive pay to the business press or to regulators ... the pressure tactics against the half-dozen or so firms that routinely provide this information seem to be working ... Some [BRT] members who are clients of Towers Perrin led that firm to conclude that it was not in its best interest to continue helping the *Wall Street Journal* prepare the executive pay survey it publishes each spring.'[15]

In fairness to the consulting profession, the BRT's efforts were not entirely effective. On 31 March, Cowan reports, four consulting firms and one accounting firm received a technical request from the FASB asking them to demonstrate how they would value five types of stock options. When all five complied, several chief executives 'said they felt betrayed by the consultants' participation in a demonstration that undermined the executives' contention that values cannot be easily placed on options'.[16]

That an 'education' program by the leaders of the nation's largest corporations would have impact goes without saying. It is a fact of life that large customers will seek accommodation from their service providers. What is of ultimate significance in this unhappy story is the public humiliation of an institution that Americans have traditionally respected for its independence.

The bullying was so unignorable as to be the subject of a speech by Walter P. Schuetze, then Chief Accountant of the SEC, to the American Institute of Certified Public Accountants.[17] In concluding his speech, Schuetze asked a critical question: 'If public companies are pressuring their outside auditors and the Accounting Standards Executive Committee of the AICPA, to take particular positions on financial accounting and reporting issues, and outside auditors are subordinating their views to their clients' views, can the outside auditor community continue to claim to be independent?'[18]

By the time that there was general recognition that the professional community had capitulated on this issue, the BRT had successfully disappeared from the scene. Bruce Atwater declined the invitation of the Senate Securities Subcommittee to testify at its hearings, and Senator Bill Bradley (D–NJ) conspicuously did not mention the BRT in his speech listing supporters for the Sense of the Senate Resolution of 3 May 1994, that defeated the measure so overwhelmingly. The organisation is not mentioned in articles describing FASB's withdrawal of its proposal in mid-1995.[19]

Substituted for the Roundtable CEOs were venture capitalists, CEOs of growth companies and various Washington lobbying organisations, some of which, like the Coalition for American Equity Expansion, had been cobbled together for this particular project. These proponents were able to change the issue from one of the very large increase in total compensation of large-firm CEOs to the 'motherhood' issues of enabling new businesses to be successful and jobs to be created. The philosopher-kings were not only suppressing the truth, they were manufacturing myths.

Warren Buffet, the premier American investor of the age and a dedicated student of accounting, submitted testimony for the Senate hearings that exposed stealth compensation as a campaign of disinformation. He attacked the notion, advanced by the BRT and its proxy army, that new companies would find new capital too expensive if they had to charge its value against earnings:

> 'In effect, the people making this argument want managers at those companies to tell their employees that the options given them are immensely valuable while they simultaneously tell the owners of the corporation that the options are cost-free. This financial schizophrenia, so it is argued, fosters the national interest, in that it aids entrepreneurs and the start-up companies we need to reinvigorate the economy. Let me point out the absurdities to which that line of thought leads. For example, it is also in the national interest that American industry spend significant sums on

research and development. To encourage business to increase such spend-
ing, we might allow these costs, too, to be recorded only in the footnotes
so that they do not reduce reported earnings. In other words, once you
adopt the idea of pursuing social goals by mandating bizarre accounting,
the possibilities are endless.'[20]

The BRT successfully defined the terms of discussion so as to avoid consideration of the reality that options are preponderantly a question of CEO
and top executive compensation. Institutional Shareholder Services (ISS)
found that, in 1992, the top 15 individuals in each company received 97%
of the stock options issued to all employees. *Business Week* wrote for all to
read that 'the 200 largest corporations set aside nearly 10% of their stock for
top executives', adding that 'in almost all cases, moreover, it's the superstar
CEO who takes the lion's share of these stock rewards'.[21]

Warren Buffett's last word to Senator Chris Dodd (D-CT), then Chairman of the Securities Subcommittee of the Senate Committee on Banking,
is a refreshing reminder that what was at stake was not a matter of principle,
but a matter of power (see box).

STOCK OPTIONS AND THE 'FIFTH LEG'

The most egregious example of let's-not-face-up-to-reality behavior by executives
and accountants has occurred in the world of stock options. The lack of logic is not
accidental: For decades, much of the business world has waged war against accounting rulemakers, trying to keep the costs of stock options from being reflected in the
profits of the corporations that issue them.

Typically, executives have argued that options are hard to value and that therefore their costs should be ignored. At other times managers have said that assigning a
cost to options would injure small start-up businesses. Some of them have even sol-
emnly declared that 'out-of-the-money' options (those with an exercise price equal
to or above the current market price) have no value when they are issued ...

It seems to me that the realities of stock options can be summarised quite simply:
If options aren't a form of compensation, what are they? If compensation isn't an
expense, what is it? And, if expenses shouldn't go into the calculation of earnings,
where in the world should they go? ...

Managers thinking about accounting issues should never forget one of Abraham
Lincoln's favorite riddles: 'How many legs does a dog have if you call his tail a leg?'

The answer: 'Four, because calling a tail a leg does not make it a leg'. It behooves managers to remember that Abe's right even if an auditor is willing to certify that the tail is a leg.

Warren Buffet, in a letter dated 18 October 1993, included with records of hearings before the Securities Subcommittee of the Senate Committee on Banking, 21 October 1993.

FROM MYTH TO REALITY

Despite wise words from Buffett and others, 'stealth compensation' won. In sporting terms, this was a game where the players disagreed with the referees, beat them up severely, and returned to play the game according to their own rules. Thanks in part to the philosopher-king and other panaceas of governance, the leaders of the BRT were able to accomplish this without leaving so much as a DNA strand of evidence behind.

This story illustrates many discouraging truths: the inability of the large accounting firms to maintain independence, the willingness of virtually the entire US Senate to opt for politics over principles, and the fragility of the self-regulatory organisations whose expertise and independence are so essential to a workable system of corporate governance – truths that continue to this day.[22] Most of all, however, the success of stealth compensation illustrates the abiding power of the CEO philosopher-king and other panaceas to cover up the need for true accountability in the corporate system.

Even today prominent voices call out for change in this regard, but to no avail. John McCain (R-AZ) and Carl Levin (D-MI) have cosponsored a bill in the 105th Congress that would limit tax deductions for options to the amount that companies report as expenses. Right now, virtually no companies report options as expenses, and virtually all of them take tax deductions for paying them. The hypocrisy is mind-boggling.

In a mid-1997 column in the *Wall Street Journal*, Roger Lowenstein asks Corporate America to 'come clean' on company stock options. His concluding line says it all: 'To argue that telling the truth risks a bad result is contemptible.'[23]

REAL ACCOUNTABILITY

For a system of 'real' accountability, corporations must be accountable to a party who is sufficiently independent, informed, motivated, and empowered to build long-term value. The question is, which of the three main participants in the corporation – directors, management (and other employees), and shareholders – fulfils these four requirements. Under the current system, each party brings potential conflicts and limitations. Of the three, only the shareholder has the potential for a future role that has all four characteristics (see Chart 4.1).

Chart 4.1

Are they now:	Independent	Informed	Motivated	Empowered
Directors*	no	no	no	no
Management	no	yes	no	yes
Shareholders	no	no	no	no
Can they be:	Independent	Informed	Motivated	Empowered
Directors*	no	no	no	no
Management	no	yes	no	yes
Shareholders	yes	yes	yes	yes

*Unless they are major equity holders, in which case they belong in the shareholder category.

Who is truly independent?

Independence means independence *from* management, so clearly management does not fulfil the independence requirement. Therefore, it will not be considered in the running for governance leadership and will not be discussed in the three categories below. Nor do employees – by definition employed by management – fill this bill. Finally, directors, whose nomination is still approved by management, are not truly independent on the whole.

Clearly the top contender for independence is the shareholder, but there are problems here. Individual shareholders are not organised, and institutional shareholders, as presently constituted, are beset with conflicts of interest. The name of J.P. Morgan conjures up a trust department with a fiduciary relationship to the pension plan beneficiaries of portfolio companies while at the same time having commercial and investment banking relationships with the company itself. This is not a situation in which the 'exclusive' benefit rule under the Employee Retirement Income Security Act of 1974 is apt to be observed![24]

Moreover, money managers who invest for public pension funds (and thus ultimately the funds themselves) are positively bedevilled with conflicts of interest via the 'pay to play' scenario. As *Wall Street Journal* reporter Charles Gasparino cogently explains, 'At issue is the messy business of money managers giving campaign contributions to elected politicians who run vast public pension funds – and have the power to hand lucrative accounts to the same money managers.'[25]

Who is truly informed?

Obviously managers (and, collectively, employees) are the most informed party when it comes to a particular corporation. Directors and institutional investors suffer from a lack of information. In the case of directors, lack of independence impedes the quest for information. Feeling beholden to the CEO who in effect appointed them, few directors have the courage to look behind the official numbers.

Shareholders have two strikes against them when it comes to information. A substantial portion of the investment by institutions in a particular company arises because of the use of 'indexing' or other market-averaging modes of investments. Buy and sell decisions are not in these cases occasioned by information about a particular company. Furthermore, many large institutions are reluctant to acquire non-public information about portfolio companies because they are afraid they might violate laws restricting transferability of non-public information.

This problem can be solved. Shareholders can become informed. Practical working rules could be developed that would encourage owners to become informed without at the same time giving them trading advantage in the market place. In aid of this, my associates and I were able to require Exxon to include in its 1992 proxy a resolution (see box) that would have permitted the organisation of shareholder groups with limited financial backing from the company.

THE EXXON PROPOSAL★

Resolved: to adopt the following new by-law.

Article IIIA
Committee of Shareholder Representatives

1   The corporation shall have a committee of shareholder representatives consisting
    of three members. The committee shall review the management of the business
    and affairs of the corporation by the board of directors and shall advise the board
    of its views and the views of shareholders which are expressed to the committee.
    The committee may, at the expense of the corporation, engage expert assistance
    and incur other expenses in a reasonable amount not to exceed in any fiscal year
    $.01 multiplied by the number of common shares outstanding at the beginning of
    the year. The committee shall be given the opportunity to have included in the
    corporation's proxy statement used in its annual election of directors a report of
    not more than 2500 words on the committee's activities during the year, its evalu-
    ation of the management of the corporation by the directors, and its recommen-
    dations on any matters proposed for action by shareholders.

2   The members of the committee shall be elected by the shareholders by plurality
    vote at their annual meeting. Elections of members shall be conducted in the
    same manner as elections of directors. Each member shall be paid a fee equal to
    half the average fee paid to nonemployee directors, shall be reimbursed for rea-
    sonable travel and other out-of-pocket expenses incurred in serving as a member,
    and shall be entitled to indemnification and advancement of expenses as would a
    director.

3   The corporation shall include in its proxy materials used in the election of direc-
    tors nominations of and nominating statements for members of the committee
    submitted by any shareholder or group of shareholders (other than a fiduciary
    appointed by or under authority of the directors) which has owned beneficially,
    within the meaning of section 13(d) of the Securities Exchange Act of 1934, at
    least $10 million in market value of common stock of the corporation continu-
    ously for the three-year period prior to the nomination. Nominations must be
    received by the corporation not less than 90 nor more than 180 days before the
    annual meeting of shareholders. The corporation's proxy materials shall include
    biographical and other information regarding the nominee required to be in-
    cluded for nominees for director and shall also include a nominating statement of

> not more than 500 words submitted at the time of nomination by the nominating shareholder or group of shareholders.
>
> 4   Nothing herein shall restrict the power of the directors to manage the business and affairs of the corporation.
>
> 5   This Article IIIA shall not be altered or repealed without approval of shareholders.
>
> *Accompanying statement*
>
> The proposed by-law would establish a three-member committee of shareholder representatives which would review and oversee the actions of the board of directors in managing the business and affairs of Exxon. We believe such a committee could be an effective mechanism for shareholders to communicate their views to the board and would serve a useful advisory function at relatively little cost.
>
> *Proposed by Robert A.G. Monks at the company's 1992 annual meeting.

Who is truly motivated?

Management may be motivated to build value for a term as long as its own tenure (ten years or so), but not for a longer term. Employees would tend to have a longer horizon, but absent strong stock ownership, they are not generally motivated to think beyond their near-term paycheques. A good case in point was the 1995 buyout effort at United Airlines. The flight attendants declined to join other employees in a proposed 'employee buy out', using all available legal techniques to bolster their situation. Their position was clearly that of disaffected employees, not owners. The pilots did become owners, taking a significant pay cut in order to 'earn' their equity, but eventually their parochial interests as employees began to preponderate over their ownership personae. The pilots' continuing claims for higher pay made plain that their interests as owners were disproportionately smaller than their interests as salaried employees.

Directors have only a weak claim on motivation to build long-term value. Even when directors are paid in stock, the stock is tied to their tenure, which is not (and should not be) much longer than that of management.

Of all the participants and contributors, long-term owners are clearly the most motivated to build long-term value for the corporation. There is nonetheless the problem of 'collective action' under which non-participants benefit from the expense and effort of participants and thus are 'free riders'.

This poses a serious problem for fiduciary shareholders, who under the present system are 'damned if they do and damned if they don't'. While they would be criticised for improper activism, they might also be faulted for failing to take necessary remedial or monitoring action to preserve value. Whereas individuals can take a cost/benefit calculation on all their holdings and couch their activism accordingly, trustees have the practical and legal problem of needing to justify their stewardship in the event of collapse of a particular holding, notwithstanding the overall success of the whole portfolio. Solutions to this problem will be introduced over the course of the next several chapters.

Who is truly empowered?

Right now, most corporate power seems to be in the hands of managements (shared, in the case of unionised companies, by employees). Director power seems to be an extension of management power and is rarely exercised in opposition to it. The recent shake-ups at American Express, Eastman Kodak, General Motors, and IBM appear to be dramatic exceptions to this more general rule. Judging from the proxy vote tallies published year after year by the Investor Responsibility Research Center of Washington, DC, shareholders are still voting more often with managements than against them.

Yet the future potential for shareholder power is enormous. According to a recent Conference Board report by Carolyn Kay Brancato, institutional investors own almost half (47.4%) of all of the equity in American corporations – approximately 4.35 trillion dollars as of the second quarter of 1996 – and they own well over half (57%) of the largest 1000 public companies.[26] In Europe, the levels of institutional holdings are even higher.[27]

Meanwhile, over the last several years several specialised institutions have developed to inform and facilitate action, including Institutional Shareholder Services, a Bethesda, Maryland, proxy advisory firm, and LENS, Inc., an activist value investment company that I cofounded. Also notable are the Council of Institutional Investors, Investor Responsibility Research Center (both mentioned previously), and Investors' Rights Association of America.

SUMMARY AND CONCLUSION

To repeat my opening point, healthy corporate governance is 'the relationship among various participants in determining the direction and performance of corporations consistent with the public good'.

Governance is a two-faceted concept in the corporate context. One has to do with competitive performance. The other has to do with power. It is the second facet that gives rise to our concern. Without denigrating the virtue of the seven panaceas, it must be said that they are incomplete as solutions to the corporate problem. While worthy both individually and collectively, they do not constitute an effective force inclining congruency of corporate and public interest.

The current system is not operating for the benefit of the public good, but this fact is masked by soothing language assuring us all of protections that don't exist. CEOs have been able to philosophise their way into wealth while selling off corporate birthrights. The standards of charters degenerate over time. Sham elections continue, and fallible experts say what their clients want to hear. The press is hailed as a force for freedom, even as advertising money mutes its voice. And with all of these forces at work, the natural mechanisms of legal, economic, and social constraints weaken. This is all happening without serious protest. One is forced to conclude that the present situation does not threaten any informed and empowered class enough to make a meaningful challenge worthwhile.

At the same time, the dichotomy between a seemingly lively and useful dialogue about governance and plain reality is perfectly satisfactory to the CEO, who continues to exercise largely unregulated power to pursue the corporate agenda of unlimited life, size, power, and license – and to benefit directly from it.

The solution is a system in which corporations are accountable to a party that is independent, informed, motivated, and empowered. Only the institutional shareholder fulfils this requirement. In the remaining chapters, we will build a case for this proposition.

5

Like all complex adaptive systems, corporations have both regularities (predictable, mechanistic laws) and dynamics (forces for change). Corporate regularities, which are shared by other manmade institutions, are the drives for unlimited life, size, power, and license. Corporate dynamics, which are shared by all CASs, are multiplicity, spontaneity, accommodation, adaptation, transcendence, and metamorphosis. These dynamics can counterbalance the four corporate dangers of unlimited life, size, power, and license – bringing instead long-term life, appropriate size, balanced power, and greater accountability to long-term owners.

5

The Corporation and the Economy as Complex Adaptive Systems

> *But the two did not sing well together, for the gold bird could sing only the same waltz over and over again, while the real nightingale sang her notes in her own natural way.*[1]

Is the corporation a mechanical structure of law and convention that will give back only what we put into it? Or is it a living, breathing entity, capable of 'singing its own notes in its own natural way'? Does the corporation dwell in the 'court' of artifice? Or does it live in the 'forest' of a self-renewing economy? The answer depends in part on how *we ourselves* see corporations and the economy. Our vision will help determine our reality.

Adam Smith saw the corporation and the economy in the language of personality or machinery – not as a unique dynamic system in its own right. This is not surprising for a man who learned his physics from Isaac Newton, but what of us? Will we incorporate, as Smith did, the scientific truths emerging in our own time?

We should and can. Therefore, in this chapter, let us take a tour of the new 'complexity' movement in science, and then apply its main findings to the corporation and the economy.

THE NEW SCIENCE OF 'COMPLEXITY'

Complexity is the state of being complex – that is, made of interrelated parts. Traceable through Latin to an ancient Greek term for 'braided', the term *complex* entered modern languages in the Renaissance and quickly attracted a myriad of meanings. Philosopher John Locke used it in the 17th century to describe ideas 'made up of several simple ones put together' (*On Human Understanding*, 1690). Adam Smith, a century later, wrote of 'the whole annual produce taken complexly' (*Wealth of Nations*, 1776). And in the 19th century, 'complexity' figured importantly in the writings of biologist Charles Darwin, who asserted life's 'tendency to advance in complexity of organisation' (*Origin of the Species*, 1859).

Now, in our own waning century, leading intellectuals are using this term in a new way, to describe a type of science that will take us not only into the next hundred years, but into the next millennium.

We turn to this new science as our only hope of understanding the modern corporation. As the corporate form has evolved, so has its potential complexity. Today the large publicly held corporation can have multiple nationalities, reporting systems, cultures, languages, and currencies. Understanding the typical large corporation and linking it to human good has become increasingly difficult. The old sciences of cause and effect, action and reaction, leverage and motion, cannot help us in this endeavour. By contrast, the emerging science of complexity – despite its unsettled state[2] – offers great promise in this regard.

This new movement (called variously the 'science' or 'sciences' of complexity) builds on many of the scientific laws discovered in the past, and uses many of the scientific methods used in the past. Its reliance on mathematics and logic give it a timeless purity. Yet this science is 'new' in approach, spirit, and thought.

Unified approach

Scientists and others working in the field of complexity pride themselves – and rightly so – on their extraordinarily *unified* approach. Laws discovered in one realm have automatic implications in all others. As a result, the new science of complexity is *multidisciplinary*. Through think tanks, publications, and conferences devoted to complexity, scientists from different fields are interchanging ideas and discoveries with mutual respect as never before.

These scientists even have a common home base for their activities – the Santa Fe Institute (SFI) (http://www.santafe.edu) in Santa Fe, New Mexico, which funds research and showcases it in publications and seminars. Like the Los Alamos Laboratories in Los Alamos, New Mexico, and the Institute for Advanced Studies in Princeton, New Jersey – both sources of genius for its endeavours – SFI has been the birthplace for some of the newest theories and proofs in the scientific field. The story of their founding years appears in Mitchell Waldrop's *Complexity,* cited earlier in this book.

The complexity scientists also have a common set of favourite topics. Like the international Cathedral scholars of the High Middle Ages, who shared the common language of Latin, SFI scientists and their peers world-wide share some favourite terms and topics. It is hard to find a book or publication on complexity that does not include Gödel's theorem, genetic algorithms, positive feedback, cellular automata, or the Turing machine.

These favourite concepts – generally from the field of mathematics and computer science – make one central point: *things are not as they seem.* Phenomena that appear to be subject to immutable, rational laws, turn out to contain random elements. Conversely, phenomena that appear to be random sometimes contain hidden orderliness. Participants in the complexity movement love these puzzles. They share a common respect for mathematics and logic, yet they are fascinated with the limits of these left-brain activities – and their link to analogy and creativity.

Complexologists love the ordinary, which, they discover, is most extraordinary. They would sooner study a backyard sandbox than the tail of the Hale-Bopp comet. John Holland – speaking of complex systems in general – puts it well: 'Even though these systems differ in detail, the question of coherence under change is the central enigma for each.'[3] Thus the object of their study is not merely the 'complex system', a phrase that may suggest merely mechanistic intricacy, but the 'complex *adaptive* system', or CAS.

Maverick spirit

Despite their shared interests, and very much in the change-orientated spirit of those interests, complexity scientists shun conformity, even when it comes to key terms. With the notable exception of their cherished 'CAS' term, each seeks his or her own mode of description. As SFI's Murray Gell-Mann has noted (when explaining why what he calls a 'schema' his SFI colleague John Holland calls an 'internal model'), 'Both of us are conforming to the old saying that a scientist would rather use someone else's toothbrush than another scientist's nomenclature.'[4]

These scientists are unified only in their search for what contradicts old complacent models that never quite worked, and they don't mind contradicting each other or themselves as they pursue this quest. They ignore problems that seem to already have good working solutions. (For example, one doesn't read much in complexity literature about the new 'unified field theory' in physics, which may be the single most exciting field in science today.[5]) They are fixing only what is broken – solving difficult problems in the physical and social sciences without posing undue limits on solutions, making simulations or models[6] in order to see what agents will do on their own without human intervention. It's not so much that they want to be right; they want to be surprised. And, the universe being as it is, they often are.

Paradoxical presuppositions

Complexity scientists have a new way of looking at the way things are. In describing this new vision, David Lane, a Santa Fe faculty member who teaches political science at the University of Modena and the University of Minnesota, has coined four aphorisms:[7]

- *Chance as cause.* This aphorism, based in part on Lane's work with economist Brian Arthur, a pioneer of SFI, says complex adaptive systems yield aggregate patterns that cannot be determined in advance. Aggregate patterns are constructed from many individual choices that can only be described as 'random'. Yet this does not mean that anything can happen, since constraints operate on the choices. Lane says that in a CAS, chance, more than any 'law', is the cause of aggregate order.
- *Winning as losing* (or 'Winning isn't necessarily winning'). This concept goes under different names. In game terms, it is a cousin of the 'Evolutionary Prisoner's Dilemma' of Kristian Lingren. Biologists might call it *punctuated equilibrium,* which happens sooner or later (usually later) when an ecology gets replaced because it fails to respond to a new challenge. Lingren proposes a 'coevolutionary' world of many evolving agents in

which 'an agent ... that defines its success by "winning" against a currently dominant rival may find itself the victim of its own success'.[8] Geologist Douglas Robertson and biologist Michael Grant, both of the University of Colorado at Boulder, find that because of the 'chaotic instabilities introduced by feedback, natural selection will commonly cause fitness to decrease, in sharp contrast to the conventional view that selection only increases fitness'.[9] So much for survival of the fittest.

- *Organisation as structure and process.* Lane goes beyond the process consultants here. Not only does he say that an organisation is process as well as structure, but he also challenges scientists to look at the interrelationship of process and structure, to see 'how they mutually determine one another'.

- *Rationality as limitation* (or 'Rationality isn't necessarily intelligent'). One can succeed as an organiser without using rational planning, says Lane. He cites the success of Cosimo de Medici as the head of the Medici dynasty. Based on the modelling work of John Padgett at the University of Chicago, it is clear that Cosimo did not engage in rational planning, but rather 'could feel the advantages his structural positioning in the network offered him, and he learned how to exploit the stream of opportunities that this positioning kept flowing in his direction'.

TRAITS OF COMPLEX ADAPTIVE SYSTEMS

Working together and separately, complexity scientists have identified many of the basic traits of complex adaptive systems – and there are many. Each scientist has his or her own list. John Holland, in *Hidden Order*, lists four 'properties' and four mechanisms.[10] Ralph D. Stacey, in *Complexity and Creativity in Organizations*, lists 13 'key features' of CASs, plus an additional four for humans. Mitchell Waldrop, in *Complexity*, suggests at least 16 basic traits of complex systems.[11]

My quest in reading these lists and others was to see how these terms applied to the modern publicly held corporation. In my experience as a shareholder activist, I had seen far too much of the predictable, mechanistic side of corporations. I turned to the complexity scientists to help me see the other side of corporate nature – the adaptive side. I wanted to see how well the language of complexity science fit the corporation, and to learn from this science what might be in store for the future of the corporation.

The news is good. It seemed that each list I encountered – not just the lists of Holland, Stacey, and Waldrop, but many others – fit my subject perfectly. I found a particularly good fit with six of the traits common to CASs, namely multiplicity, spontaneity, accommodation, adaptation, transcendence, and metamorphosis. These are not the only traits of CASs, but they are among the most important, and for this reason I have highlighted them.

Each of these traits characterises *all* facets of corporate and economic life – facets such as management, innovation, information, finance, resource allocation, and identity, and many more too numerous to be listed. Chart 5.1 shows how the traits of complex systems can help explain the many facets of corporate life, from management to … you name it. This chart, and the chapters that follow, represents my best effort to explore a *terra incognita* – the corporation as a complex adaptive system.

Chart 5.1

Complexity is everywhere in corporate life							
	Mgt.	*Innov.*	*Markets*	*Finance*	*Res. Alloc.*	*Identity*	*Etc.*
Multiplicity	TYC	★	★	★	★	★	★
Spontaneity	★	WX/CBS	★	★	★	★	★
Acommunication	★	★	MSBHY	★	★	★	★
Adaptation	★	★	★	DAI	★	★	★
Transcendence	★	★	★	★	GE	★	★
Metamorphosis	★	★	★	★	★	FUBNA	★
Etc.	★	★	★	★	★	★	★

All six traits of complex adaptive systems apply to all six activities of corporations and the economy. Furthermore, there are more than six traits and more than six activities. Therefore, the corporate cases in this chapter (see ticker symbols) show only part of the whole picture.

A FIRST EFFORT

To my knowledge, although scholars (notably Stacey) have studied the 'organisation' as a complex adaptive system, no one has attempted to study the *corporation* per se in this light. When attempting to apply science to the corporations in scientific terms, business observers have assumed economic equilibrium with fixed supply and demand, and have spoken easily of 'winners' and 'losers' in the 'fight' for 'dominance' in various domains. Waxing Darwinian, they have spoken of the 'survival of the fittest'.

Few corporate observers, if any, have looked at the stranger side of Darwin, in particular his discovery of apparent mutations – sudden, irreversible changes – in the life of species. Nor have they delved into the emerging science of complexity – a collective effort to explain mutation in the broadest sense of the term.

As a corporate activist I have felt a prolonged sense of dissatisfaction with prevailing terminology. With this book, I hope to create a new lexicon for describing both corporations and the economy, starting first with the important question of perspective.

TWO VIEWS

So how are we to apply these concepts from complexity science to corporations and the economy? Let's start by establishing our perspective – or, more properly, perspectives. Every scientific discipline has a close view/distant view distinction. Economists would call the first view corporate 'microeconomics' and the second view corporate 'macroeconomics'. Physicists might call these two approaches the study of corporate 'particles' versus 'condensed matter'. For biologists, the closer view would be corporate 'biochemistry', the second, corporate 'biology'.

To achieve congruity with these important classifying activities, and to borrow from their allure, it would be tempting to borrow one of these terms. But our subject is already intricate enough, and surely it is best to be simple whenever possible. Therefore, we will call the two perspectives 'close' and 'distant'.

Viewed from the perspective of a participant, a corporation is a complex adaptive system. Seen from a distance, the corporation is an agent in the complex system of the economy. We need to maintain *both views* to understand the corporation as a vital creature of our economic life.

With this distinction in mind, let us now review the traits of corporations – both as complex adaptive systems themselves *and* as agents within a complex adaptive system. If we are looking up close at a single corporation, we can see that it is a *complex system* linking several agents, including owners, managers, and other participants. Taking a more distant view, we can see that the corporation is itself an *adaptive agent* operating in the larger system of the economy.

But the corporation is more than a 'box' within the larger 'box' of the economy. The two systems interact in manifold ways, with some primary agents of the corporation also acting in their own individual rights as agents within the economy. The corporation and the economy are like three-dimensional Chinese boxes that nest and cross-nest and then nest some more. They co-evolve.

With these principles in mind, let us now review the six main traits of complex systems, to see how they apply to various aspects of corporations and the economy. In the process, we will show through 'sketches' how even very large companies can possess – to some degree – the dynamic qualities described in this chapter. Of course, any effort to characterise a huge company in monolithic terms is preposterously bold, and doomed to self-contradiction. Nonetheless, we offer this gallery for the reader's consideration.

Multiplicity

Complex systems have a great number of agents interacting with each other in a great many ways. One of the best descriptions of this multiplicity comes from Lee A. Segel, a US-born mathematician who teaches at the Weizmann Institute in Israel. He says that a complex system is 'typically composed of a large number of elements whose interaction is nonlinear'. The system seems 'hierarchically organised with disparate space and time scales and a variety of intercommunicating functional layers'.[12]

One of the most significant aspects of multiplicity studied by complexity scientists is the concept of *multiple equilibria*. When something grows by leaps and bounds rather than declining because of diminishing returns, it is clear that there are many forces at work, not just one. But although this phenomenon is common in nature and in the economy, it was ignored because it was inconvenient to scientists, says above-mentioned pioneer Brian Arthur, who quotes Joseph A. Schumpeter: 'Multiple equilibria ... are not necessarily useless, but from the standpoint of any exact science, the existence of a uniquely determined equilibrium is, of course, of utmost importance, even if proof has to be purchased at the price of very restrictive assumptions.' (The quote brings me back to my days studying economics, when we all had to learn the fiction of *ceteris paribus* – all else being equal – which of course it was not.)

Multiple corporate agents

Certainly corporations have many agents interacting in many ways. The agents that comprise a corporate system include:

- owners (majority)
- directors (management)
- employees
- customers
- suppliers
- lenders.[13]

All of these agents are internal to the corporation, in that without them the corporation would not exist. Also, legally (for example, in defining 'insiders' under US securities laws) they are considered 'insiders' who are not entirely independent of management. Our close view reveals that each of these agents has interconnections with the other agents through the corporation.

Multiple economic agents

When we look at the corporation from afar, seeing it as one of many enterprises interacting, we see again the trait of multiplicity. We see corporations interacting with outside forces including:

- owners (minority)
- directors (non-management)
- other corporations
- the general public
- regulators
- the environment.

Notice that owners and directors appear on both lists. This is because owners are deemed 'insiders' of the corporation if they have automatic control over it, and 'outsiders' if they do not. The same applies to directors, who may be members of management, or independent outsiders. (Note, though, that even directors considered 'independent' in spirit or in fact are still by definition 'insiders' under US federal securities laws.)

Multiplicity in management – corporate and economic examples

We mentioned earlier that corporations have many agents interacting in many ways. One such area of interaction is ordinary business – what one makes and sells where. A good corporate example of this is Tyco, a company that has diversified with great success (see box).

For economic multiplicity, one need go no further than the examples of positive feedback provided in the works of Brian Arthur. Looking back on a decade of research, he describes a dawning realisation that 'if several similar-sized firms entered a market at the same time, small fortuitous events – unexpected orders, chance meetings with buyers, managerial whims – would help determine which ones achieved early sales and, over time, which firm dominated.' He concludes that 'economic activity is quantified by individual transactions that are too small to observe, and these small "random" events can accumulate and become magnified by positive feedbacks so as to determine the eventual outcome'.[14]

Niche marketing is a good example of multiplicity at work in the economy. Probably the most profitable category of products in the world are 'the unintended consequences' of the most rational development and marketing programs. The permutations of diversity are beyond the power of humans to extrapolate, so out of the most explicit of programs emerge the niche – those proprietary economic islands where profit margins are highest.

Multiplicity = Many agents interacting in many ways
Multiplicity in management

TYCO INTERNATIONAL

Dennis Kozlowski, the Chief Executive Officer of Tyco International, believes that the sky is the limit for an effective manager's compensation potential. The $10 billion Bermuda-based Tyco is emerging as the international exemplar of corporate multiplicity. It is:

- a world-wide force in a host of businesses having to do with the flow of liquids – sprinkler systems for fire protection, valves for all uses, pipes for all kinds of flow
- a major contractor on some of the largest building projects in world history in south-east Asia
- owner of the principal 'security business' in the world and a dominant factor in every component of the fire protection business
- manufacturer and seller of branded medical products
- manufacturer of complex computer circuit boards
- a major player in the packaging business
- a veteran in cable and a new entrant into fibre optics.

What is the logic of all of this? Who can manage such a conglomeration? The quick answer is, very few people indeed: Jack Welch of GE in the 1990s, Harold Sydney Geneen in the heyday of ITT before him, and Tex Thornton and Roy Ash of Litton Industries before him.

Notwithstanding the thousands of products and markets Tyco goods must compete in, company employees are rewarded by a single compensation system – one that rewards them for success in changing markets. Tyco ultimately believes in the ingenuity of the manager in the field. As Kozlowski puts it, 'The financial interest of our managers, who have unusual autonomy, and of our shareholders are identical. The more managers earn for shareholders, the more they earn for themselves.'

So diversity comes together in a diverse number of ways; there is no commonality between the management challenges, each is different, each requires different solutions. What is consistent is the self-interest of the manager. In effect, Tyco has found a way to turn managers into agents of positive change.

Diversity begets diversity, but it can lead to unity – that is, uniformly good results for shareholders. Because the company is grounded on the simple theme of identifying and motivating highly competent managers, Tyco is open to diverse new input. There is a willingness to hear, to adapt, and to act. In itself, this gives the company great advantage in competition with others who are tied to a more traditional sense of industrial logic.

Spontaneity

The richness of interactions among agents enables the system as a whole to act spontaneously; agents do not react to changes in rigid, predictable fashion. In their spontaneous responses to events, the agents in complex systems show sudden bursts of self-organising (and reorganising) activity.

This organisational ability distinguishes complexity from chaos, which may be a stage on the way to complexity, but which is not equal to complexity. Indeed, one noted complexologist – Murray Gell-Mann, a founder of SFI – has said that the effective complexity of an entity is equal to the 'length of a concise description of the entity's *regularities*'.[15] As our perception evolves, so will our appreciation of these 'regularities' within what seems to be merely random or chaotic. Life is dynamic, but it is also repetitious. Karl Sigmund, of the University of Vienna's Institute of Mathematics, defines life as 'replications with slight variations'.[16]

The spontaneous self-organisation of complex systems may be gradual or sudden – as when units that were polarised regroup in a new way. Physics professor Ricard V. Sole, of the Universitat Politecnica de Catalunya, writing with colleagues at the Complex Systems Research Group, has described this process aptly: 'It is well known, from the theory of phase transitions, that a given system (possibly made of many subsystems) can undergo strong qualitative changes in its macroscopic properties ... At critical points, fractal structures, complex dynamical patterns, and optimal information transfer appear in a spontaneous way. Observing such properties in those systems which we call "complex", we can conjecture that complexity tends to appear close to instability points.'

The spontaneous *self-organisation* of complex systems occurs, in the insightful words of Waldrop, 'without anyone being in charge or consciously planning it'. It is as though the agents involved are responding to higher laws, not just one but many, as well as to random circumstances. The point is, they are not forming and pursuing rational plans. Rather, they are part of a larger whole.

This is not to say that systems somehow have personalities that make beautiful holistic choices (as the term spontaneous may suggest). Rather, the spontaneity of a complex system has to do with its low susceptibility to simple probabilities. Key traits are *randomness* and *nonlinearity* (traits obviously related to the multiple equilibria mentioned earlier). Brian Arthur is the master here. As economist Kenneth J. Arrow of Stanford University notes in his introduction to *Increasing Returns and Path Dependence in the Economy*, a collection of Arthur's papers, 'One outstanding characteristic of Arthur's viewpoint is its emphatically *dynamic* nature. Learning by using or doing plays an essential role, as opposed to static examples of returns to scale … The object of study is a history.'[17] In studying the history of phenomena over longer terms, Arthur has seen 'the importance of random deviations for long-run tendencies'.

But be warned: This emphasis on the 'dynamic' does not mean that everything in a complex system is unpredictable. During 'lock-in', as mentioned in the previous chapter, systems are all too predictable. Lock-in happens when a product or service gets an early advantage and, on the strength of that advantage alone, experiences increasing success over the long term, and becomes almost impervious to the consequences of its own flaws. One challenge in living with corporations is the reconciliation of those traits with other more dynamic possibilities.

Corporate spontaneity

Like all complex adaptive systems, corporations act in their own styles in response to stimuli; not merely react in a predictable way. Writing on 'Nonlinearity in Human Networks', Ralph D. Stacey writes of the coexistence of a 'legitimate' and a 'shadow' network in the typical organisation, including corporations. The first network is linear in intent, he says, but can be nonlinear under certain circumstances, while the second is 'quite clearly nonlinear'.

Evidence of spontaneous corporate self-organisation is overwhelming. Anyone who has worked with a corporate enterprise over time knows how true this is. Slow decline – such as the decline of the 'dinosaur' US giants such as General Motors and IBM – can be followed by sudden, dramatic recovery.

One could make a study of such spontaneous behaviour by studying the 'beta' of stock behaviour. ('Beta' is the term mathematicians use to describe volatility of an agent compared to volatility of a system – chiefly with respect to stock prices, but theoretically elsewhere.) Or one could study sudden changes in a company's 'core business' – often signalled through changes in company names – such as US Steel to USX. My own favourite example of corporate spontaneity is the recovery of Westinghouse, renamed CBS (see box) through its use of innovation.

Economic spontaneity

Spontaneous economic self-organisation seems to be an obvious occurrence as well. An industry may seem to be in shambles, and then suddenly show promise. This change is often referred to through the Phoenix myth of a bird rising from ashes, and countless small consultancies have used this logo on their business cards.

The idea of busts and booms based on supply and demand is long gone, along with myriad curves taught in business school. Random inputs proliferate, and we have seemingly spontaneous swings and lulls, where the 'best' conditions can cause declines in 'indicators' and the 'worst' conditions can send indicators up. The most striking recent example was the stock market rally prompted by the world's largest mass firing at AT&T.

Spontaneity = Sudden bursts of self-organising activity

Spontaneity in innovation

WESTINGHOUSE/CBS

Westinghouse has been one of the proudest names in American industry and innovation; and, yet, to be blunt, the company has been disaster-plagued and mismanaged for decades. The company was poised on the edge of bankruptcy in the late 1960s when uranium prices turned against its fixed price positions. A legal twist of fate – an extension of the idea of *force majeure* to commercial impracticality – got the company out of that scrape. In the early 1980s Westinghouse took advantage of the booming economy by creating a new real estate financing unit. Principal officers were compensated by the extent to which their loan revenues exceeded a targeted return on equity. No adjustments were made for bad credits – or for the geometric expansion of parent company liability for the new debts.

The inevitable downturn drove the company into such discredit that on one memorable day in the early 1990s CEO Paul Lego held a press conference in New York City to deny that the company was going into bankruptcy. Lego was in the unhappy position of trying to deal with a problem he did not understand. He knew little about the real estate division because of an ill-conceived and executed decision by the board of directors to split CEO responsibility into two stages over a half-dozen years.

The directors pulled themselves together, accepted Lego's resignation, hired an executive consulting firm, and within six months engaged the clever Michael Jordan. Bursting with energies from Yale, McKinsey, Pepsi-Cola, and the venture capi-

---

tal world, Jordan spent several months surveying his domain and conceived of the brilliant and risky strategy of using the credit from the traditional businesses to leverage the company further into the communications business. This idea was just the 'small input' that the Westinghouse system needed to produce a 'major output'.

Many months of negotiation and successful persuasion of government agencies later, many billions of dollars of financing richer and hundreds of millions of fees poorer, Westinghouse acquired CBS and a host of new radio properties to emerge as one of the premier factors in this exciting new industry. On 1 December 1997 Westinghouse renamed itself CBS.

Jordan had felt that the only area in which the company's experience was both excellent and susceptible of high future growth was communications. He ignored all the commonsensical suggestions that he sell this division at the high prices then prevailing to pay down the company's huge debts and pension fund liabilities. His vision was that only through *transformation of the company into virtually a new enterprise* would he be able to create the long-term value enhancement for the company owners that is the accepted challenge for managements.

So the company that began the century as the cynosure of technological innovation is ending it – in downward fits and upward starts – as the reborn creature of strategic and financial innovation.

Accommodation

Agents in a complex system seek to accommodate one another; serving their collective selves in the long term, not their individual selves in the short term. Accommodation, put simply, means letting others win sometimes.

This process of accommodation is often modelled through what programmers call 'cellular automata'. As noted by Harold Gutowitz, a mathematics professor at the Ecole Supérieure de Physique et Chimie Industrielle in Paris, cellular automata are models that describe the 'interaction of a multitude of simple individuals ... such as when ants interact to form a colony or water molecules interact to form a fluid'. This type of model 'chooses an initial state of the system and observes the resulting sequence of states'. This approach 'permits descriptions of natural processes in computational terms (computational biology, computational physics) but also of computation in biological and physical terms (artificial life, physics of computation).[18]

In this process of accommodation, agents are continually changing, giving rise to new states of being that were previously unpredictable. This quality of 'becoming' or 'emergence' is the most obvious result of removing equilibrium as an assumption. In the words of mathematician Martin Shubik, of Yale University, the old notion of equilibrium 'killed the role of time'.[19] Complexity scientists have restored that role.

SFI's Murray Gell-Mann has highlighted this important feature of complex systems. 'Life can perfectly well emerge from the laws of physics plus accidents, and mind, from neurobiology. It is not necessary to assume additional mechanisms or hidden causes. Once emergence is considered, a huge burden is lifted from the inquiring mind. We don't need something more in order to get something more ... At each new level new laws emerge that should be studied for themselves; new phenomena appear that should be appreciated and valued at their own level.'

In their accommodation, complex systems can achieve *balance* between agents within a system, between two systems, and between order and chaos itself. Balance, ironically, means equilibrium – the very factor that the complexity scientists have targeted as naïve. Yet the balance sought and found in complex systems is not a static one, but one that is evolving and changing. It does not mean symmetry in the old sense.

Symmetry describes a sameness or equivalence on two sides of a dividing point or line. In math, an equation is symmetrical, as are perfect geometric shapes such as circles or squares. In nature, there are many symmetries – the two wings of a butterfly, the two halves of a snowflake. The role of 'tagging' in a complex system is to *create new aggregates by breaking old symmetries.* 'In general, tags enable us to observe and act on properties previously *hidden* by symmetries.' [20]

Corporate accommodation

The agents within corporations and economies seek to accommodate one another; serving their collective selves in the long term, not their individual selves in the short term. This shifting does and should occur constantly in any corporation, a phenomenon that has recently taken on the name of 'teamwork'. At the same time, corporations seek accommodation in their environment, serving the free market economy as a whole rather than their individual corporate good. For a good example of corporate accommodation, we would cite the trials and tribulations of Mitsubishi (see box).

Economic accommodation

Economies evince accommodation as well. Consider mergers. Their returns are good if various interests are accommodated, but they are poor when there is little or no accommodation.

Economists have long preached that the risk of a 'hostile takeover' is a necessary discipline to ensure that management effectively focuses on competitiveness and maximising long-term values for shareholders. The hostile takeover translates poorly from theory to practice. It involves needless loss to several constituencies: employees, communities, uninformed shareholders, to say nothing of the taken-over managers. These interests need to be accommodated.

Fortunately, the takeover discipline has been adapted during the 1990s into the practice of 'shareholder activism'. Failing companies that used to be prey to hostile takeovers can improve performance without such intervention. And when mergers do occur, there is better accommodation of stakeholder interests. Institutional shareholders controlling a majority of the stock of the largest public companies have taken over the legendary role of 'monitors' and have provided the necessary oversight. As a result, returns from mergers have been better in this decade than in the previous one. Recent research from Mercer Management Consulting has found that the mergers of the 1990s are substantially outperforming those of the 1980s. A study of 215 large transactions ($500 million-plus) shows that 52 percent of the 1990s deals are achieving above-industry returns to the merged companies' shareholders, versus only 37 percent of the 1980s deals.[21]

Accommodation = Putting the interests of others first
Accommodation in markets

MITSUBISHI

From the time of the Emperor Meiji in the mid-19th century, the Mitsubishi Company, operating under the three red diamonds (*mitsu bishi*) in the crest of its founding Iwasaki family has been at the service of Japan's changing needs. The fundamental rule of Mitsubishi Corporation is 'Corporate Responsibility to Society'.

Corporate responsibility to society

It is our ultimate goal that we, as a trading firm, should contribute to the nation and the society through commerce. Hence, by utilising capital resources, considering the supply demand situation, and by capitalising on the time difference, we should promote business as much as possible to keep our operations afloat generating reasonable profits; however, because our ultimate goal is to contribute to the public well-being of the nation and society, our selection of business, our modus operandi, etc. should be based on this fundamental understanding and we must always keep in mind that our real raison d'être *exists in activities based on such primary objective.* *

'Export or perish' was the chief corollary of this rule in a Japan not blessed with the natural resources essential for the level of industrialisation Mitsubishi was committed to achieve. To build a base for exporting, the company sent its employees abroad to learn foreign customs and languages.

For three-quarters of a century the corporation loyally and competently instrumented the policies of its native country – through great prosperity to the utter destruction of World War II. In the post-war years, the Mitsubishi group strove for greater commercial success, but without losing its nationalistic ties. On 3 July 1954, a newly reorganised – indeed reformed – Mitsubishi group restored its long-time mission (first articulated 20 years before):

- To work for the common good of the nation and society
- To trade internationally, both as exporters and importers
- To retain a fair and impartial attitude.

Today these goals are understood as:

- Corporate responsibility to society
- Integrity and fairness
- International understanding through trade.

The first goal is of special interest: The problems of rebuilding a world-wide business when physical assets had been destroyed and financial assets confiscated required continuing close cooperation between business and state. Only through a cooperative system of credit availability and the creation of stock values through interlocking holdings was Japan able to create an equity and debt capability sufficient to finance its expanding needs.

Mitsubishi succeeded in creating an economic dynamism that was the envy of the world thanks to one central factor: accommodation to the national purpose – incredibly hard work, unbelievably low pay, unfailing discipline, and long years away from home. (Japanese manufacturing company executives did not relocate their families, because of the impossibility of raising children to be Japanese in foreign climes.) All in all, the company's managers lived out the immortal words of Rudyard Kipling (in 'The White Man's Burden', 1899): 'Send forth the best ye breed – Go, bind your sons to exile, to serve your captives' needs'.

It was a viable exchange: the government would provide loan capital, while the company would pursue avenues of identified national interest. When times were bad, there would be no layoffs of employees. Money would always be available to finance appropriate ventures, while the time and skill of key executives would be available for national purposes.

The schizophrenic requirements of running a world-wide business at the same time as complying with the accounting, capitalisation, and staffing requirements of the Japanese world were a continuing challenge. In order to be real 'players' in world commerce in the 21st century, companies need access to capital on the most favourable competitive terms.

The final accommodation to the requirements of international investors at the same time as retaining the essential commitment to Japanese objectives has temporarily eluded MC's managers: 'Mitsubishi said it no longer planned to list on the NYSE in 1998, although it wanted to do so eventually. A listing on the NYSE has been a goal of Mr Minoru Makihara, Mitsubishi's president, who sees it as necessary to be acknowledged as a truly international company.'★★

Over a century's experience in accommodation have imbedded this mode into the genetic code of the Mitsubishi group. No one should bet against this firm's ability to achieve its desired objectives.

★   Thanks to Toshio Kitazawa of Georgetown University for this translation.

★★ Michiyo Nakamoto, 'Mitsubishi Drops Plan to List in New York Next Year', *The Financial Times*, May 20, 1997, p. 23. The company has decided to 'wait until it raises its return on equity to at least 8 percent, a target it has set for 2000'.

Adaptation

Agents in complex systems adapt to events, acting in response to them. They try to turn events to their advantage. For example, in the plant and animal kingdoms, species evolve in an attempt to improve their chances of survival in a changing environment. The interaction among agents causes complex systems to change.

Ralph D. Stacey's description of complex adaptive systems in *Complexity and Creativity in Organizations* describes this process of adaptation succinctly. The complex adaptive system, both human and non-human (for example, organisational), has a basic purpose of performing tasks and surviving and consists of networks of large numbers of interacting agents, Stacey begins. He follows these observations with several on the theme of adaptation:

- *interacts* with an environment consisting of other complex adaptive systems and therefore *co-evolves*
- *interacts* in an iterative, nonlinear manner
- *discovers* – that is, acquires information about the systems constituting its environment and information about the consequences of its own interactions with those systems by employing feedback
- *chooses* – that is, exercises a kind of free will to identity and select regularities in the feedback information it acquires and then condenses those regularities into a schema or 'model' of this world
- *acts according to its schema* rules in relation to the systems that are in its environment
- *discovers the responses* its action provokes, as well as the consequences of

those responses
- *uses* this information to *adapt* in behaviour, that is, to perform simple or single-loop learning
- *revises* its schema so as *better to adapt*, that is, to perform complex or double-loop learning.

This is not to say that adaptation always leads to the 'survival of the fittest' – mentally or physically. In a sense no system can be considered permanently 'fit' or 'unfit'. Fitness is relative to adaptation, and the rewards of adaptation vary. Sometimes the adaptive traits a system develops to survive in one environment fail it in a new one. Winning, as stated above, can mean losing.

Corporate adaptation

As quintessential 'organisations', corporations certainly adapt to external change. This is perhaps most obvious in the endless ways companies find to finance and refinance their endeavours. There is debt, equity, and hybrid financing. Within each of these categories there are many different instruments and many different types of sources for those instruments. We see an endless stream of creativity from the corporate community in finding ways to attract capital. In a complementary way, the finance community is endlessly creative in finding ways to provide it. Daimler–Benz is an excellent example of the role of adaptation in financing (see box).

Economic adaptation

The economy adapts because its many agents, including but not limited to corporations, adapt. Brian Arthur observes that the economy is a 'collection of activities, technologies, and needs, all interacting through a market system peopled by decision-making agents such as firms, banks, consumers, and investors'. But it can also be seen as 'a collection of beliefs, anticipations, expectations, and interpretations, with decision-making and strategizing and action-taking predicated upon these beliefs and expectations'.

Perhaps the greatest example of the principle of adaptation can be seen in the world of post-gold finance – a world that came into being when in July 1971 President Richard Nixon made the un-Republican announcement that the US was going to abandon the effort to maintain a parity between its currency and the price of gold. Some years later, the successes of the Organisation of the Petroleum Exporting Countries (OPEC) in raising prices increased the prospect that the petro-dollar surplus could not be financed. Notwithstanding former Citibank CEO Walter Wriston's boast that no sovereign nation had ever been allowed to go broke, it appeared that third world debt in general and the Mexican bailout would literally destroy the world's banking system. Today's banking system is a monument to the durability of an institution whose governing principal is adaptability to real events.

Adaptation = Responding to external change
Adaptation in financing

DAIMLER–BENZ

The photograph of obviously professional-class men pushing wheelbarrows full of currency notes to the grocery stores of Germany in the late 1920s has a permanent place in the collective consciousness of more than a few of today's political and business leaders. Yet the mark that was worth almost nothing then is strong today – despite the catastrophic events toward which those barrows were wheeling. Thanks to penance, hard work, a succession of 'miracles', and a disciplined focus on the fundamental technologies of machinery, chemicals, dyes, and automobiles, Germany's social and economic redemption has been the envy of the world over the past half-century.

Mercedes–Benz, one of the most prestigious cars in the world, incarnates this history, while displaying just those qualities that Germans like to believe about themselves. This most expensive vehicle has traditionally been among the most profitable in markets all around the world. One reason for this has been its bold new way of financing its endeavours.

In the early 1990s, after being the pride and joy of the industrial banking complex that had owned and financed half a century of its prosperity, Daimler–Benz (DB) found itself at a financial turning point. While investment and loan funds were still abundantly available through the German system, by far the largest and the cheapest capital in the world was available in New York. DB saw the handwriting on the wall: a world-wide company could not afford to function without access to the most favourable sources of money.

So DB made an adaptive decision to list its shares on the New York Stock Exchange and to comply with the governance and accounting standards of the SEC.

This took courage. During its first year of listing DB posted a billion-dollar loss in its financial statements filed in New York, while the traditional statement would have indicated a marginal profit. If the ultimate measure of a business is its ability to earn the highest marginal rate of return, then businesses all over the world will need adapt to this reality.

DB's decision and its short-term results wounded German pride, but showed corporate executives everywhere how crucial it is to be willing and able to adapt to new realities, no matter how unexpected or how unwelcome.

Transcendence

As part of a larger whole, agents in complex systems 'somehow manage to transcend themselves, acquiring collective properties such as life, thought, and purpose that they might never have possessed individually'.[22] One way they achieve this shift is through *lever points*. A lever point, poetically called the 'butterfly effect', is the ability of a small input to produce major changes. (The butterfly image comes from the delightful example mentioned in the preface to this book – the connection between the flapping of a butterfly's wings and the creation of a major weather system on the other side of the globe.)

Corporate transcendence

In their mutual accommodation, corporations transcend themselves. When corporations work together, their efforts have two effects, one linear, the other transcendent. When a group of corporations works together to set voluntary standards in anticipation of rulemaking, they may experience initial success or failure, but there are other long-term results from the act of collaboration – results they cannot predict or control. A famous example is negative lock-in through benchmarking, where a minimum standard becomes a new maximum, or a maximum standard becomes a new minimum, driving down the ethical impulse at the individual corporate level. On the positive side, we can see corporate transcendence in resource allocation. An exemplar here is General Electric (see box).

Economic transcendence

The economy in general also has 'transcendent' traits, although the changing levels of 'life, thought, and purpose' of the economy may defy analysis at times. The point is that there seems to be a dialectic going on, with each result leading to further results at a geometric rate.

Resource allocation in energy is a good example. In this arena, there are constant shifts to new realities. As a result, it seems that no one can ever outwit others. In the world of energy, everybody is always wrong.

> *'Oil is going to hit $100 a barrel next year.'*
> *'We have to ration the amount of foreign oil coming into the United States.'*
> *'Natural gas reserves will only last another ten years, so gas may no longer be used for power generation.'*
> *'Most electric power in the future will be generated by nuclear energy.'*

Each of these eventually absurd statements has informed American energy policy at some time in the last half-century. And none has been 'right'. The rapidly changing political situations, both worldwide and domestic, and the emergence of hugely productive new technologies conspire to create massive, across-the-board shifts in the energy field not just year-by-year, but second-by-second.

Transcendence = Shifting to new behaviours across the board
Transcendence in resource allocation

GENERAL ELECTRIC COMPANY

Founded as one of the several progeny of the genius of Thomas Alva Edison, General Electric Company was on the Dow Jones list of most important companies at the beginning of the 20th century. As the century ends, it is still on that list – and it may well be the most valuable commercial enterprise in the world.

German-born engineer Charles Proteus Steinmetz ran his Schenectady labs with no budgetary constraints, and a cornucopia of products flowed during the first half of the century. Then, as America's post-World War II commercial dominion melted into the realities of world-wide competition in the 1960s, something happened. The

---

Great GE dropped out of the 'core businesses' in its traditional franchise. No GE in computers! No GE in nuclear power!! No GE in television sets!!!

These were not voluntary decisions. They represented management failures – sometimes blamed on 'unfair' foreign competition. Then the company took stock of the traditional excellences that could be preserved, and made a 'cast' of these for posterity. Light bulbs, turbine engines, household appliances, and defense work would remain staples for a time – but not forever.

When Dr Jack Welch became CEO in the 1980s, he established a new policy, highly mechanistic in nature. Each business would be number one or number two in its field – or would be sold off. Under his leadership, GE abandoned even more of its few remaining core businesses.

Over the past two decades, Welch has continued to think more like the graduate of a traditional engineering school than like a student of the new way of management in a complex world. His famous dictum, 'Be number 1 or number 2 or don't compete', leaves little room for risk and failure – the drivers of learning and change. Not surprisingly, the latest Welch hagiography, *Control Your Destiny or Someone Else Will*, abounds with mechanical images – from 'business engine', to 'leverage', to 'mechanisms to show best practices'.★

Yet paradoxically, even while pursuing a machine-like strategy, GE has overcome what it refers to as the 'Old Way' or 'mechanistic' corporation.★★ Even as it reallocated resources from 'losers' to 'winners', GE has cast off restraints:

- large physical locations
- multiple management layers
- 'doing it by the book'.

And so the GE *medium* of change (a more dynamic way of structuring the business) has transcended the Welch *message* of change (win or die). GE has thrived as a complex adaptive system despite the simplistic logic its surviving managers have been forced to follow during the Welch era.

★ Noel M. Tichy and Stratford Sherman, *Control Your Destiny or Someone Else Will* (New York: HarperBusiness, 1994). Tichy, a professor at the University of Michigan, has been a consultant with GE since 1982.

★★ From 'Creating the Competitive Organization in the 21st Century: The Boundariless Corporation', by Mary Anne Devanna and Noel Tichy, *Human Resources Management*, Winter 1990, Vol. 29, pp. 455–71.

Metamorphosis

As a result of all of these attributes, complex systems are subject to sudden, dramatic changes that are difficult to predict. Mitchell Waldrop's vivid description of complex systems, begun in the prologue to this book, deserves to be completed here.

> 'The edge of chaos is where life has enough stability to sustain itself and enough creativity to deserve the name of life. The edge of chaos is where new ideas and innovative genotypes are forever nibbling away at the edges of the status quo, and where even the most entrenched old guard will eventually be overthrown. ... where eons of evolutionary stability suddenly give way to wholesale species transformation. The edge of chaos is the constantly shifting battle zone between stagnation and anarchy, the one place where a complex system can be spontaneous, adaptive, and alive.'

Corporate metamorphosis

Finally, both corporations and the economy are subject to sudden, dramatic changes that are difficult to predict. These changes at first occur imperceptibly but then perceptibly as 'strong qualitative changes in its macroscopic properties', to repeat Ricard Sole's apt phrase. In the corporation, we can see this type of change in Fortune Brands, formerly American Brands (see box).

Economic metamorphosis

As for the economy, we know all too well how sudden changes can be. I am reminded of a story of two brothers in the late 1920s – one thrifty, the other profligate, and a drunkard to boot. The thrifty one kept a savings account. The drunk one passed out daily in a heap of bottles. After the Great Crash of 1929, the thrifty brother had nothing. The drunkard had an inventory of bottles that he was able to sell for enough to keep body and soul together, and wound up supporting his brother.

In our time, consider the metamorphosis in economic identity that has occurred in the former Soviet Union, which has changed from a planned socialist economy to an unplanned – seemingly anarchistic – one. Is there a hidden order in the seeming disorder now in that region? We can only hope.

Metamorphosis = As a result of all of the above, changing radically in form and nature
Metamorphosis in identity

FORTUNE BRANDS, INC.

Tobacco was the first and largest industry resulting from the European settlement in the Americas in the early 17th century. No company had a more prominent position in this industry than George Washington Hill's American Tobacco Company. Founded in the 1800s, this company flourished for a century. Eventually, however, it faced a need for change. Even as profits flowed in the post-World War II years, counter-currents were developing. Eventually, evidence that tobacco was injurious to health became overwhelming.

The company's first response was to fight. Canute-like ATC and its peers joined to fight in the courts, in the polls, in the halls of government, and in the press. With huge tax payments to state, city, and federal government and with billions of dollars dispersed to aid the arts and other concerns of community leaders, they succeeded in staving off government intervention, allowing a half-million Americans to meet untimely deaths every year.

But then the tide turned. Such giants as R.J. Reynolds and Philip Morris finally began to enter into negotiations with all of the constituencies who had a claim against cigarettes: state governments who claimed that tobacco caused inflated medical, welfare, and unemployment costs; individuals who claimed suffering and diminished lifespan; and the various federal agencies who are involved in the effort to protect the health of the citizenry.

With speed and dexterity American Tobacco transformed itself into American Brands, disposing of all of its US tobacco holdings (but retaining its Gallaher cigarettes in the UK) and acquiring liquor, insurance, residential hardware, office supply, golf, and leisure products businesses. It converted its huge tobacco cash flows into flows from an amalgam of consumer products – just in time to avoid the claims of the plaintiffs and bar.

Rarely has a company that was so prominent in one industry voluntarily turned itself inside out to assume an utterly different corporate form. Rarely has a management strategy so conspicuously changed the nature of the risks and rewards to be expected by its owners. And it has lived happily ever after, so far anyway. American Brands – renamed Fortune Brands in June 1997, does not even function as an operating business, with factories and employees and relationships with real people. Rather, it exists in a quiet building in a Connecticut town as a holding company, possessing the shares of the companies from which its profits derive.

SUMMARY AND CONCLUSION

Human enterprises and the human economy have always been complex adaptive systems. But as enterprises and the economy have evolved, their complexity has grown – with a greater number of variables – including random inputs to determine outcomes. In complexity economics, *there is no single equilibrium*, so we cannot be certain of a positive outcome based on natural economic forces such as supply and demand.

This key point is made by George Soros in his profound essay on 'The Capitalist Threat', which has provoked predictable and unjustified outrage since its appearance in the February 1997 *Atlantic Monthly*.

'The main scientific underpinning of the *laissez-faire* ideology,' says Soros, 'is the theory that free and competitive markets bring supply and demand into equilibrium and thereby ensure the best allocation of resources. This is widely accepted as an eternal verity, and in a sense it is one. Economic theory is an axiomatic system. As long as the basic assumptions hold, the conclusions follow. But when we examine the assumptions closely, we find that they do not apply to the real world.'[23]

The reason the assumptions do not hold is that the economy is forever affected by our beliefs about it, says Soros. For example, in financial markets, 'instead of tending toward equilibrium, prices continue to fluctuate relative to the expectations of buyers and sellers'.[24]

I find this observation extremely important. It tells me that if the corporate form poses dangers, these will not be solved by the magic of equilibrium. Solutions in the Newtonian system were steady-state; in complexity, they are provisional.[25]

In our newly perceived world, solutions require sustained human effort – particularly in the realm of beliefs and perceptions. Only by understanding the corporation as a lifelike system – not as a person and not as a machine – can we curb these drives and restore this form to the integrity and vitality the framers of the original corporate concept surely intended.

This is not to say that we should or can somehow 'go back' to a golden era of corporate good. That time never existed. Name a corporate-like form, trace it to its origins, and you will find problems. Why? Because by its very definition, the corporation, a structure enabling limited liability, separates ownership and management, accountability and action. *This golden bargain, this alchemy, is the very essence of the 'corporation'.*

The question here is whether and how this magic can move from the realm of sleight-of-hand and become something truly creative. To restore integrity to the corporate form, we must reconcile its programmed, mechanical drives with its nature as a lifelike system in touch with human needs.

How can we do this? In my view, there are two steps to this process, one mental and the other practical. The mental step will be to see corporations as they are: not as people, not as machines, but as a form of dynamic system – 'artificial life' in the broadest sense of the term. The practical step will be to encourage the changes we need to make the corporation more lifelike.

Instead of unlimited life, we must encourage long-term life. Instead of unlimited size, we must encourage appropriate size. Instead of unlimited power, we must encourage balanced power. And instead of unlimited license, we must encourage greater accountability to long-term owners – for accountability. For without accountability, no living system can thrive and evolve.

This encouragement will not require passing new laws. Nor will it require widespread conflict and struggle. Rather, it requires only that we stop resisting the solutions that are all around us – solutions that will become clearer as we seek them. Things won't get better by themselves. They need two types of action – one by individuals and one by government.[26] Our search will continue in the following chapters.

Chart 5.2

Four Corporate Solutions
~~FOUR CORPORATE DANGERS~~

Long-term life
~~UNLIMITED LIFE~~

Appropriate size
~~UNLIMITED SIZE~~

Balanced power
~~UNLIMITED POWER~~

Accountability to long-term owners
~~UNLIMITED LICENSE~~

6

Agent-based computer modelling can advance our inquiry. Our 'Brightline' model represents, among other factors, the dynamics of externalisation in interactions among four key agents in the large publicly held corporations: customers, corporations, government, and shareholders. Companies compete for customers by reducing their liabilities through externalisation; an aggressive management that is compelled by its shareholders to function within government-determined limits on externalisation will generate superior values over the long term.

6

Modelling Corporate Accountability

> *And the music master praised the bird very highly – yes, even assured them that it was better than the real nightingale ... But the poor fisherman, who had heard the real nightingale, said: 'It sounds pretty enough and it is similar too. But something is missing. I don't know what it is.'*[1]

The previous chapters have led us to an important question: How can corporations achieve greater accountability? In Chapter 1, presenting a synopsis of 'The Nightingale' by Hans Christian Andersen, we faced the eternal question of ordered predictability versus dynamic change. In Chapters 2 through 5, we saw this tension at work in the modern corporation, which has two distinct aspects: on the one hand, it relentlessly pursues the goals of unlimited life, size, power, and license; on the other hand, it continues to evolve as a complex adaptive system (CAS) that is capable of evolving beyond its original, simple 'programming'. And we said that the best hope for greater accountability lies in independent, informed, motivated. ˌıd empowered shareholders.

In the present chapter, we seek to explore this last idea more fully via agent-based computer modelling – a relatively new technology that can reveal the interactions present within complex systems. We are fortunate to have worked on this project with a programmer from the 'SWARM'[2] team at the Santa Fe Institute, who created specifically for this book a useful and effective tool for modelling the interactions of shareholders and corporations based on our views of corporate accountability. We call this modelling project 'Brightline'.[3]

MODELLING COMPLEX ADAPTIVE SYSTEMS

Thinking about the corporation as a complex system operating *within* a complex system can quickly become intricate – so much so that it qualifies as an 'intrinsically difficult problem', one that requires for its full solution a 'computer as large as the universe running for at least as long as the age of the universe'.[4]

Can the dynamics of corporate complexity be accurately modelled? Even the great John Holland of the Santa Fe Institute admits the limitations of his peers and forbears in this regard. 'After more than a century of intensive effort, we still cannot model many basic capabilities of the central nervous system.'[5] Ecosystems likewise defy easy analysis: 'Matter, energy, and information are shunted around in complex cycles … Even when we have a catalogue of the activities of most of the participating species, we are far from understanding the effect of changes in the ecosystem.'[6]

Similar challenges awaited us, we knew, in modelling corporate complexity. To quote John Holland again, the quest of the complexity scientists is to identify 'coherence under change', which is the 'central enigma' to each complex adaptive system. I would like to pause here at the word 'enigma' because I think it says a tremendous amount about the challenge of modelling.

An enigma is a puzzle. A puzzle is something that appears disordered but that has a hidden order subject to decoding. In this book, we have wanted to 'decode' certain aspects of corporate structure to find the potential for dynamic life within it. At the same time, we have wanted to see the economy in the same light, focusing on the corporation's role in the 'living' economy.

MODEL DESCRIPTION

Ultimately we decided to focus our efforts very narrowly on the externalising practices of *large publicly held corporations,* specifically those corporations where a substantial proportion of stock is held by institutional investors. The ability of these firms to access capital at attractive rates is directly dependent on their stock performance, which in turn is dependent on their ability to draw and maintain customers. We also decided to focus on the manner in which these corporations persistently externalise costs, one of the key concerns of the long-term owner, as described more fully below. We then built our model specifically around these mechanisms and the impact that active shareholders might have in responding.

We also designed the model to allow multiple runs using a wide range of variable settings, and will eventually include the capability of then showing and comparing the results of multiple runs against one another. The result is a basic modelling program for exploring these fundamental issues of corporate accountability from a number of different perspectives. In particular we wanted to show how *active shareholder involvement*, by imposing new standards of accountability, might ultimately affect the long-term value of these large corporations. Previous studies have shown or suggested a link between shareholder activism and improved long-term corporate performance.[7] In creating our model we sought to reveal at least one of the mechanisms involved.

Further, by comparing runs we can compare the results attained both with and without the presence of active shareholder involvement, what might be called the 'governance gap'. From an active shareholder's perspective, the ideal corporation should either be fully internalising or fully disclosing – indeed 'transparent' – in its accounting for the real costs of doing business. We believe that only the fully transparent corporation will maximise shareholder value over the long term, and that this is the central goal towards which all such reforms must be directed.

Where existing corporations externalise costs and even seek to influence the regulating mechanisms of government (i.e. taxation and penalties for illegal activities), the ideal corporation must accept full accountability for *all* of the costs of doing business – and active shareholders will seek to ensure this. Thus we chose to model corporate agents that seek to externalise costs in order to maximise short-term market gains and profitability. We also sought to show how the countering influence of active shareholders might impact this behaviour in the interest of longer term and persistent value. (For more about the Brightline model, see the Appendix to Chapter 6.)

ON EXTERNALISATION

In the age of instant information, diminishing tariff barriers, free movement of currency, interchangeable domiciles for optimum production, and the universal availability (at least in theory) of management talent, much of the traditional 'competitive advantage' that one company enjoyed in competition with others has disappeared. Given these difficult competitive conditions, how can one company undersell another?

To paraphrase a political button in a past US presidential election, 'It's the externalisation, stupid!' Around the globe, with the national interest turning from war to commerce, large corporations are now able as never before to *pass on the costs of their operations to society as a whole* – all the while convincing elected officials that the corporate interests are congruent with the public good.

And so the values that government has traditionally given to business – patent protection, enforcement of 'property rights', and all manner of patents and franchises – now have an important new supplement. Business has become more competitive in the short term by externalising its costs. The specific manifestations of this cost transfer vary from country to country. In one nation, we might see high unemployment, in another, high medical costs, and in yet another inadequate pension reserves. As the corporate cause of these social costs becomes more obvious, shareholders begin to see profits for the shell game they are, and adjust the value of stocks (see box, 'Tobacco Road: A Sermon', in Chapter 10).

In sum, short-term competitiveness, purchased at a high social cost, cannot last. As we hope to show in the Brightline model, extreme externalisation eventually causes a corporation to cease being competitive, a condition that can only be corrected by active shareholder involvement.

THE AGENTS

After carefully considering the minimum number of agents needed to effectively model our intended range of behaviours, we implemented the following interactive agents:

- customers
- corporations
- government
- shareholders.

The customer agents

The customer agents represent the purchasers of the products and services offered by the corporations. The corporations are assigned a variable number of customer agents at the beginning of each run, reflecting real-world variations in age and size. Customer agents may then choose to continue to 'buy' the goods or services of their original assigned corporation, or to jump ship to another as the run progresses. (See Fig. 6.1.)

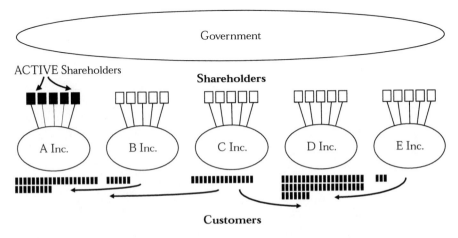

Fig. 6.1 Brightline model sample run showing movement of agents.

The loss of customers translates directly into a decline in cash flow, a measure of short-term performance; this is the first of two standards we will use to 'value' each corporation. The second is the accumulated total number of customers held over time, a measure of the corporation's persistent value. We want to see what relative changes in valuation will occur between the beginning and end of the run, and to then gauge the impact of ACTIVE shareholder agents on these valuations.

While we acknowledge that real-world customers often can and do play an activist role in affecting corporate behaviour, we felt that any effort attempting to model this role was beyond the scope of the present effort. We note, however, that real-world customers and shareholders, particularly the beneficiaries of the institutional shareholders of these large publicly held corporations, are increasingly one and the same.

The corporation agents

The corporation agents begin each run having been assigned an equal share of the available customer agents, whose movements from corporation to corporation then provide the basic measure of each corporation agent's performance over the course of each business cycle. (See Fig. 6.2.)

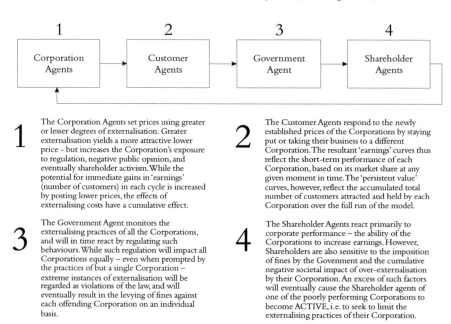

1 The Corporation Agents set prices using greater or lesser degrees of externalisation. Greater externalisation yields a more attractive lower price – but increases the Corporation's exposure to regulation, negative public opinion, and eventually shareholder activism. While the potential for immediate gains in 'earnings' (number of customers) in each cycle is increased by posting lower prices, the effects of externalising costs have a cumulative effect.

2 The Customer Agents respond to the newly established prices of the Corporations by staying put or taking their business to a different Corporation. The resultant 'earnings' curves thus reflect the short-term performance of each Corporation, based on its market share at any given moment in time. The 'persistent value' curves, however, reflect the accumulated total number of customers attracted and held by each Corporation over the full run of the model.

3 The Government Agent monitors the externalising practices of all the Corporations, and will in time react by regulating such behaviours. While such regulation will impact all Corporations equally – even when prompted by the practices of but a single Corporation – extreme instances of externalisation will be regarded as violations of the law, and will eventually result in the levying of fines against each offending Corporation on an individual basis.

4 The Shareholder Agents react primarily to corporate performance – the ability of the Corporations to increase earnings. However, Shareholders are also sensitive to the imposition of fines by the Government and the cumulative negative societal impact of over-externalisation by their Corporation. An excess of such factors will eventually cause the Shareholder agents of one of the poorly performing Corporations to become ACTIVE, i.e. to seek to limit the externalising practices of their Corporation.

Fig. 6.2 The business cycle.

To improve its performance, a corporation must attract new customers. It does this by 'posting' a more attractive 'price' for its 'products', but in this instance it may do so only by externalising more of its 'costs'. The greater the degree of externalisation, the lower the price; the lower the price, the more attractive the corporation becomes to potential customers. But while the customer agents react to such price changes on a per cycle basis, there are other effects of externalisation that are cumulative and are monitored by both the government and shareholder agents. *Thus while a corporation may improve its 'performance' in a given cycle by externalising more of its costs, the long-term effects of such behaviour will have a cumulative negative impact on performance.* The corporation must always weigh the benefits of any short-term gains against this long-term cost to its value.

In a given business cycle each corporation agent must consider its current market share, existing price position, and the current impact of past externalising practices in order to set a new price for attracting new customers. Ideally, this new price will be low enough to attract new customers without increasing the externalisation of costs – because (as we shall see) externalisation lowers the long-term value of the company.

The government agent

The government agent responds to the effects of such externalisation, either all at once or cumulatively over time, by imposing taxes and legal constraints upon the corporation agents. While one or more of the corporations may be responsible for such behaviours, it is important to note that as long as such behaviours fall within the law, the resultant governmental constraints generally apply equally to all the corporations.

Thus while 'taxes' effect all corporations and their shareholders more or less equally, governmental fines and legal settlements in response to extreme instances of externalisation (described together for purposes of our model as 'fines') impact corporations individually. Furthermore, these penalties will then increase the likelihood that the shareholder agents attached to that corporation will become active. In this way our model reflects the long-term 'costs' to society of such externalising behaviours, and the potential sensitivity of long-term shareholders to such mounting costs.

The shareholder agents

The shareholder agents have but a single variable attribute – they may become more or less ACTIVE in seeking to limit the externalising practices of their corporations. As all of our shareholder agents represent long-term, value-directed investors, with concise and consistent needs for the future, they remain fully invested in a single corporation throughout the run of the model. (See Fig. 6.1.) We did not make any attempt to model the market behaviours of shareholders, something far beyond the scope of this project.

Instead, we programmed several typical shareholder tendencies into the model. Passive shareholders are 'satisfied' with their corporation's performance – and thus remain passive – whenever such performance improves or at least holds steady. They become 'unhappy', i.e. more likely to turn ACTIVE in response to decreases in performance.

In each run, however, the shareholders of one corporation are given the capacity to become ACTIVE, in response to excessive externalisation by their corporations, particularly if such behaviour reaches illegal levels, providing a much needed balancing mechanism. Eventually such ACTIVE shareholders, acting in concert – to become effective at least three of the five shareholders must become ACTIVE at the same time – then limit subsequent externalisation by their corporation to insure that such practices will remain within the law, on the one hand limiting management's ability to seek the highest possible levels of short-term performance, but on the other effectively shielding the corporation from future intervention and fining by government.

While we felt it was beyond the scope of these efforts to examine or even fully describe the role of employees in relation to our corporation agents, it is nevertheless worth noting once again that in many real-world instances the interests of shareholders and employees are identical. In fact, pension fund beneficiaries now in effect own as much as 26% of the outstanding stock in America's publicly held corporations, plus another 8% through other mechanisms such as employee stock ownership plans.[8]

We similarly chose to ignore the existence of the various other classes of shareholders, such as market speculators. These short-term holders, while having their place in the overall economy, are simply not relevant to our discussion here.

RUNNING THE MODEL

Thus the model includes a total of five corporation agents, and seeks to describe the impact of no more than five shareholder agents for each of the corporation agents. There is just one government agent, and there are 100 customer agents. These numbers reflect a not-uncommon number of competitors in a single market, a sufficient number of sizeable shareholders needed to directly impact such corporations, and a large enough pool of customers to clearly show market share trends and patterns. We wanted to keep the model small enough to be run on commonly available desktop computers, yet sufficiently complex to do its intended work, in hopes of facilitating further study.

At the beginning of each run a number of attribute variables (see Appendix to Chapter 6) are set by the run-time user. The typical run covers an elapsed time period of 300 cycles of activity. In the course of each cycle (see Fig. 6.2) the corporation agents post prices for their 'products' using greater or lesser degrees of externalisation of costs. While more externalisation may yield a more attractive lower price, it also increases the corporation's exposure to government taxation, negative public opinion, and eventually fines against performance – which will in turn increase the likelihood of shareholder activism.

Following the posting of new prices, the customer agents then react by staying where they are or moving to a different corporation.

Next, the government agent examines the cumulative externalising practices of all the corporation agents and reacts accordingly. Too much accumulated externalisation will result in the application of more taxation, making further externalisation more difficult and 'costly' for the corporation agents. And genuinely excessive externalisation by any one corporation will result in the levying of penalties against that corporation, further inhibiting its ability to lower prices and compete more effectively.

Finally the shareholder agents react to this latest round of corporate 'performance', responding to changes in market share, the imposition of penalties against their corporation by the government, and the cumulative negative societal impact of over-externalisation. Any excess of such factors will eventually cause certain shareholder agents to become ACTIVE, and thereafter seek to limit further externalisation by their corporation.

A SAMPLE RUN

We present here (in Fig. 6.3) a run of the Brightline program to show competition between five companies over a 300-cycle time span. In this run, the companies compete for customers by reducing their liabilities through externalisation. They externalise within the constraints of government intervention and fines, as well as shareholder intervention. What this particular run illustrates is that an aggressive management that is compelled by its shareholders to function within government-determined limits will generate maximum values over the long term. This provides initial evidence that directors and other fiduciaries can use to require management restraint in various relationships with society. It is important to be able to project the long-term implications of particular patterns of corporate conduct. Corporate decisions can and should have a long-term beneficial impact – one that lasts after the retirement of most current officers and directors.

This sample run of the Brightline model illustrates both the advantages of corporate externalisation in maximising short-term performance and the longer-term advantages of a more controlled approach to externalisation, motivated in the Brightline model by the presence of ACTIVE shareholders in one of our corporate agents. It is interesting to note, however, that the presence of ACTIVE shareholders alone cannot possibly have this effect, as our ACTIVE shareholder agents can only insist that the corporation act within the legal limits established by the government agent. In the absence of government standards our model will either crash completely due to over-externalisation, or result in complete monopoly by the most aggressively externalising corporation. Similarly, in the absence of ACTIVE shareholders, the government agent alone will eventually prove ineffective, with the typical result being that the model will cycle endlessly between 'winning' corporations until eventually one gains monopolistic status.

One interesting twist on this variation, which need not be demonstrated using Brightline, is the kind of situation we now see in the tobacco industry, where government steps in ostensibly to address excessive externalisation, but is utterly ineffective in doing so, merely resetting its own standards to a lower level, and in effect encouraging the previously existent unregulated cycling between competitors to continue. In Chapter 10, we will explore this problem more fully (see box, 'Tobacco Road: A Sermon').

In this particular run we can see clear examples of most of the interactions possible in Brightline. It is important to note, however, that this particular run is but one of a very great many possibilities. While we have presented this example as a somewhat 'typical' Brightline run, readers should note that each and every run is different, given our beginning parameters, and it is only by comparing a great many such runs that the truly emergent patterns and possibilities presented by the model can be fully understood.

The run begins with all five corporations having an equal share of customer agents. Although it is too soon in the run to tell, C Inc. has been chosen as the potential focus company, but its shareholders remain passive at this point as its performance is still quite high. E Inc. is the first corporation to begin externalising aggressively, and assumes the earliest lead. By cycle 48, however, B Inc. has become even more aggressive, and has overtaken E and assumed the lead. Not only have all five corporations begun externalising in an effort to attract customers, but all of them are now externalising at 'illegal' levels. At the same time, the government agent has noted the rise in overall externalisation and is preparing to begin fining the most aggressive companies.

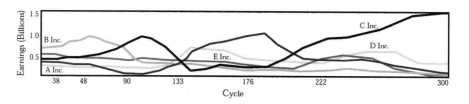

Fig. 6.3   Brightline sample run showing relative company performance.

Late in the run, company E is in the midst of value destruction caused by its externalising practices. The market will not value E at levels comparable to the earnings, cash flow, and assets multiples accorded other companies. As soon as sustained and effective shareholder involvement emerges (which is eventually possible), positive valuation will resume.

For companies that have risky products (asbestos, silicone, or tobacco) or that generate environmental hazards (nuclear energy, oil), sudden public awareness has triggered retaliation and consequent loss of values. In some instances, the companies have failed to disclose what they knew about the impact of their functioning in society. In others, the companies have egregiously subverted the election and other political processes – sometimes in violation of the law.

Corporate contumacy predictably invites public retaliation in the form of fines, new restrictions, or even a trend toward socialisation. The time frame in which this occurs in likely to be beyond the tenure of a single CEO, management team, or board of directors. Therefore, it is most likely to be addressed – if at all – by long-term owners.

By cycle 90, C Inc. has been able to assume the lead because both B and D have been fined by the government for their earlier high levels of externalisation. C's shareholders remain passive, in light of C's performance, but C will now be next in line for government action.

The shareholders of our focus company, C Inc., do not in fact become ACTIVE until cycle 176, by which time C has already been fined and A has been able to take over the lead in current earnings. It is interesting to note that at this point all five corporations can claim roughly the same amount of accumulated earnings, our measure of long-term performance.

By cycle 222, however, the model has begun to stabilise, with C Inc.'s ACTIVE shareholders effectively limiting C's externalisation to the legal limit. While all four of the other corporations now continue their cycles of over-externalisation and consequent government action, C now has the advantage of complete freedom from government intervention, and its current earnings consistently surpass its competitors, even though total accumulated earnings continue to be fairly evenly balanced.

At the end of the run at cycle 300, moreover, not only has C retained its current cycle advantage, to dramatic effect, but can now claim the highest level of total earnings as well, by a factor of nearly 2:1. In this particular run, at least, the actions of ACTIVE shareholders have provided a clear competitive advantage.

Of course, not every run is so clear cut. In each run the interactions are different, with government intervention coming sometimes much earlier in the run, and sometimes much later, depending on the relative aggressiveness of the corporate agents. If the designated focus company is able to assume a large enough lead early on in the run its shareholders may become ACTIVE too late in the run have any real impact. Conversely, absent at least some degree of aggressive management in externalising to gain greater customer share the focus company may never be able to gain enough advantage to 'win' by run's end. Over numerous multiple runs, however, some variation of this sample scenario emerges as the one most likely to occur, with the ACTIVE shareholder corporation turning in not only the best current performance but the best total performance as well.

Clearly then, at least in our Brightline model, it is a combination of factors that makes for the highest performance:

- a corporation agent with an aggressive management style
- an effective government agent with clear standards for externalisation
- ACTIVE shareholders able to hold their corporation to these standards.

SUMMARY AND CONCLUSION

We know that the real economic environment within which corporate entities operate is itself a complex, adaptive, self-organising system. Thus the overall trends and behaviours of the economy are aggregations of individually directed behaviours, exhibiting non-linear dynamic relationships. Real-world economic trends and behaviours are based on the interaction between individual corporations, boards, shareholders, customers, the government, and other stakeholders. These trends and behaviours change over time as each individual entity seeks to gain a more advantageous position.

We have sought to model some of these interactions to explore the impact of responsible shareholder activism on the long-term performance of corporations. We have also sought to more fully explore the mechanisms whereby it is possible for one relatively small change in agent attributes within such a complex system – the shift of the shareholder role from passive owner to active participant – to impact the overall patterns and trends of the larger system.

Our sample run illustrates how existing, typical corporations, lacking in active shareholder involvement, cannot effectively be regulated by government alone. The unreformed corporation seeks to maximise short-term profitability by externalising as much of the true costs of doing business as possible, as we have seen both in our models and in the current case of the tobacco industry. But long-term shareholders, the actual owners of our public corporations, whose tenure over the generations will far exceed that of any given management/director term, can take action in the their own interest and in the interests of long-term value. We are not talking here about 'social investing', but rather best business practices – the maximisation of long-term value.

Fiduciary shareholders and other participants in corporate life need structure and language with which to evaluate the relationship of current functioning and long-term value optimisation. The Brightline model can help owners and boards understand and communicate the impact of externalising behaviour on corporate competitiveness. Preliminary results from model runs indicate that a high level and/or rate of externalisation will bring – within a decade – substantial loss of competitive position. Owners, directors, and managers will want to consider these findings as they make decisions for the near and long term.

A great deal remains to be learned about the relatively new economic phenomenon of active shareholders. We offer here one useful tool for improving our understanding of their emerging role – explored more fully in the following chapters.

7

Analogising to 'cellular automata', we see that there may be 'classes' of corporate life: doomsday (Class I), stagnation (Class II), chaos (Class III), and true orderliness (Class IV). In many runs of an automata model, only the first three classes emerge. From time to time, however, true order imposes itself at the brink of chaos. Is the corporate world poised for positive change in this sense? Will our 'Class II' stagnation be followed by 'Class III' conditions, or by true order, the desired 'Class IV'? To make such a shift, active shareholders may be the agent needed.

7

Intermezzo: The 'Four Phases' of Corporate Life

> *But one evening, when the bird was singing its best and the Emperor was lying in bed listening to it, something gave way inside the bird with a 'whizz'. 'Whirr' went all the wheels, and the music stopped.*[1]

In the previous six chapters, we built a case for shareholder activism, step by step. We began by using humankind's oldest form of communication – storytelling – to present a pressing modern problem: lack of accountability in the large publicly held corporation. Then through the eyes of Adam Smith we faced the dangers inherent in the basic corporate form. Next, we described the corporation as an artificial life form, using the language of complexity science. Finally, after dispensing with several common panaceas about the corporation, we presented an agent-based model that shows how long-term shareholders can effect corporate reforms in the interest of long-term value.

In this chapter, we call for an 'intermezzo' – a midway break from our continuing line of argument – to indulge in some broad speculation. In this intermission, we will look at the 'big picture', stretching the notion of the corporation as an 'artificial life form' to its limits – and perhaps a bit beyond. Our argument here is simple but bold. If the corporation is an artificial life form, then we can learn about it from the models used to simulate life, namely 'cellular automata'.

Unlike the careful modelling work in the previous chapter, this is not a discovery; it is merely an analogy. But in the words of John Archibald Wheeler, a noted physicist cited earlier in this book, 'analogy gives insight'. He said this in 1955 in a talk at Princeton University on the question, 'Can a unifying concept from one field be applied in another?' Wheeler answered his own question with a resounding *yes*, noting that a correlation between the shape and activities of the polymer molecule and the nucleus helped advance the entire field of nuclear physics.

> *'Passing from one analogy to another, saying always X is to A as B is to C, asking always what this implies for X, we suddenly realise what Confucius meant when he said, "I show the student three corners of the subject, and if he cannot find the fourth, I do not repeat the lesson". Not an easy taskmaster! But what principle can guide one more quickly than analogy into the first trial ideas of a new subject? This is for today, the day of optimism and creation. Forget that there will be a tomorrow of criticism and reevaluation!*

In the spirit, then, of 'optimism and creation', then, let us continue this analogy between the corporation and other forms of life, to see what the future may hold....

THE CORPORATION AS AN ARTIFICIAL LIFE FORM

One of the most important things to remember about any complex system, particularly an extension of our humanity like the corporation, is that although it may be 'alive' as we are alive, it is not us. We humans seek our own image and patterns in everything. This anthropomorphic instinct is natural and sometimes appropriate. Indeed, leading thinkers in the natural sciences – notably R.H. Dicke and B. Carter[2] – have given this impulse dignity and meaning. Sadly, however, in the case of corporations, our human projections can work against us. Corporations, as complex adaptive systems, are like us. Yet as systems in their own right, they are different from us as well. They are their own species.

Earlier in this book (Chapter 2), we said that people do not fear the growing power of corporations because of the 'human camouflage' that corporations can wear. We tend to think of corporations as 'big people', or as 'big machines' made by people. Therefore, we think we can manage them. The truth is that corporations are complex adaptive systems with rules of their own. The are, in this sense, forms of 'artificial life'. But what exactly does this mean?

The World Wide Web now contains thousands of definitions of artificial life ('A-Life') – and related terms such as 'artificial intelligence', 'artificial reality', and 'artificial systems'.[3] In simple English, though, 'artificial' means constructed through human effort – as opposed to naturally arising from conditions. And life – to paraphrase the *New Shorter Oxford English Diction-ary* (1993) – is first and foremost the condition, quality, or fact of being a living organism – the condition that characterises animals and plants (when alive) and distinguishes them from inanimate matter. In a general biological sense, 'life' can also mean animate life dependent on sustenance or favour-able physical conditions. Finally, life is something one has until one dies.

Corporations clearly do not have and cannot seek life in this sense. These terms place us firmly in the realm of biology – not economics. This is not surprising; the field of artificial life has been so dominated by the biological model that one complexity scientist (Lee Segel, of the Weizman Institute in Israel) has suggested that we rename artificial life as 'artificial biology' – and go on to create other artificial disciplines, such as 'artificial physics', and so forth.[4]

But there are other definitions of 'life' that do not involve biology in the sense of plants and animals. 'Life' is also (again drawing from *Oxford*) a 'be-ing marked by a capacity for growth and development and by continued functional activity, and the activities and phenomena by which this is mani-fested'. Life can mean the cause or source of living, or an *animating principle*. In this very broad sense, a dynamic, self-perpetuating system can be said to have 'life'. A Web site at the University of Brunel in the United Kingdom puts it this way:

> '*A major step toward understanding how artificial creatures might be considered alive, is in realising that the essence of a machine lies in the logic of its organisation; the material is not important. There's nothing implicit about the material of anything – if you can capture its logical organisation in some other medium you can have that same machine.*'[5]

In this sense, 'life' is the ghost in the machine, not the physical machine itself. In this sense, a corporation can have 'life' – albeit a kind of life con-structed by humans, and hence artificial. Importantly, the corporation as artificial life goes beyond the predictable equilibrium of if/then decisions to incorporate a certain amount of randomness and surprise.

CELLULAR AUTOMATA

When artificial systems take on a 'life of their own', it means that their behaviour has the traits of complexity defined earlier – including multiplicity,
spontaneity, adaptiveness, accommodation, transcendence, and – ultimately
– the capacity for total metamorphosis. Our modelling results so far indicate
that corporations behave like the classic CAS scientists call 'cellular automata',
models developed over 30 years ago by the physicist John von Neuman at
the Los Alamos Laboratory in New Mexico, with the help of his colleague,
Polish mathematician Stanislaw Ulam.

In the words of A.A. Tsonis of the Department of Geosciences at the
University of Wisconsin-Milwaukee, cellular automata are 'mathematical
realisations of physical systems in which space and time are discrete, and
physical quantities take on a finite set of discrete values. They are constructed
from many identical components, each simple, but together capable of complex behavior.'[6]

Complexity scientists use the cellular automata model as a basic proxy for
complex systems in the real world. Although primitive (much more primitive than the model presented in Chapter 6) cellular automata can proxy the
corporate form, piece by piece, in a physical and relational sense (see Chart
7.1). Although the corporation begins its life as a mere legal construct, it lives
its life as a dynamic ensemble of people, places, and things. Cellular automata
models can show us the different shapes this very real ensemble can take.

Chart 7.1

Agents interacting with each other and with variables (V) = CAS★

For example:

cell 1 + cell 2 + cell 3 ... + V = person (CAS)

person 1 + person 2 + person 3 ... + V = constituency (CAS)

constituency 1 + constituency 2 + constituency 3 ... + V = corporation (CAS)

corporation 1 + corporation 2 + corporation 3 ... + V = economy (CAS)

★CAS = complex adaptive system.

Stephen Wolfram, a young British physicist working at the Institute of Advanced Study in Princeton, New Jersey, discovered that cellular automata
rules fall into four classes:

- Cells in *Class I* systems follow doomsday rules. They all converge on a single point that leaves all cells dead in a short time frame.
- Cells in *Class II* systems do not die, but stagnate. They form groups but then stay relatively frozen.
- Cells in *Class III* systems act randomly, showing no stability or predictability. They degenerate into chaos.
- Cells in *Class IV* systems show true orderliness – forming groups and splitting apart to form new groups in patterns that show symmetry and predictability. In this sense, they are very much like the 'Game of Life', a 'miniature universe' invented by English mathematician John Conway.[7]

It does not take much imagination to see in these four classes the four types of interaction that can occur in any system over time. In the governance world, we have all seen corporations that have died out because of extreme short-termism (Class I), that have let affinities override higher purposes (Class II), and that have degenerated into anarchy (Class III). Also, from time to time, we have seen corporations that have lived up to their true nature as complex adaptive systems (Class IV).

The most common type of corporation is the Class I, II, or III corporation. Most corporations die in one or two human generations. Few survive a century. Of the 20 largest companies in existence at the beginning of this century, only two remain pre-eminent today: AT&T and General Electric. All the others have failed, been merged out of existence, or have diminished significantly in size. Speaking on this point 25 years ago, then–IBM Chairman Thomas Watson observed, 'Figures like these help to remind us that corporations are expendable and that success – at best – is an impermanent achievement which can always slip out of hand.'[8]

Even in the short term, mortality rates can be high. In the 13 years between 1970 and 1983 – a relatively quiet period in corporate history – one third of the *Fortune* 500 disappeared, merged, were acquired, or broke asunder.[9]

In Chapter 5, we provided sketches of six companies that exhibit the traits of complex adaptive systems, namely multiplicity, spontaneity, accommodation, adaptation, transcendence, and metamorphosis. There are other such companies. Arie de Geus, in *The Living Company* (Boston: Harvard Business School Press, 1997), writes about 30 companies that have lived long lives thanks to their 'living' traits. He defines these traits as sensitivity to the world around them, tolerance of new ideas, awareness of their identity, and (surprisingly to this author) conservatism in financing.[10] James C. Collins and Jerry Porras, in *Built to Last: The Successful Habits of Visionary Companies* (New York: HarperBusiness, 1997) name 17 corporations that have survived the tests of time (and add two dozen more companies in their 1997 edition). These traits include 'clock-building, not time-telling', to 'try a lot of stuff and see what works'.[11]

Will 'Class IV' corporations become more common? Is the entire corporate system on the verge of greater multiplicity, spontaneity, accommodation, adaptation, transcendence, and – ultimately – metamorphosis? Yes it is, I believe – that, or an utter breakdown.

Chris Langton, a fellow at the SFI, has discovered that Class IV behaviour happens not after Class III (after chaos) but before it as a superior alternative to it. For each run, he set a certain probability (or 'lambda') that cells would be alive after the first run. Here is Waldrop's description of this discovery: 'At very low values around 0.0 he found nothing but the dead, frozen Class I rules. As he increased the values a little more, he noticed that the Class II rules took longer and longer to settle down. Then if he jumped all the way to 0.50, he found himself in the total chaos of Class III, just as he expected. But right there in between Classes II and III, clustered tightly around this magic "critical" value of lambda (about 0.273), he found whole thickets of complex Class IV rules.'[12]

Langton, drawing on other work in the physical sciences, likened this to the kind of 'phase transition' one sees in the realm of matter. The lambda parameter was like a temperature that led to radical changes in physical properties: 'Then the Class I and II rules that you found at low values of lambda would correspond to a solid like ice, where the water molecules are rigidly locked into a crystal lattice. The Class III rules that you found at high values of lambda would correspond to a vapor like steam, where the molecules are flying around and slamming into each other in total chaos.'[13]

Between Class II and III was a 'phase transition' on the 'edge of chaos'. Something orderly and self-generating very much like life itself. Langton had 'an irresistible vision of life as eternally trying to keep its balance on the edge of chaos, always in danger of falling off into too much order on the one side, and too much chaos on the other. Maybe that's what evolution is, he thought: just a process of life's learning how to seize control of more and more of its own parameters, so that it has a better and better chance to stay balanced on the edge.'

Could the 'lambda' necessary for corporate reform be increased involvement from independent, informed, motivated, and empowered owners? It is not far-fetched to assert this.

It seems to me that the corporation stands at a decisive turning point in its history. In the next few years, I predict – possibly by the turn of the millennium – the corporation will move either toward greater orderliness – or toward utter chaos. The outcome will depend on whether or not long-term shareholders begin fulfilling their roles as agents of change.

This kind of change is not unique to the corporation, of course. It is potentially true of all complex adaptive systems, including all the major institutions through which human life seeks order. Just as corporations arise from our economic activities, so organised religions emerge from our spiritual activities, and governments arise from our political acts. These entities are not mere abstractions; they take on a life of their own. Consider the rise of Islam as a dynamic force in modern geopolitics, or the tremendous sway that Communism held over mankind for much of the 20th century.

But these artificial life forms are already recognised as such – not so the corporation. For centuries, human observers have puzzled over the relationship of 'Church' and 'State'. With the rise of the multinational corporation in this century, it may be time to add the 'Corporation' to this list.

APPLICATION TO CORPORATE LIFE

In corporate life, we might say that 'Class I' governance occurs when participants share single, short-term goals. Nobody wins. In 'Class II' governance, players form differing affinity groups, but remain short-term orientated. In 'Class III' governance, players separate entirely, pursuing different goals. This leads to chaos. Only in the rare event of 'Class IV' governance do we see orderliness. This requires that the system be set at a particular value. In our case, the value would be a shared commitment to long-term viability – a commitment most likely to be held by the owners we have described.

Using cellular automata to understand corporations may seem overly simplistic, but consider these wise words from Yale mathematician Martin Shubik: 'Frequently even very simple models manifest complex properties.

A safe rule of thumb is: do not reject the simplest models because they are *a priori* too simple. Reject them when a quick investigation shows that the phenomenon of interest to you cannot appear at this level of simplicity ... I evolved a simple rule in economic modelling: "Do not believe in any economic model which cannot be played as an experimental game".[14]

Even accepting the use of models, a critic is likely to question their significance. Comparing cellular automata to the vast expanse of corporate history may seem to be a leap. So be it. The quest for knowledge requires no less. We can learn from our experience, from mathematics and logic, and from computer programming. Each of these methods of inquiry has validity – even if at times they seem separate and apart.

I am reminded here of an excellent article E. Atlee Jackson recently wrote in response to those who argue that science as we know it has come to an end.[15] Jackson says that in the physical or natural sciences, 'knowledge' requires 'understanding', a process that includes three steps:

- to gather information through physical observation, a mathematical model, or computer experiments;
- to discover correlations within these sets of observables; and
- to apply an accepted scientific method involving formal reasoning to these discoveries.

Because the types of observables in the first step (observing, equations, and programs) are separate and apart from one another, they are not 'susceptible to any logical proof' concerning limitations of their relationships with one another, says Jackson. Rather, it is the human mind that has limitations.

In this chapter, we are taking what we have learned from our *experience* as shareholder activists, combining it with the findings from our computer *model*, and – to cite Jackson – 'applying formal *reasoning* to these discoveries'. Our reasoning is as follows:

- Corporations are complex adaptive systems.
- Cellular automata models can be used to make discoveries about complex adaptive systems.
- Therefore, cellular automata models can be used to make discoveries about corporations.

And why not? To quote Lee Segel again, a complex system is 'typically composed of a large number of elements whose interaction is nonlinear'. The system seems 'hierarchically organised with disparate space and time scales and a variety of intercommunicating functional layers. The iteration of the system components gives rise to higher-level emergent properties that are often not apparent in the lower levels.'[16]

In the great laboratory of life, too, we are seeing such changes. Like the cellular automata that go into 'phase transition', our corporate system could experience widespread, dramatic change toward greater orderliness.

In our view, the current system is poised for change through self-organisation on the part of the relatively 'simple' agents called institutional shareholders. Ralph Stacey has described this process well: 'nonlinear feedback, operating at critical points in system parameter values, causes spontaneous self-organization among agents, which in turn causes new patterns of behavior.'[17]

To cite just one example, we can already see this at work in annual meetings. There is a certain 'order' to the process of proxy voting by both law and convention, and there seems to be a kind of bell curve at work in how many proposals are put forth on what topics from year to year. The Investor Responsibility Research Center rarely reports wild swings. Excluding the obvious statistical outliers of extreme high and low performers, there are so many opportunities via activism that choices can be virtually random! But this is just the beginning. What appears to be random is moving toward richer behaviour, as shareholders become more independent, more informed, more motivated, and more empowered.

SUMMARY AND CONCLUSION

William Greider, a proponent of shareholder activism, has expressed doubts about the likelihood of owner-based capitalism. 'The great unanswered question is whether an economy in which almost everyone was an owner might also eventually alter the irresponsible behaviour engendered by capitalism itself. The capitalist process, by its nature, encourages infantile responses from every quarter, as people are led to maximise self-interest and evade responsibility for the collateral consequences of their activities, the damage to other people of society or the natural environment.'

Despite his doubts, however, he expresses hope for the future. 'New laws might grant favoured status to "responsible owners" – the employee or community stakeholders who are closely connected to their holdings and willing to serve as active stewards of enterprise ... The idea of "responsible owners" also offers at least a possibility for establishing greater social accountability in the stateless corporations. This is far beyond the present reality certainly, but imagine that employee and community owners existed on both ends of the global system, exerting the influence of local values on the multinational firms. If this were the case, it might provide a viable bridge for connecting the mutual social values across the global system ..."[18]

Is this possible? Similar events occur in other complex systems, according to Ricard V. Sole of the Universitat Politecnica de Catalunya in Spain: 'It is well known, from the theory of phase transitions, that a given system (possibly made of many subsystems) can undergo strong qualitative changes in its macroscopic properties ... At critical points, fractal structures, complex dynamical patterns, and optimal information transfer appear in a spontaneous way.'[19]

This is precisely what we predict for the future of the corporation in the 21st century. As mentioned, the present corporate system appears to be approaching a period of transition. The key to a positive outcome will be involvement from independent, informed, motivated, and empowered owners. In their unique nature as long-term stakeholders, they provide the single element needed for change. And the changes they bring can be as sweeping as the ones seen in any system at the 'edge of chaos'.

For the remainder of this book, we will anticipate Class IV corporate life from several different perspectives, starting with a case study of shareholder activism, moving on to a description of the New Owner and the New Language, and then the 'biography' of a future governance pioneer who has 'lived' the changes proposed in this book.

So now, back to the show! Intermission is over.

8

The Stone & Webster story shows how apt the cellular automata analogy can be in a single company. In this case, stagnation (Class II) could have been followed by chaos (Class III). Fortunately, active shareholders moved the company toward orderliness (Class IV).

8

8

Stone & Webster: A Journey to the Edge of Chaos

> *A new emperor had already been chosen, and the people stood out-*
> *side in the street and asked the Chamberlain if there was any hope*
> *of their old Emperor getting well again.*
> *'Peh!' said the Chamberlain, and shook his head.[1]*

In the words of its fleeting-termed CEO Bruce Coles in the company's 1994 annual report, 'Stone & Webster is a century-old group of integrated and interdependent engineering, construction and consulting businesses. We have, for more than 105 years, been providing technological vision and innovative solutions to the changing world of energy, petroleum, petrochemicals, environmental responsibility, and infrastructure.'

At the time these reassuring words were written, few people realised that their object was on the brink of dramatic change. After all, wasn't Stone & Webster one of the great business provenances in 20th-century America? It had impeccable credentials – principal contractor for the Manhattan Project during World War II, designer of more than 70% of the world's installed ethylene plant capacity, leading investment banker for the utility industry, one of the 'brain companies' from the proud university environment of Boston … The noble epithets seemed endless.

In addition to its excellent reputation, Stone & Webster had all the other accoutrements of success – a prestigious board of directors, rich physical assets, highly skilled employees, professionally audited accounts, and a traditional share of a vibrant and expanding market. It also had what appeared to be a sophisticated structure, with a holding company headquarters staff centrally located in New York City. Records were duly kept and legal requirements diligently complied with. People were hired and people retired. Stone & Webster seemed to be a permanent part of the landscape. Indeed, it seemed to be too much a part of the landscape, and not enough part of the future.

The fact of its decline was particularly clear in hindsight. By the mid-1990s, the company's permanent staff had dropped to 6000 – less than half of the 15,000 level it enjoyed in the 1980s. As lucrative 'cost-plus' work in the nuclear power industry phased out, the company had lost its ability to make competitive bids. Profits flattened, and stock prices plummeted from the mid-40s to the high 20s at a time of general price advances. Upon close examination, it became clear that although the company reported profitable operations during this time in statements certified by independent auditors, it had in fact been losing money in its principal engineering and construction businesses for several years.

BURIED TREASURE

A substantial portion of the value attributed by the market to Stone & Webster was based on its surplus passive assets (as of 31 December 1993). The company had miscellaneous real estate assets with a book value of $169.6 million, plus an even greater amount of wealth tied up in liquid assets. In inverse order of size, these were 700,317 shares of Tenneco worth $38.2 million, US government bonds worth $55 million, and a 'prepaid pension asset' worth $115 million. The company had no plans to invest these, using them instead to defray ongoing operating losses. Like the foolish man in the biblical 'parable of the talents', Stone & Webster chose to bury its coins rather than invest them.

Of all these assets burials, the stowing away of the company's prepaid pension asset was perhaps the most dramatic, as the following mini-history should show. In the 1970s and the early 1980s, the company was performing a large volume of cost-plus work. As its workforce grew, Stone & Webster began making substantial contributions to its employee benefit plans, especially its pension plan. Indeed, the more the better, as pension payments were part of the 'cost', which increased the ultimate percentage fee paid to Stone & Webster. Participants in the plan did not become fully vested until they had worked for the company for ten years and few jobs lasted that long.

As the company's workforce dwindled in the latter half of the 1980s, the plan grew. Large sums deposited earlier for pensions of terminated employees remained in the plan and became available for the company's relatively few ongoing employees. Because the plan was overfunded, the trustees were able to take risks and invest substantially all of the assets in equity securities at just the time of the largest bull market in history.

In the late 1980s, the plan passed the $100 million mark – far more than needed for existing employees. The company amortized a portion of this surplus to cover current accruals and to reduce its reported operating expenses. This adjustment consisted solely of an entry on the books of the company and did not represent the receipt of any cash from the pension plan. Nonetheless, it increased the company's reported earnings by an average of $14.4 million per year for the years 1988 to 1994. This inflationary strategy transformed loss into significant gain for the engineering operations for all of those years (except in 1991, when there was only a nominal profit).

The company, although restricted by pension laws from some uses of the pension surpluses, could have liquidated the plan and paid the excess to the corporation either for growth or for distribution to shareholders. Or it could have merged with a company having a pension fund deficit. It pursued none of these courses.

BEHIND THE SCREEN

The question that arises at this point is: Where was the board? Directors should have noticed the decline in the company's core business and asked the company to reflect it in their financial statements – and, more important, to address it. This is supposedly one of the main reasons companies have boards of directors. But as the Stone & Webster story illustrates, boards are rarely enough. Behind the screen of the independent board acting as a monitor of management was the reality of a self-perpetuating dynasty.

As of year-end 1993, Stone & Webster had a board of directors composed of three corporate employees and nine others considered to be outside directors. Despite the appearance of independence, however, the Stone & Webster board was not equipped to respond to the company's situation. Aside from the redoubtable Peter Grace, then in his 50th year of service as a director, none of the outsiders had more than a nominal stake in the company. Indeed, the eight of them together owned only 1,900 shares, worth at that time just $50,000 – or approximately the amount of the consulting fee that director Kent Hansen received in addition to his director's pay.

The outside directors at the time had an average tenure of 16 years. Mr Grace at age 80 was the Dean of the Board, followed by Howard Clark, former CEO of American Express, at age 78, and bankers Bill Brown and John Hooper in their mid-70s. Bill Allen, the retiring CEO, was 74 and completing his 46th year in the company's employ. Phasing off the board for a promising career as a United States Senator was Fred Thompson, a Tennessee Republican.[2]

The overall impression was one of extreme stability – even stagnation – all the while Stone & Webster was in the throes of systemic collapse. Some force for ordered change needed to emerge – but who and how?

SHAREHOLDER ACTION

At the time of these developments, I was a relatively new shareholder in Stone & Webster. As a principal of LENS, an activist fund, I am always on the lookout for companies where there is a 'governance gap' that can be closed by shareholder activism. LENS had bought over 90,000 shares at under $30 per share in the summer of 1993.[3] We knew that the company's share price could return to the 40s, but this would require concerted action. So in late 1993, I contacted another shareholder, Joseph Blasi, a leader in the field of employee stock ownership plans (ESOPs). Blasi and I submitted our names as candidates for the company's board of directors.

The Stone & Webster nomination process at this time of systemic collapse illumines the essential difference between a mechanical obedience to legal rules and the alive reaction to interrelating agents characteristic of healthy organisms. When we wrote the company in January 1994 asking to be added to its slate of board nominees, we were told – for the first time – that a nominating committee had been formed in the previous September. We learned also that this committee, almost like the full-grown Venus of Botticelli's famous painting, arrived armed with traditions, rules, and practices with which we could not possibly comply!

Our letter to the newly discovered nominating committee chairman, Kent Hansen, elicited the following response:

> *'The Nominating Committee, both on an informal basis prior to its formation in September and since its formation in September, has been giving careful consideration to a number of proposed candidates for nomination by the stockholders. Prior to our consideration of any nomination we review detailed written information about the background and qualifications of the individual being proposed together with the type of information that would be required to be disclosed in the Company's proxy material.*
>
> *'Although it is very late in the process of our consideration, we would be pleased to receive proposals made by you with such information. Quite frankly, in view of the necessity of our finalizing the Company's proxy materials within the next month, I am not certain that the Committee will have sufficient time to give your proposed nominations the kind of consideration we typically give to nominees so as to realistically be in a position of presenting them to the Board and including them in our proxy material for this year's annual meeting.*
>
> *'It does not appear to me to be necessary for us to have a meeting until the Committee has had an opportunity to review the background and qualifications of the proposed nominees that you would make.'*

While this letter might not pass muster with the SEC's newly created 'plain English' program, its message was clear: 'We have the power to control the director selection process. You are at liberty to waste your time contesting that simple truth, but we won't meet with you in any event.'

We got the same answer when we wrote the trustee for the employee stock ownership plan, Chase Manhattan Bank:

> *'Chase has evaluated the information provided in your letter as directed Trustee of the Stone & Webster plans. The resources available to Chase enable us to fulfill our fiduciary responsibilities through internal means. Accordingly, we thank you for your interest in this matter but do not feel that it is necessary at this time to meet with your company.'*

In simple English, this letter says: 'We know the law. We are not legally required to meet with you. So long as we work for the management of Stone & Webster, we choose not to meet with you.'

The governance implications of this answer are worth exploring. Clearly, it is the owners of a public company who have the greatest incentive to be concerned about such matters – and the highest degree of independence to act on their concern. Whether this concern is translatable into action depends on many things, including the following:

- Does the shareholder have a large enough financial interest to justify spending the funds necessary to address the problem effectively?
- Can other shareholders be expected to share the same concerns to the point of cost-free voting support, if nothing else?
- Are the principal shareholders free from other commercial relationships that could be more important to them than their holdings in the company?

At least one major shareholder failed on all three of these points. The progress of shareholder effectiveness in Stone & Webster was delayed and inhibited by the existence of Chase Manhattan Bank as trustee for the employee benefit plans, which had 35.7% of the total outstanding voting shares for the 1994 annual meeting.

When a company consistently loses money in its principal business, it normally provokes harsh discipline from the marketplace. In debt markets, it finds it increasingly difficult to borrow at favourable rates. In equity markets, its stock loses value, and it becomes more and more vulnerable to takeover. Stone & Webster immunised itself from full marketplace accountability through its relationship with Chase, which could function as both a generous lender and, through its role as trustee of the company's employee stock ownership plan, as an uncomplaining investor.

There had been (and there continues to be) a long-standing and close business and commercial relationship between Stone & Webster and Chase. Chase was appointed trustee by the management of the company, receiving significant compensation for its services as both a commercial and investment banker. Interlocking directors strengthened this bond. One of the directors of Stone & Webster, John Hooper, was formerly a vice chairman of Chase. In an earlier time, Stone & Webster CEO Whitney Stone was a member of Chase's board of directors. As a practical matter, no outside candidate for election to the board of Stone & Webster could expect to be successful without the support of Chase. At the time, the company did not have confidential proxy voting, so it was unlikely that Chase would join our cause anonymously or otherwise.

Given all these circumstances, it is not surprising, then, that Chase rebuffed our efforts to meet with them as fellow shareholders.

We finally did get a meeting with the three senior officers of the company – CEO Bill Allen, CFO Bill Eagan, and COO Bruce Coles – but it was most disappointing. When we asked, 'Why does the company hold on to almost $40 million in the common stock of Tenneco?' the soon-to-depart CFOs response had the virtue of novelty: 'Because it didn't cost anything.' From the grand days of its long-abandoned strong position as investment banker to the utilities business, Stone & Webster had acquired its stake as part of the fee for putting together the modern Tenneco some 30 years ago. Although the holding had no 'cost basis' in the parlance of the Internal Revenue Service, it was clearly an asset of value, which could be easily converted into cash and used for corporate or shareholder wealth creation.

When we asked about the bonds and the overfunding, Eagan and Coles, joined by Allen, took the position that the engineering and construction business had a lot of risks, that reserve assets were absolutely essential in order to get business and particularly bonding; anyone saying anything else was both ignorant and dangerous. When we asked: 'Can you quantify that? How many assets, etc.', we learned only that 'Goldman Sachs advises us and approves of the way we do things'.

My partners and I left the meeting with the same impression: none of the three had even a twinge of regret about letting significant assets lie fallow. It was a striking case of corporate stasis. Contrast this to the way Microsoft reacted to its owners' concerns about the growing competitive threat posed by the Internet in the spring of 1995. The company could have rested on its laurels (it had just launched Windows 95 to great acclaim) but instead it jumped into motion, becoming dominant in the new field. Microsoft is the epitome of a company with active owners who are capable of refocusing the enterprise's energy.

'CLASS II' GOVERNANCE

In the Stone & Webster situation, all of the conventional theories for holding corporate management accountable to an 'independent board' dissolved in the determination of management to abuse its control over corporate resources. The corporate mechanism was transformed from its intended role as the guarantor of a dynamic interrelationship of the various corporate constituencies to a mechanical stasis of centralised power preserved by dominion over the rule-setting capabilities.

This was 'Class II' governance at its worst. Stone & Webster strove to preserve power rather than using corporate resources to adapt to the challenges of the changing world – a drive that inclined Stone & Webster into a spiral of diminishing returns on all levels. With none of the agents in a position of power being effectively accountable to anyone else, the corporation persevered on the path of 'eating its own seed corn'.

What could we do? Unfortunately, the law is not available as a remedy for shareholders in a situation like this. On the contrary, the law can be – and has been – used as a device to entrench the incumbents. Our suit filed in the Federal District Court for the District of Massachusetts requesting judicial intervention into this situation of mismanagement and entrenchment was unsuccessful. Courts are traditionally loath to involve themselves in matters they consider private. The company, for its part, continued to rebuff our attempts to hold a meeting to discuss changes at the company. That such resistance metastasises the vital energies of a complex adaptive system is of only secondary relevance to those whose primary concern is the retention of power.

In the end, neither Blasi nor I became nominees to the company's board of directors. Our efforts to change, however, did have an impact. Emergence from this year-end 1994 miasma is attributable to the seemingly spontaneous generation of new forces, which slowly but surely ushered in true progress:

The company's CEO Bill Allen retired after 46 years at the company and ten years at its helm, hand-picking Bruce Coles as his successor. Those who appeal to powerful mentors frequently lack leadership qualities themselves, and so Coles lasted only months, leaving the board a free hand to go 'outside' to find a permanent successor.

As the passage of time tolled the end of Peter Grace's 49 years on the board, it tolled for Howard Clark with 25 years, for Bill Brown with 24, and for John Hooper with 20. Fred Thompson left to serve the people of Tennessee, and Meredith Spangler resigned immediately after being re-elected at the 1995 annual meeting. New directors were added with no institutional memory of the glories of the past and little protection from the realities of the present precarious situation.

With the company's stock selling at little above the cash value of the corporation's assets for several years, new shareholders had acquired significant equity positions – notably Cilluffo Associates of Portsmouth, New Hampshire, with holdings up to 12% and our LENS group, which increased its holdings to 1.5%. Frank J.A. Cilluffo was elected to the board of directors and did not hesitate to express his dissatisfaction with the corporate direction.

Stone & Webster changed its method of reporting the company's 'pension surplus', dissolved its holding company shell, moved out of New York City, and sold most assets unrelated to its principal business, making commitments to sell the rest.

The company adopted a policy of confidential voting as part of overall governance reforms that succeeded in earning the trust of its most critical shareholders. (The Chase Bank treated the changes with its time-honoured indifference.)

In 1996, under the direction of new CEO H. Kerner Smith, the company appointed and elected three new directors, including especially entrepreneur John P. Merrill, who has an outstanding record of realising values for shareholders. With no previous ties to the company, these individuals could chart a new and better course.

The new board engaged the services of professional executive recruiters in 1997 to find a new 'outside' CFO.

Share prices rose. They are now hovering around 50.

SUMMARY AND CONCLUSION

Could Stone & Webster have moved from stagnation to vitality without the involvement of the activist shareholders? I, for one, don't think so. There were too many illusions at work. Somebody had to say, not once, but repeatedly: 'The Emperor has no clothes.' It was not the auditors, or the investment bankers, or the traditional directors; it was the shareholders.

The system almost short-circuited from the presence of a single, interest-conflicted trustee who controlled almost one-third of the votes. Fortunately, however, the superior energy of other shareholders prevailed. The persistence of independent, informed, motivated, and empowered owners provided the energy needed to transform a dying enterprise into a vital one. The result was a restored corporation; one ready to meet the growing need for skilled and reliable engineering around the globe, and to give back more to society than its managers ever received. At the end of the day, Stone & Webster's elaborate efforts to entrench its failing status quo created such a pervasive imbalance that it attracted new elements – active shareholders that became the agents of its successful future.

9

Institutional shareholders, the key agents in fiduciary capitalism, are not monoliths. Institutions elect, pay, and work their trustees in different ways. Conflicts of interest and investment horizons also vary. Of all institutional shareholders, private pension funds show the most promise. They and other funds need to find their 'voice' as New Owners.

9

The New Owners

> *'She's a plain little thing, isn't she?'*[1]

The existence of investment funds large enough to acquire, hold, and exercise control over any company or industry will define national strength in the 21st century, much as nuclear weapons did in the 20th century and naval superiority did in the century before. With the end of the Cold War and the break-up of the old 'military industrial complex',[2] geopolitical warfare has waned in importance. Rising in its stead is a new dynamic: competitive battles among nation-sized public corporations. What these companies do, and how they do it, is perhaps the most important question that civilisation now faces. Who will ensure accountability in these behemoths?

AN OVERVIEW OF INSTITUTIONAL INVESTORS

The guardian of corporate accountability in the next century should be a participant who can be independent, informed, motivated, and empowered. Comparing directors, managers, and institutional shareholders earlier in this book (Chapter 4), we said that of these three main groups, shareholders have the highest potential. In the present chapter, which proposes a system of *fiduciary capitalism* based on shareholder involvement, we will ask another important question: *which shareholders* and *why*?

As mentioned in Chapter 4, institutional shareholders (as opposed to individual shareholders) together own nearly half (47.4%) of all of the equity in American corporations – approximately $4.35 trillion worth as of the second quarter of 1996. Even more impressively, they own some 57% of the largest 1000 public companies. And over half of this equity – 30% of the total – is owned by public and private pension funds.[3]

Institutional investors are not 'monoliths', as former SEC Commissioner A.A. Sommer, Jr, aptly observed nearly a decade ago.[4] There are many different types of institutional shareholders, namely public pension funds, private pension funds, money managers (also called investment advisors), mutual funds (more formally called investment companies), insurance companies, banks, trust companies, and foundations.

Comparing various types of investors (except for money managers, which we will consider as a separate case), we can see that fund groups are different in the way they elect trustees, in the amount they pay trustees, in the amount of time trustees spend in fulfilling their fiduciary duties, in the potential conflicts of interest they face, and, most important, in their investment horizons.

Public pension funds

Public pension funds elect their trustees in several different ways. These run a gamut from the Federal Employees' Retirement System (FERSA), where trustees are selected by the President,[5] to state and local plans, where the governor makes appointments. In some state and local plans, certain officials are designated *ex officio* to be trustees; in others, participants elect trustees. And finally, in some public plans (such as New York) the public elects the fiduciary. Public fund trustees receive modest pay for their fiduciary functioning.[6] Many are civil servants who receive virtually no extra pay for their services, which are extensive. For example, trustees of the California Public Employees' Retirement System (CalPERS) are expected to read some 26,000 pages of material per year.

In California, pursuant to statute, the governor makes appointments of representatives of various private sector interest groups as trustees. The problem is that they don't get paid much, and the first-class private-sector people simply cannot afford to take on the full schedule adopted by the trustees currently serving on the fund, many of whom are former white-collar union officers.

Compared with other investors, public fund trustees tend to have the greatest level of independence from corporate management, because their primary goal is to build the assets of fund beneficiaries. Admittedly, however, this independence is not absolute in every case. As discussed in Chapter 4, they do have some constraints on their freedom to promote beneficiaries' rights. As Barry Rehfeld noted in a recent issue of *Institutional Investor*, 'It's easy to imagine the public outcry that would result if CalPERS were seen to be using taxpayer funds to help a corporate raider throw thousands of California voters out of work by downsizing a local company.'[7]

The investment horizon of public pension funds is long term. Their large stakes in companies, combined with the practice of indexing, make them virtually permanent owners. For them – unlike individual investors and most other institutional investors – there can be no 'Wall Street Walk'; it is too costly to divest holdings.[8] Pension plan investments – particularly with defined benefit plans – fund known commitments. The commitments are to retirees during their natural life; and everyone knows actuarially how long people will live. Thus, investment planning can be based in certainty.

Private pension funds

Private pension funds are retirement funds created for the benefit of employees of corporations. As mentioned in previous chapters, these funds are governed by the Employees Retirement Income Security Act of 1974 (ERISA).

At private pension funds, trustees are chosen by plan sponsors – that is, the corporations that set up the funds for their employees. These corporate sponsors pay pension fund trustees very little for their work as fiduciaries. They usually perform it as an adjunct to other corporate work. For example, the members of the finance committee of General Motors, which is its 'named fiduciary' under ERISA, get no special compensation for their trustee function; it is considered ancillary to their main corporate responsibilities. Not surprisingly, given these conditions, the trustees of private pension funds spend little time fulfilling their duties.

Private pension funds are clearly beholden to their sponsors. Indeed, the fundamental contradiction in ERISA, as others before me have noted, is the control of the trustees by the company sponsoring the employee benefit plan. How can one expect corporate employees – with normal appetite for advancement – to be 'independent' of those who hire them, notwithstanding the unmistakable language of the statute requiring that trust assets be administered 'for the exclusive benefit of plan participants'?

The investment horizon of private pension funds is as long term as the horizon of public funds and for the same reason. This long-term holding pattern is an extremely important qualification for new ownership, as we shall see.

Insurance companies, banks, and foundations

Insurance companies, banks, and foundations select fiduciaries pursuant to local law, their charters and by-laws. Insurance company and bank employees receive only modest pay for their fiduciary work, which is superimposed on (and secondary to) existing duties. Like the employees acting as trustees of ERISA funds, these hired hands are none too likely to 'bite the hand that feeds them'. Trustees of large foundations and universities, with few exceptions, define the 'establishment'. They receive comfortable pay for their work, which grants them desired prestige and power.

In this area, there can be interlocks. The same individuals seem to end up as trustees of the Ford Foundation, directors of AT&T, and directors of Cummins Engine. There is a world of 'top people' who serve on each others' boards, thus ensuring both prestige and compliance. The foundations and the universities would not dream of offending 'the great and the good'. They would rather vote with management on proxy issues than side with activists (or act themselves) even if action is in the interests of their fund owners.

The investment horizon of all these institutions is relatively short term. In particular, insurance companies (particularly casualty companies) may need money 'tomorrow' – not ten years from now – if disaster strikes today.

Mutual funds

In mutual funds (more formally known as investment companies), the 'independent directors' are chosen under the provisions of the federal Investment Company Act of 1940. They are paid extremely well for services that basically consist of deciding whether to ratify the investment management contract (with a firm whose principals invited them to serve as directors!), and they almost invariably vote to do so. In other words, mutual fund trustees are paid so much too much for doing so little that they are unlikely to disturb their sponsors.

These funds, too, have a short-term perspective. Moreover, they must place a high priority on liquidity in order to meet the threat of redemptions. Suppose that all the investors who have been pouring money into equity mutual funds decide to redeem. The funds have very few days to pay them – and they must pay in cash. In order to raise this cash, they must sell portfolio securities, selling even stocks that they would ideally like to keep for the long run.

MONEY MANAGERS: THE 'FLYWHEEL OF PROFITS'

Although all institutional investors act through trustees or other fiduciaries, many of them delegate out investment management responsibilities to other professionals. This distinction between *assets held in trust* and *assets managed* will be critically important as we explore the nature and potential of the 'New Owners'. Chart 9.1 shows how this distinction varies according to fund type.[9]

Chart 9.1

Percentage of Total US Institutional Assets – Held and Managed		
Type of Institution	Assets held	Assets under management
Pension Funds	47.2%	20.7%
Money Managers	0.0%	4.8%
Mutual Funds	19.0%	28.0%
Insurance Companies	19.5%	26.3%
Banks and Trust Companies	12.3%	19.0%
Foundations	2.0%	1.2%

Chart 9.1 covers only the primary types of institutional investors. Beyond these primary types, there are many others. Any investing group that rises above individual status by forming a partnership or corporation to invest jointly is an institutional investor. As such, the percentage of equities owned by 'institutions' may be even higher than the scholars estimate – perhaps as high as 60%.

The odd man out in this list is clearly the pension funds. Their percentage of total assets held is higher than their percentage of assets under management. They hold nearly half of all assets, but manage only 20%. Private funds have an *even greater tendency* in this direction. Yet it is precisely private pension funds that offer the greatest hope as the New Owner.

Having seen the various types of institutional investors, let us now look at the people to whom they often delegate investment decisions: money managers. Although as independent organisations, these institutions manage less than 5% of corporate equities in the United States, their impact is in fact broader, since other types of institutions, such as banks, insurance companies, and mutual funds, own money management companies – sometimes through a complicated layering of subsidiaries.[10]

These managers receive a small percentage (typically 1%) of these assets as their compensation. This can amount to substantial sums at very high profit margins. One percent of $4.35 trillion (the amount of equity held by institutional investors, as mentioned above) is $43.5 billion per year. Yet nowhere near that amount is necessary to manage these investments. After a manager has staffed adequately to manage the first billion dollars' worth of assets, the incremental costs for additional business are virtually nothing.

In the course of NBC's widely acclaimed television special, 'The Biggest Lump of Money in the World', shown first in July 1985, Bob Kirby, then CEO of the Capital Group, dramatically called the world's attention to the new profit cornucopia when he said: 'I don't know why everybody is pointing at movie stars and basketball players, when the people I know who are making over $5 million a year are in the money management business.'

Management fees are not only large, they are predictable. In good times and in bad, they accrue daily (and nightly for that matter). Money management has become the profit flywheel on which all modern financial conglomerates are built. Take, for example, the traditional Mellon Bank in Pittsburgh. Through aggressive strategic acquisitions – the Dreyfus Mutual Funds, The Boston Company – Mellon built a money management foundation underneath its banking structure. In its 1996 annual report, Mellon reports that the return on average common shareholders' equity for their corporate institutional investment services was 24%, up from 23% in 1995. This compared favourably with the bank's other operations for that year.[11]

Beyond the appeal of generous margins, money managers have not had to demonstrate performance results significantly in excess of what an investor could achieve through purchase of an index fund. Why haven't trustees of funds tried to negotiate management fees directly tied to value added? The obvious answer is a conflict of interests between their fiduciary duties as the trustees of beneficiaries, and their ongoing relationships with plan sponsors.

PENSION FUNDS: A SPECIAL KIND OF OWNER

In the previous sections of this chapter, we have seen that no one type of investment fund is perfectly suited to take on the role of the New Owner. Considering their long-term perspective, though, pension funds may be better suited than other types of funds to assume the independence, information, motivation, and empowerment of the New Owners we envision. Private-sector pension funds may have conflicts of interest, but they are ideally suited to take on the role of the New Owner. They have an easily defined class of beneficiaries to whom they are accountable – people who are going to retire in an average number of years. All other institutions have the entire spectrum of beneficiaries with all different interests and needs, thus blunting the sharp definition of fiduciary obligations.

At this juncture, some background on this sector may be appropriate.

In the years immediately following the devastation of World War II, countries in the prosperous West set policies to provide for retirement income. This activity was particularly pronounced in the countries belonging to the Organisation for Economic Cooperation and Development, where retirement programs took two different paths: public and compulsory versus private and voluntary. France, Germany, and Italy made retirement obligations a commitment of the state (one of many unfunded ones). Canada, Japan, the Netherlands, the United Kingdom, and the United States, by contrast, devised systems encouraging individuals and employers through tax incentives to save in advance for retirement needs. (The annual 'tax cost' of pensions is one of the largest items in the American federal budget.)

Governments in all these countries mandated that the funds be held in trust, where they are available for investment and not for consumption. And these trusts quickly became the largest repository for savings in the developed world.

The traditional mandate of trustees is to 'preserve capital; don't take risks'. And so for generations, through much of the 19th and 20th centuries, this meant: buy bonds. Indeed, for many years in the United States, state governments specifically limited trustee investments to bonds and then gradually expanded to the 'legal list' of permitted equities. This changed in 1974, with the passage of ERISA, which importantly expanded the common law investment standard of the prudent man by allowing a trustee's performance to be evaluated by the performance of the whole portfolio and not by individual stocks.[12] One by one the states repealed restrictive legislation; the last to join the modern anglophone world was Indiana in 1997.

Thus by the end of the 20th century, by which time funds were holding upwards of $7.5 trillion, most fund holdings (65%) were in equity securities.[13] The involvement of these enormous trust funds in equity markets is having a profound impact – they are analogous to a great mountain that creates its own weather system.

For example, a recent trend towards investment of US pension fund assets outside of the country has created an unexpectedly powerful 'export' of shareholder activism. The numbers involved are impressive. Consider that the principal US institutions making foreign equity investment (chiefly pension funds) *tripled* their foreign equity holdings in the first half of the 1990s – increasing them from $97.5 billion in 1990 to $281.7 billion in 1994. The 25 largest pension funds held a total of $85.3 billion in international stocks (up to 10.5% of their total equity portfolio in 1994). And many of these funds have been trying to influence the governance of the companies they own – communicating with managements and actively voting their proxies.

These 'activist' funds – free abroad from the constraints of retaliation that hampered them at home – voted substantially all of their foreign proxies based on the best interests of fund beneficiaries, in accordance with the US Department of Labor's increasingly specific guidelines to do so. The combination of rapidly escalating holdings and virtually total participation were in contrast to the somnolence of local institutions. For example, in the United Kingdom, the most recent studies show that only about 35% of corporate stock is represented at annual meetings (or in UK parlance, annual general meetings – AGM).

The New Owners have made an indelible mark on the landscape of governance around the world. Lord Hanson had to withdraw a resolution at the AGM of the company that he had founded; the Saatchi brothers were fired by the company with their name on the door – all on account of the presence of pension funds in the governance of modern corporations.

CHALLENGES FOR OWNER ACTIVISM

The notion of a special class of independent, informed, and motivated share-holders as the 'monitors' of corporate management has great appeal. There are several impediments to this idea, however – namely, lack of independence, the 'free rider' challenge, de facto control, bureaucracy, and what I call the 'Buffet Phenomenon'.

Lack of independence

As discussed in Chapter 4, the trustees of private pension plans are appointed by the plans' sponsoring companies, which are anxious to avoid a reputation for activism – as are the money managers to whom the trustees often delegate their buying decisions. In extreme cases activism invites reprisal; in more moderate circumstances it would tend to make them 'unclubable' in a world where lucrative management contracts are available only to those who 'go along to get along'. The internationalisation of pension fund investments (and eventually management) may diminish the problem of conflicts of interest in time, but meanwhile laws go unenforced.[14]

Neither regulators nor courts have been willing to enforce statutory provisions of ERISA that require trustees to administer plans 'for the exclusive benefit of plan participants'. The trustee function, although increasingly lucrative, is ancillary to the traditional commercial ties between financial conglomerates and most plan sponsor corporations. Institutions are reluctant to give up banking, insuring, underwriting, and other service functions for which they are well equipped unless they literally have no other choice. *Thus, one of the strongest potential monitors has been permitted to do nothing.* Similar patterns exist in other private-sector funds such as mutual funds, insurance companies, banks, trusts, and foundations.

Only the public pension funds are free of this conflict of commercial interest. They are not trying to sell anybody anything. That factor, rather than any particular competency in the commercial area or any real capacity for sustained involvement, is why funds such CalPERS have been the most conspicuous of monitors. Unfortunately, however, their limited business experience, combined with their low salaries and high exposure to ultimate political restraint (mentioned above), places severe and perhaps permanent limitations on their suitability for monitoring.

The 'free rider' challenge

In a well-known 1994 *Harvard Business Review* article, 'Institutional Investors: the Reluctant Activists', Robert C. Pozen, then general counsel of Fidelity, expressed concern with the so-called 'free rider' problem, whereby non-participants are carried by the energy of the initiators. Pozen, who is now CEO of this leading investment company (which has scores of mutual funds) noted that 'as a practical matter, it is virtually impossible for the activist investors to force all other benefiting shareholders to contribute to the effort'. If the managers of mutual funds take an activist approach in the companies they own, said Pozen, the unreimbursed costs for this activity would exceed their fee levels, which are calculated on the assumption of passivity.[15] In other words, they would have to spend more money than they make.

The same problem applies to other institutional investors. Indeed, there is a vast scholarly literature on this topic. When my company, LENS, hosted a contest for corporate governance papers, many of the 103 studies we received made mention of the 'free rider' and the related problem of 'agency costs'. In the parlance of financial economists and corporate lawyers, 'agent' means a secondary actor – someone who takes action on behalf of someone else. (This definition is very different from the one used by computer modelers, who use 'agent' to indicate a *primary* 'actor' – very simply, someone who takes action.)

Control

Control is another agency problem – one that arises when a particular type of capitalisation gives voting control to one class of equity holders while other classes represent a majority of the invested capital. The problem is not bad if the class with legal control represents the interests of others. Ultimately, the suitability of a voting class as 'monitor' depends on whether it represents a spectrum of ownership interest broad enough to give confidence act as a reliable proxy for *all* of the beneficial owners.

A recurrent pattern in the American experience is a 'voting class' that functions as a device to ensure that specific individuals, and their heirs, retain control of a corporate enterprise. For example, as mentioned in Chapter 4 (see box, 'The Phoney Freedom of the Press'), many publishing companies – New York Times, Washington Post, Dow Jones, Los Angeles Times (now part of the Times Mirror media giant) – have traditionally entrenched voting control in 'founding families'. This pattern is disingenuously justified as being in aid of a free press, when it has more to do with the simple mechanics of perpetuating power in a special minority.

A creative twist on this same phenomenon is the Reader's Digest, where the majority owner of voting shares is a charitable foundation established by a founding family. The question that needs to be asked in all cases is – does the existence of a controlling class of equity stockholders enhance the position of all owners? (See box.)

PAIN IN PLEASANTVILLE FOR READER'S DIGEST

The publisher's scary story: Lower profits, fewer readers.

… Although investors have been hit hard by the troubles, their lack of voting shares means it's hard to press for change. After Wallace's death, he left 71% of the company's voting rights to two charities, the DeWitt Wallace Reader's Digest Fund and the Lila Wallace Reader's Digest Fund. Most of the rest is held by an employee stock ownership plan and former executives.

It's a tight-knit group. Many of the funds' board members also sit on the company board, including the funds' President M. Christine DeVita, Reader's Digest general counsel Melvin R. Laird, and Chase Manhattan Bank CEO Walter V. Shipley. Ex-CEO Grune has chaired the funds' board since 1984. 'This is the coziest relationship between a corporation and its investors I've ever seen', says Bob Monks of LENS, an activist investor fund. 'It will make it impossible for the company to turn around.' The company says these relationships have been fully disclosed. Board members wouldn't comment on the structures.

The setup has kept Monks and other shareholder activists at bay. 'I examined investing, but came to the conclusion that there's nothing we can do', he says. Michael Price, chief executive of Franklin Mutual Fund Advisors, agrees. He was the prime suspect when the volume of Reader's Digest shares skyrocketed in May, but he says he was golfing that day and has no interest. 'It's been run poorly', he says, 'and there is nothing anybody but the funds and the board can do.'

Source: *Business Week*, 14 July 1997.

The challenge of bureaucracy

Will the trustees themselves become 'just another bureaucracy'? This obvious risk merits exquisite attention. The last thing the world's corporations need is the addition of another group to whom to be accountable. My point is not that corporations need to be accountable to trustees; rather it is that *corporations, their managements, and their trustees need to be accountable to pension fund beneficiaries and, through them, to the general public.*

The New Owners – a broad class of activist investors – are uniquely equipped to ensure corporate accountability in this broad sense, and they can do this without creating a bureaucracy. The technology of the Internet now permits free, instant, and interactive communication between and among beneficiaries and their trustees. This communication will enable trustees to create protocols and procedures by which they can inform beneficiaries and obtain whatever level of ratification or consent they may deem appropriate.

The 'Buffet phenomenon'

Finally, there is the 'Buffet phenomenon'. By negotiating the creation of a special class of security, not available to others, Warren Buffet has ensured that the undoubted benefits of his involvement in companies will not entirely pass to others. Buffet's fame and skill make his involvement in a company value-adding for all owners. The question is whether it is appropriate for Buffet and the management to negotiate the terms of his involvement without consultation or consent of the other owners.

Consider Buffet's involvement in Champion Paper, for example. While it is clear that what is good for Buffet – a rising stock price – is good for all the shareholders, what is bad for all the shareholders is not so bad for Buffet, who continues to collect a very expensive (from the company's perspective) preferred stock dividend in bad times as well as good. This tends, of course, to depress the earnings and the value of the common stock. Even though Buffet has sufficient incentive and integrity to act as 'monitor' for all owners, it is worth noting that he sets his own price. In a person less motivated and less scrupulous than Warren Buffet, such an arrangement could be abusive. There would be an overwhelming temptation for management to give stock with particularly attractive characteristics to a 'White Squire' in exchange for job security.

LENS: A 'SPECIAL PURPOSE' INVESTOR

These challenges are not insurmountable. Investors can be independent, informed, motivated, and empowered. Each type of investor has its own way of arriving at these goals. The following discussion outlines what we have done at LENS towards these ends.

LENS is a special-purpose activist partnership that invests its own and clients' money in underperforming companies. As the optical nature of our name suggests, we have a focus – identifying and closing the 'governance gap' at underperforming companies. As discussed in Chapter 6, that gap can be wide indeed. Over the last dozen years, we have been very much involved as an 'activist investor' in many of the great companies of America – American Express, Westinghouse, Eastman Kodak, Sears, Scott Paper, Stone & Webster, Tenneco, Corning, and WMX among them.

At first with the investment of our own money and eventually with over $100 million of clients' funds, we have brought about real improvements in many of these companies. In our five years of existence, we have outperformed the conventional market indexes with an annualised return of 23.8% against 19% for the Standard & Poor's index. This record of achievement is a real-life experiment proving that a company having independent, informed, motivated, and empowered owners is worth more than one without – as discussed in previous chapters.[16] (Full details about LENS are available on the Web – http://www.lens-inc.com.)

Clearly, LENS has received superior returns from its policy of investing in underperforming companies susceptible to improvement through the involvement of their owners. Given our success, why haven't other institutional investors done the same? Why have so few institutional investors emerged as activists? Why have so many retained their customary passive posture?

One reason is the free rider phenomenon: activism is expensive; why pay for it if someone else is doing it and others get the benefit? Also, many institutional investors are poorly equipped to be activists. They do not have people with the necessary specialised experience; they are afraid to antagonize present or potential customers; and they do not want to acquire the image in the market place of being hostile to management. With the widespread adoption of 'confidential voting', however, investors like LENS can be confident of getting the support of other institutions on critical voting matters.

A ROLE FOR GOVERNMENT?

In this area, as any other area of public policy, a question presents itself. Is there a role for government involvement? In my view, given the need for owner independence, information, motivation, and empowerment, the answer is yes.

Every credible analyst of the desirable scope of government action – from Adam Smith and John Locke centuries ago to Frederick Hayek and Milton Friedman in our day – agrees that government *must* set standards and enforce compliance with them in order to encourage action for public good and discourage actions for public harm. One recalls Adam Smith's famous statement that without a civil government to protect property, owners cannot 'sleep a single night in security'.[17]

It is within the authority of the present government to declare (without passing any new laws) the existence of a *federal standard of ownership*. This would represent a finding by government that the existence of independent and informed owners in the governance of public companies is in the public interest.

In this way, the federal and state governments would simply enforce existing conflict of interest and disclosure statutes. Such a standard would permit institutions to monitor their portfolio companies without the competitive repercussions that are now inhibiting such action. An inter-agency group could be created to ensure enforcement of existing law in a consistent manner.

It must be stressed that *no new authorising legislation* would be necessary to justify federal involvement in this area. The laws creating trustee authority and responsibilities *already exist* under the various banking laws, securities laws, the Investment Company Act of 1940, and, of course, ERISA.

Despite the existence of these laws, at present there are no *working* governmental incentives for appropriate action on behalf of fund beneficiaries. Under current conditions, trustees can jeopardise their position in the marketplace just *because* they are doing what is right. To cite just one example, Batterymarch Financial is believed to have lost substantial business because of the outspoken activism of its founder and CEO, Dean LeBaron.

Government, through its inaction, is encouraging antisocial conduct by corporations. Clearly, change is urgently required – and, one hopes, imminent. Every requisite law is now in place, every necessary agency is functioning; all that is needed is for government to *recognise officially and explicitly the value and necessity of shareholder involvement.* This is already in effect for corporations that have ERISA funds; it should be declared for all other fiduciary funds. This will put trustees on notice that the government will take action across the board – in mutual funds, banks, insurance companies, foundations, and money-management firms – to enforce existing laws, starting with conflict of interest laws.

A clear government stance in favour of activism – indeed, a government standard of activism – makes particular sense when it comes to pension funds. After all, they exist in large part because of a national policy of subsidy, so their functioning is ultimately susceptible to monitoring and suggestion of their creating authority. Pension funds are a public issue.

All countries today are struggling with the problem of financing the retirement years of a longer-living population; those countries who have encouraged individuals to make provision for their own needs are thrice blessed. The extent of demand on the public treasury is diminished, the nation acquires the invaluable resource of long-term capital funds for investment, and the pension fund beneficiaries comprise a legitimate and effective ownership to whom managements can be accountable.

Critics may protest this proposed federal standard of ownership as creeping socialism, yet it is precisely the opposite. Putting owners in charge of what they own is the purest form of capitalism. Government involvement in protecting property rights is hardly socialistic. Indeed, government is already substantially involved as a monitor of corporate ownership, so this area is clearly in its domain, and should be.

NOTES ON FERSA AND ERISA

Government involvement in pensions need not mean government interference. Consider FERSA, mentioned earlier. Under FERSA, new federal hires are not automatically given the traditional cost of living adjustment (COLA) to their promised pension payments. Instead, they are allowed to accumulate savings on a tax-aided basis in a defined contribution trust – the substantial equivalent of the 401(k) plan. The equity index tranche of the trust is administered by a private-sector bank (now BZW), which decides how to vote portfolio securities.[18] This first entry of government into the private equity markets did not elicit howls of protest against the entering wedge of 'socialism', even though state, local, and federal pension plans now own over 10% of total outstanding equity.

ERISA is an even more well-known example of successful, non-intrusive government involvement in pension markets. Over the past dozen years, the Pension and Welfare Benefits Agency of the Department of Labor has developed a careful exegesis of the ownership responsibilities of fiduciaries with respect to portfolio companies. The Department of Labor concludes that ownership rights are 'plan assets' that must be administered with the same level of prudence as is required in managing other assets. How they are administered is left to the discretion of the particular fiduciaries and the law of the controlling jurisdiction. The other government agencies can either adopt the Department of Labor standards or develop their own.

As mentioned earlier, however, conflicts of interest often prevent trustees of ERISA plans from following either the letter or the spirit of ERISA in this respect. If the government would outline clearly the existence of a federal law of ownership, as I am proposing, courts could (and surely would) require that any fiduciary having multiple relationships with a plan sponsor take on the burden of proving that no harm is caused beneficiaries on this account. Readers may wish to look ahead to the epilogue.

The current level of management fees is fully adequate either to justify giving up other business relationships with the plan sponsor or to support a new stand-alone, special-purpose 'ownership fiduciary' institution. There is no economic reason therefore that trustee ownership should not be fully functional at the present time. What is lacking is the sense of commitment that can only come from government.

It is not reasonable to expect private sector firms to voluntarily place themselves at competitive disadvantage. On the other hand, if the government makes clear its determination that ERISA fiduciaries should operate within the 'exclusive benefit' rules, there will be a high level of compliance. Many managers would like to discharge their responsibilities today, but are inhibited in doing so because their competitors not only would make more money but would be in a position of unfair advantage in the market place.

The government needs to establish uniform standards and enforcement practices to pull together the institutional fiduciaries, the scope of whose responsibilities come within federal purview under existing laws. When one aggregates the pension funds under the Department of Labor, the mutual funds under the SEC and the various bank trusts under the Federal Reserve, the Controller of the Currency and the FDIC, it is startling to reflect that *today* a majority of the equity of American public companies is held by federally created trustees, the realm of whose responsibilities respecting ownership of portfolio securities is within the realm of existing legal authority.

SEPARATION OF POWERS

The creation of an informed and effective ownership to whom management is to be accountable would constitute a separation of powers in the civil side of American government. Just as the views of legislative, judicial, and executive competencies differ with respect to laws, so too do the views of owners and managers differ with respect to companies. Owners, as those at ultimate economic risk, have a capacity for ambiguity and a disposition for the long term different from managers, with their need for specific goals and the realities of time limited personal tenure.

There is no more thought of owners 'running' corporations than of the 'judiciary' running the government. There is the need for power to be contained and channelled so that its ultimate expression accords with the public good. There is the belief that this Hegelian process – one party having the responsibility to direct being effectively accountable to another informed and independent structure – is most apt to generate corporate functioning that accommodates a high present standard of living with the future needs of the planet.

The New Owners are therefore fiduciaries representing a broad cross section of the population with permanent investments in the largest worldwide companies. What should trustees do? Who are they? What are their qualifications? Gradually, this little-known class of individuals known heretofore for their propensity to avoid risk of all kinds is being thrust to the fore. The New Owners are trustees whose present disinterest in broadening the scope of their responsibility is matched by their lack of qualification to do so.

We must recognise that the existing ERISA fiduciaries are in most cases utterly unsuitable for their needed role as corporate owners. We will either need change or new institutions, but in any event a very different informing energy. In addition to independence, trustees will need to have an understanding of the theoretical basis of governance. This will require an educational system that has only begun to be developed. The range of study will necessarily involve law, economics, management, accounting, ethics, and such other disciplines as may be helpful in understanding the role of commercial energy in a civil world. This is not a simple task. For now, these simple guidelines must suffice.

Once institutions invest in a company, they must do two things:

- *Stay informed.* Corporate boards should insist that managers provide clear operational (not just financial) information. Ideally, the operational measures would include benchmarks against global best practice firms. For financial information, investors should press for clearer reporting requirements so they can be sure they are getting the full story.
- *Take action.* In our experience, corporate governance never forces real change until or unless a firm's performance has already substantially deteriorated. Owners should not wait that long. When company information reveals serious performance lags, greater pressure should be applied on managers to change their behaviour. The ultimate sanction investors have is to remove management.[19]

BENEFITS OF ACTIVISM

Too often the importance of shareholder involvement is dismissed because of their unwillingness and lack of qualification. The ultimate question is – can we *afford* a system in which owners are *not* required to be responsible for the consequences of their ownership? Between the individual and the shareholder mode of ownership, responsibility appears to have disappeared – to have become externalised, to become a cost of society. The absence of responsible ownership has created an unacceptable capitalism. Now that the elements exist for rejoining ownership with responsibility, we must take advantage in order to secure the continued benefits of a healthy capitalist system.

Clearly, owner activism has been responsible for the improved competitiveness of American companies over the last decade. The list of American companies where significant change was stimulated by owners is almost an enumeration of the traditionally great names – General Motors, IBM, Eastman Kodak, Westinghouse, and Sears Roebuck. Moreover, funds having informed and effectively participating trustees are worth more to beneficiaries than funds without them.[20]

Much is written about running corporations for the benefit of 'stakeholders' rather than for 'stockholders'. These writings ignore the reality, touched on in Chapter 6, that increasingly the two are one and the same! Today employees, through their employee benefit plans as well as employee stock ownership plans, already are the largest class of owner. The involvement of institutional investors really involves the interests of over one hundred million Americans, all those with retirement plans, trust interests and mutual fund holdings. It is worth quoting the observations of Michael Useem in his 1996 book *Investor Capitalism: How Money Managers are Changing the Face of Corporate America:*

> '*The average citizen, however, is as likely as not to be a party to the struggle [for corporate control]. Of those who are gainfully employed, most participate in a private or public pension plan. Of those who have accumulated assets, most invest in a mutual fund or the market directly. In 1990, state and local retirement systems included 2.4. million participants, mutual funds more than 23 million households (one quarter of all households), and private pension plans some 77 million participants. Most Americans derive a substantial fraction of their current or future livelihood from the performance of companies whose stock they directly or indirectly own.*'[21]

New ownership is most likely to be found among private pension funds, but it is potentially everywhere there is freedom from conflicts of interest, a long-term perspective, and a commitment to activism. At LENS, as a special-purpose activist investor, we hope to be a model of this type of ownership. In the Epilogue, we will present a larger model – one that embraces all types of investors.

Can all institutional shareholders strive to be active as independent, informed, motivated, and empowered owners? Can they bring modern capitalism to what we have earlier called 'Class IV' governance? I believe that they will – in due time in the next millennium.

For now, each must struggle with impediments to at least some of these goals. Of all shareholders, however, private pension funds have the characteristics most suitable for ultimate responsibility. As significant shareholders of the principal publicly held companies in the world, these funds could have a profound and positive impact on the performance and governance of the world's leading businesses in the coming century. But this will happen only if these funds and others can free themselves from conflicts of interest and find their 'voice' – the subject of our next chapter.

In the meantime, one stands and watches in horror as the management of several large blue-chip companies continue to destroy the value of holdings by countless shareholders, individual and institutional. Perhaps the most poignant example of this trend is AT&T (see box). The problem here is that everybody – every institution – owns AT&T, so nobody owns it. There are no shareholders that hold a level of AT&T shares that is significantly larger than the amount they would hold if all of their equity assets were in a passive index fund. This scattered ownership defines dispersion – or to borrow a term from physics, entropy. (AT&T is another example of 'Class III' governance, to recall a term introduced in Chapter 7.) By negative example, AT&T's failure proves the necessity of fiduciary capitalism through activist shareholder involvement.

WHERE WERE THE OWNERS? THE DECLINE OF AT&T

The American Telephone and Telegraph Company paid a dividend all through the depression of the 1930s. It was reputed to have the finest research laboratories and engineering capability in the world, with more PhDs and Nobel Prize winners than any university. It had only one class of capital stock and more shareholders than any company in the world. 'Ma Bell' appeared to be the 'beneficent monopoly' with leadership great enough not to abuse its power, scientists proud and self motivated enough to define the state of communications art, and a system of state regulation that ensured affordable service. Its Madison Avenue headquarters, with its tri-storied open arcades, was a virtual Versailles for the people. AT&T was a truly great company.

In the Monks family, one spoke of AT&T with reverence. My great-grandfather was one of the original investors in AT&T, and my uncle and great uncle were board members for a combined total of 50 years earlier in this century. By the time my generation came along, however, things had changed.

In the 1980s, the federal government had wrestled with the applicability of the antitrust laws to even this loveable colossus. Without any of the rancour and publicity accompanying the parallel government efforts to 'break up' IBM, AT&T adapted to the political pressure of the times and consented to spin out its local telephone service into seven so-called 'baby bells'. The Sheraton Sideboard Headquarters building was sold, and management retrenched to cinder blocks in New Jersey.

The break-up, imposed from without, shocked the system beyond repair, or so it seemed. There followed a dizzying succession of acquisitions and reorganisations, but all failed. In one downsizing, AT&T management fired 50,000 in one blow, with negative repercussions in communities around the country. Thus AT&T showed that it was accountable neither to beneficial shareholders nor to the general public.

The board of AT&T, considered the epitome of commercial accomplishment in America, made a disaster of the most hostile of hostile takeovers of National Cash Register Company – this notwithstanding that half a dozen of the AT&T directors in their 'real' lives as corporate leaders had conspicuously fought against 'hostile' takeovers when they were the targets. AT&T overpaid by bidding against itself. The takeover destroyed much of the value in the company, leading to another spin-off – this time out of necessity. AT&T spun off NCR and Lucent, heir to the old and venerable Bell Laboratories. Perhaps, Lucent, with AT&T director Henry Schacht serving as CEO, will turn out to be the only remnant of AT&T's noble past.

It was almost as if the 'great lady' having been immune from the pressures of outside forces for so long, simply had not had the opportunity to develop a 'change gene' ensuring the vitality of corporate life – with its multiplicity, spontaneity, accommodation, adaptation, transcendence, and metamorphosis.

Owner activism was needed to provoke this, yet all attempts to stir this failed. *Clearly, the widely dispersed holdings of AT&T made organised shareholder activism virtually impossible.*

In a letter to me dated 12 September 1997, Robert Allen admits as much. He writes:

> *'While there is no doubt that our performance has lagged, given the size of AT&T's market capitalization, well over $60 billion, a 3% stake represents close to a $2 billion investment. This is a huge investment for even a large institutional shareholder to make in a single company.'*

Too often when things go wrong in corporate America, boards respond by pointing to a CEO and saying 'off with his head'. Not surprisingly, the AT&T board applied this sanction to CEO Robert Allen's understudy, John R. Walter, who by all credible accounts was doing a perfectly good job as president and COO. The nine months he spent trying to correct decades of poor decisions now appear to have been a waste of everyone's time. The AT&T board has it all wrong. Clearly, heads must roll, but not 'out there'. The directors need to look in the mirror.

10

The New Owners are universal, long-term, global, and humane fiduciaries. They can use their unique status to follow three important imperatives, identified 20 years ago by David Engel: (1) obey the law, (2) inform the public about the corporation's impact on society, (3) minimise corporate involvement in politics. Laws are not perfect, but they are the corporation's best proxy for justice. The New Language of ownership takes this justice into account, even as new idiom continues to evolve in dialogue with management's more traditional language of profit optimisation.

10

The New Language

I shall sing about those who are happy and those who suffer. I shall sing of good and evil, which is kept hidden from you. The little songbird flies far, to the poor fisherman, to the farmer's roof, to everyone who is far from you and your court.[1]

Pensioners in the private sector, the leaders in the class of New Owners identified in the previous chapter, are unlike any other owners in the corporate world past or present — and they may well usher in a new corporate world in the future. This new world of fiduciary capitalism will restore ancient values of ownership that preceded the corporate form, and that seem to have eluded corporations in the long modern era. These restored values will be expressed in a new language, *the language of ownership.*

What will that voice be? What kind of information do these New Owners need to fulfil their role as the ultimate monitors of management? To answer this question, we must reflect on several facts.

The New Owners are:

- *universal* in the sense of owning all public companies in all industries;
- *long term* in holding period (indeed, the pattern of indexed holdings indicates virtually permanent ownership);
- *global* in outlook, with increasingly similar expectations for financial performance and reporting (consider that the largest companies in all countries are being privatised with multinational 'transparency' – disclosure and governance safeguards equivalent to the requirements of the New York Stock Exchange for listing); and

- last but not least, the New Owners are fundamentally *humane* in the sense that they have a perspective closely tied to the public interest.

Indeed, in a very real sense, they *are* the public. Like all ordinary people, pensioners not only want to receive payments sufficient to afford a decent standard of living, but also to live in a world that is civil, clean, and safe. In these important respects, the new owners are capable of speaking a new language we humans collectively can understand. It is beyond the scope of this discussion to analyse existing funds against the criteria set forth here. Suffice it to say that more than one is close to our ideal.

TWO CULTURES

In this chapter we will examine how all owners – particularly the New Owners described in the previous chapter – can communicate best with the world and with management, which has an idiom of its own. Explaining the differences in these two languages – the language of ownership and the language of management – requires a brief tour of fundamentals.

In the corporate equity marketplace, owners and managers alike take risks in the hope of returns, and neither risks very much. Owners risk *their own money* (and no more, thanks to limited liability). Managers, on the other hand, to reiterate the words of Adam Smith, risk *other people's money.*

As we have seen in earlier chapters, myriad problems have grown from this fundamental split between ownership and management. These problems are even more profound and pervasive than those identified by Adolf Berle and Gardiner Means in their famous 1932 treatise, *The Modern Corporation and Private Property*. The ownership-management split goes beyond lack of accountability; in many important ways, it defines the very essence of the corporate form, giving it systemic life – a life that truly comes into its own with the involvement of independent, informed, motivated, and empowered owners.

But it is one thing to say that we need these New Owners to take charge and quite another to design a world in which this can occur. Many factors must be worked out, starting with the fundamental question of the role of the corporation in society.

THE CORPORATION AND SOCIETY

What role should the corporation play in society? Should the corporation's resources be dispensed according to the wishes or whims of a CEO philosopher-king? We have already (in Chapter 4) dismissed that as a panacea – yet it persists as an unfortunate practice. Corporations spend hundreds of millions of dollars a year in advertising the many positive ways in which they impact society. There is nothing wrong with this so long as we remember that in a democracy power belongs to the people, and the people have not elected a single corporate director or officer, nor have they ever authorised any specific corporate activity. Ultimately, questions as to the quality of air or the safety of transportation must be made pursuant to power conferred on officials elected by the people.

Frederick A. Hayek provides the keystone in an essential foundation for a governance system in explaining why corporations – no matter how well intended – cannot be permitted to define their role in society beyond that prescribed by law.

> *'So long as the management has the one overriding duty of administering the resources under its control as trustees for the shareholders and for their benefit, its hands are largely tied; and it will have no arbitrary power to benefit from this or that particular interest. But once the management of a big enterprise is regarded as not only entitled but even obliged to consider in its decisions whatever is regarded as the public or social interest, or to support good causes and generally to act for the public benefit, it gains indeed an uncontrollable power – a power which could not long be left in the hands of private managers but would inevitably be made the subject of increasing public control.'*[2]

The relatively unacclaimed work of David Engel 20 years ago[3] provides our second building block. In the late 1970s, the post-Watergate climate had revealed many examples of unlawful corporate conduct, including involvement in political activity both in this country and abroad. There was public outcry for more responsible corporate behaviour. This was reflected in The Business Roundtable's statesmanlike manifesto, *The Role and Composition of the Board of Directors of the Large Publicly Held Corporation* (1978) and the passage of the Foreign Corrupt Practices Act in that same year. A vast literature on the subject of corporate social responsibility resulted, the premises of which Engel challenged with Occam-like rigour.

Without pausing to point out the obvious threats to a free society from unrestrained corporate 'benevolence', Engel asked plainly: what activities should a corporation be free to do outside of the scope of profit maximisation? Very little, he answered (following the 'Kew Gardens' principle, which says that corporations should act when failing to do so would clearly injure society).[4]

Engel found only three permissible corporate activities beyond profit maximisation:

- obey the law
- inform the public about the corporation's impact on society
- minimise corporate involvement in politics.

We suggest that the New Language of corporate accountability can be developed by moving Engel's principles from the realm of the permissible to the domain of the expected. In requiring that corporations obey the law, disclose socially important information, and exercise restraint in political involvement, we are – consciously – investing in the legitimacy of democratic government. This 'Engel Triad' actually forms an interrelated and self-reinforcing conceptual basis for corporate accountability. Corporations are required (1) to obey the law, which is based on (2) informed action by a legitimate government that has (3) not been improperly influenced by corporate power.

Governments composed of elected officials may not always act 'perfectly', for in this world there is no perfection, neither in markets nor in nations. But governments in a very real sense will always act properly, assuming a free and fair election process. Moreover, government determinations, as expressed in law and administrative action, represent an optimal balance between public and private interest. The Engel Triad thus provides a stable, coherent, and universal base of standards that are susceptible of verification and enforcement – indeed certification by independent auditors. Given this base, entities will find it easier to organise themselves so as to reward executives for maximising long-term value.

Obviously, the Engel Triad requires us to face certain complex realities. There will never be a perfect law – indeed, some laws are unjust and should be repealed. Nor will there ever be agreement as to appropriate mode of compliance with the law. Mandating disclosure has its side effects; it automatically creates two classes of information: 'public' information versus 'non–disclosed non–public' information; since trading on the basis of the latter (so-called insider trading) is illegal, this creates concerns of the timing and distribution of information, among other issues.[5] Finally, opinions as to the appropriate level of corporate involvement in politics will be limited only by the number of people asked. Different answers will be correct at different times.

None of these potential objections to the Engel Triad invalidates it, however; each merely signals how carefully we must proceed in using the triad to develop policy. The three dimensions of the triad – legal compliance, full disclosure, and political restraint – foster a realistic perspective in equity markets.

DIMENSION 1: LEGAL COMPLIANCE

Corporations should obey the law. This imperative may seem absolute, but in current reality it is relative: from the perspective of company management today (as discussed in Chapter 3) the decision whether to obey the law is simply a cost/benefit calculation. The corporation in effect asks whether the costs of disobedience – discounted by the probability of being discovered, prosecuted, and fined (there is almost no risk of jail) – equal the costs of compliance.

In many cases, the costs of disobedience are lower than the costs of compliance, and so many corporations find it to their economic advantage to break the law. In this action, corporations are effectively ignoring the signals that society has sent out in the form of laws. We need to think seriously as to whether a society so constructed can – or should – long endure.

What is the solution? *Remember, corporations are not people; they have no conscience.* Although corporate acts are carried out by individuals, even individuals with high moral standards often find themselves caught up in a corporate action that is beyond their control – or even, in some cases, their knowledge.

Corporate America does not need sermons (our 'Tobacco Road' homily below notwithstanding); it needs systemic solutions. These are obvious. Society must either lower the cost of compliance, increase the penalties of non-compliance, and/or increase the rewards for compliance. The first of these options is virtually impossible. There is no easy way to lower the cost of compliance; indeed, if corporations are to become more effective in combating non-compliance, then the cost of compliance could rise. There-fore, the solution is obviously to increase the cost of non-compliance and/ or to increase the rewards for compliance. If either or both of those occur, corporate compliance with the law would increase, thus benefiting the public.

It is well within the scope of current law not only to encourage but to *require* companies to put in place strong legal compliance programs, exacting penalties for failure to comply with this requirement. The Organizational Sentencing Guidelines (enacted in 1987 and revised in 1991) already obli-gate judges to penalise corporations for poor compliance systems and to reward them for having strong ones. Commenting on the guidelines *In Re Caremark International Inc. Derivative Litigation* (1996), Justice William T. Allen, then-Chancellor of the Delaware Chancery Court, commended Caremark for having programs to ensure compliance and control, but directed the company to do even more in this domain. A board's failure to ensure legal compliance may 'render a director liable for losses caused by non-compli-ance with applicable legal standards', declared Chancellor Allen.[6]

Given the importance of legal compliance, it would not be unreasonable to require corporations to have an independent auditor certify the existence of their compliance systems and to report periodically on the auditor's find-ings. This would be very much in the spirit of the sentencing guidelines as interpreted by Chancellor Allen. If penalties were imposed for failure to com-ply with this requirement, this would decrease the allure of non-compliance.

(It must be stressed here again, as we said in Chapter 9, that no new authorising legislation will be necessary; this is a matter of enforcing existing laws.)

Finally, the equity marketplace should and someday will *place a higher value on law-abiding companies than on companies that disobey the law.* The joint effect of these changes – higher fines for non-compliance and greater mar-ket rewards for compliance – will be to encourage respect for the law and thus to enhance the public good.

The OECD announced in May 1997 that its 29 members would intro-duce laws in their national legislatures by April 1998 that would subject their companies to criminal penalties for bribing foreign officials while soliciting business. 'We're very pleased', said Fritz Heiman, chairman of the US chap-ter of Transparency International, an organisation that monitors global corruption and presses for anti-bribery measures. 'The OECD member states are the home bases of practically every major international company around the world.'[7] The New Owners from every country own stock in all of these companies. When we consider the different lawmaking and enforcement processes in 29 different ethnic, cultural, and national bodies, the underlying importance of an ownership-based governance system becomes clear.

DIMENSION 2: FULL DISCLOSURE

Accounting statements can only reflect information about corporate impact that is known. To the extent that managements see fit to limit disclosure about what they *know or strongly suspect* about the 'costs' of their functioning on society, the financial statements will be defective. There are laws that detail what information is required to be disclosed. When should companies venture beyond what is legally required?

We encounter daily newspaper discussions of the research reports of various tobacco companies disclosing harmful impact of smoking over many decades. This impact is not limited to smokers but to others working or living near smokers; and it has affected the general public by raising healthcare costs for all those affected by smoke. Should these companies disclose this information publicly? The proposed $368.5 billion tobacco agreement pending before the US Congress includes such a recommendation for tobacco companies. What about companies in other industries with products that contain risks to consumers or to the general public? For example, what about nuclear power companies?

There are occasions when it is plainly in society's interest that companies disclose social costs. One has to question the utility of GAAP if the information on which it is based is incomplete. Are the income statements of a tobacco company or a nuclear power company misleading if there is no reference to reserves arising out of future liabilities suggested by the company's own research work? The market cannot work without access to better information than this. Silicone showed signs of risky side effects when used as an implant, but its makers were slow to recognise and disclose these risks.[8] Dow Corning, the principal supplier of silicone products, paid billions of dollars in damages before going bankrupt. Will its parent companies – Dow Chemical and Corning – be liable for damages? If so, their own survival would be in question. From a public policy/cost-benefit standpoint, what is the relevance of that risk? Existing US disclosure regulations (the SEC's SAB 92 and SEC Regulation S-K, Item 301) already require such disclosures. The key is to enforce them. (See Fig. 3.1.)

At all stages – from the earliest research to the most sophisticated legal pleadings – the question of information disclosure has been paramount. At this point of life-and-death litigation, no one really is free to say anything without causing unknown consequences. Corporate employees are put in the impossible position of either being silent or of the painful, lonely, and expensive choice of becoming 'whistle blowers'. This was the fate that befell Jeffrey Wigand, former director of research at Brown & Williamson Tobacco Company, who first blew the whistle on tobacco companies, revealing industry-wide knowledge of the harmful effects of smoking.

It is not always easy to estimate the risks of litigation; yet this must be done. In the words of Sir Adrian Cadbury, there should be no less than full disclosure in this area, however uncertain. 'If companies do have any doubts about the effects of their products on people or on the environment, they have a duty to share their concerns with the appropriate authorities as soon as they become aware of them.'[9]

To strike the right balance in this domain requires commitment to the cause, an articulation of the goals, and an organisation of the enterprise so as to ensure that information and motivation are aligned to achieve those goals. It also requires a compensation system based on results. This may seem daunting, but it can be done. The linearity of the GAAP-based corporate 'score card' needs to be supplemented by the dynamic process of commitment to modes of conduct.

In the terminology of the law, the 'burden of proof' is on the corporation to demonstrate that it has taken all reasonable steps to achieve compliance with law, disclosure of material information and restraint in dealing with the political process. In the words of The Business Roundtable, spoken two decades ago, 'It is the board's duty to consider the overall impact of the activities of the corporation on (1) the society of which it is a part, and on (2) the interests and views of groups other than those immediately identified with the corporation.'[10] The emergence of the New Owners makes possible the continuous and effective pursuit of these norms.

While the seeming precision of numerical evaluation is beguiling, we must pause to consider that corporations have wide impact on the society in which they function that extends well beyond those items that are generally included within GAAP. Referred to by economists as 'externalities', these range from the costs of training, medical and disability expenses arising from work, unemployment, and impact on the environment.[11] The fundamental question is: will the Private Sector – the corporation, its shareholders – bear the cost of externalities or will they be borne by the public? This is a political question, and it has been answered in dramatically different ways in different countries.

Many competent professionals have invested time and ingenuity in the effort to identify and quantify 'externalities'. There is no precise formula; there is even difficulty in being confident that the right elements are being considered and that causality is real. In brief, there is need for disclosure, open consideration, and implementation in good faith knowledge that adjustments will be inevitable. 'For those who accept the conceptual basis of stakeholder theory, however, there is a fundamental difficulty over accountability. Neither economists nor accountants have come up with an adequate system of measuring and reporting the intangible values on which stakeholder theory is built. It follows that any move to stakeholder-type corporate governance will have to bottom from the existing shareholder framework to ensure that incumbent management does not end up with more discretion and *less* accountability.'[12]

As a starting point, corporations can help the process by initiating their own disclosure of impact on society. More than a quarter of a century ago (1971–2), Abt Associates, a Cambridge, Massachusetts, consulting firm, published annual 'social balance sheets' and 'social income statements' along with an analysis of the social audit as a decision-making tool. Here is an excerpt from a book that two principals of Abt wrote about their work:

> 'Management needs the tools to assess the financial consequences of social investment and policy decisions and the social consequences of financial decisions which in turn lead to further financial results.
>
> 'The financial earnings of the company result from both the financial and the social assets. Therefore, the integrated financial and social statements ... recognize a net social asset which together with financial assets affect the company's financial return. Calculation of the return on social investment of net social asset thus becomes feasible, offering a new performance measure to use as a policy guide for maximizing overall return on investment.'[13]

Many other companies prepared social audits that focused on the different aspects of the company's impact on society. Eastern Gas and Fuel Associates focused on the employment area; ARCO focused on its impact on the environment. In more recent times, Ben & Jerry's and The Body Shop have issued comprehensive annual social reports. The US Department of Commerce prepared a model form of social accounting.[14] This is the 'good' side of the disclosure coin. Companies can and should disclose all the benefits they are bringing to society.[15]

DIMENSION 3: MINIMAL POLITICAL INVOLVEMENT

The involvement of corporations in politics took a giant leap forward in 1977 when the Supreme Court declared (wrongfully, in my view) that because corporations are 'persons', they have a right to political expression. Earlier (in Chapter 3) we quoted Chief Justice (then Justice) Rehnquist in dissent. An additional citation from that opinion may be useful here.

> *'I would think that any particular form of organization upon which the State confers special privileges or immunities different from those of natural persons would be subject to like regulation, whether the organization is a labor union, a partnership, a trade association, or a corporation.'*[16]

The majority of the court supported the conclusion that while corporate power could indeed threaten the integrity of the civil state, it was not doing so at the time the decision was handed down. One wonders how the court would feel today – some 20 years later – with the increase in lobbying, corporate welfare, and political action committees, as described in Chapter 3. As mentioned in that chapter, the US federal government has created a gigantic federal corporate welfare state through an amalgamation of trade policies, selective tax breaks, and spending programs that has resulted in what one group (The Cato Institute) calls the '$80 billion dole'.

In terms of the 'third dimension' of the Engel Triad – the need for restraint in dealings with government – the area where restraint is most urgently needed is soft money. Even corporate executives want reforms (but ironically, not for the right reasons). In March 1997, *Business Week* reported that:

> *'For the most part, executives are joining the chorus calling for curbs on soft money because they're tired of endless appeals for funds that may not serve their interests. The unrestricted millions supposedly support party building activities, but in practice are often funneled to candidates through-*

out the country. With soft money, donors still buy clout. But they don't
get the direct access that comes from making contributions to politicians.[17]

In other words, business isn't getting its money's worth and wants a more
cost-effective system. Yet we should be slow to encourage changes that
would merely help businesses increase their control over business. The real
solution, of course, is not to increase the efficiency of political influence,
but to channel it appropriately. While commercial interests are an important consideration in the governing process, it should work for the public
good or not at all – and never in a way that compromises the integrity of the
political process.

The Business Roundtable has emerged as the most sophisticated and efficient user of the existing system. As *The Weekly Standard* reported in early
1997, 'Republicans have long complained that corporate America's flagship
organisation "will not fight to re-elect members of Congress who advocate
and vote for free enterprise".'[18] Big business has its own agenda to which par-
tisanship is irrelevant. In other words, today's business lobbying does not
represent 'free enterprise' versus 'big government'. If it did, I for one would be
all for it! Rather, it represents a move by the corporate form to achieve unlimited life, size, power, and license – four dangers we cannot afford to nurture.

By incorporating the Engel Triad into the 'mission' energy of a corporate
enterprise, corporations can put a wrench in these works. In place of the
mechanistic urge to overpower, corporations can return to a state that is
closer to the nature of people and societies. By obeying the law, telling the
truth, and leaving politics to the people, corporations will create new and
better economic values. These in turn will subsume the short-term costs of
corporate responses to social concerns. Taking on such costs willingly will
become second nature. This will take time however – so much that time
itself may seem like a 'fourth dimension' in the process of corporate change.
Yet a shift in this direction is already occurring as recent events in the US
tobacco industry indicate (see box).

TOBACCO ROAD: A SERMON

Phillip Morris has reported profits growth over the last ten years from $3.3 billion for
the year ending December 1987 to $11.3 billion for the 12 months ending June
1997. In deciding on a value for the stock the market has accorded to these earnings

multiples of between 10 to 14, while the multiples for the S&P 500 companies have ranged during the same period from 15 to upwards of 22. This is a striking reversal of the market's usual pattern of placing a premium on companies with rapidly growing earnings. Why did this happen?

The 'disconnect' between profits and stock values happened because Philip Morris had been externalising *too many* of the costs of those profits for *too long.* Just as 'the wages of sin is death', so the wages of externalisation is value destruction.

The behaviour of the tobacco manufacturers violated all three of the basic requirements for effective corporate accountability, namely legal compliance, full disclosure, and minimal political involvement. This enabled the companies to externalise their costs. Eventually, however, events forced a change in this behaviour.

For decades, tobacco lawyers overwhelmed the judicial process and averted damages. This party at the public expense ended when several recent Medicaid recovery suits revealed that violations of law had occurred and the only question remaining would be the extent of the damages.

For decades the industry denied that nicotine was addictive. It refused to disclose information in its own files that made clear that managements had *knowingly* marketed addicting products at the same time as publicly denying that they were doing so. This cover-up ended with the stunning testimony of RJR CEO Steven Gladstone in connection with the Florida litigation in August 1997.

The tobacco industry has reduced to a science the co-optation of leadership groups and levels of government through the adroit funneling of profits from the sale of addicting products.* When New York City threatened passage of an anti-smoking ordinance, the performing arts community panicked. Eventually, it had to reevaluate its dependence on tobacco dollars.

It is ironic that the industry would be brought to the table of accountability not by government, not by public outcry, not by messianic leaders, and not even by the entrepreneurial energies of the plaintiffs' bar – despite its most imaginative role of 'off budget' (contingent fee) counsel for various State Attorneys General. Instead, the agent of change was a concerned shareholder.

It was Princeton's *summa cum laude* philosophy graduate, Carl Icahn, who, acting as *homo economicus,* threatened proxy contests in 1996 and 1997. He correctly sensed that the social costs of tobacco – in the broadest sense of the term – would eventually return to haunt the company, and he was right. Icahn was not alone.

Long-term investors have been abandoning tobacco stocks in droves because they see the writing on the wall. And its says – no more politely than a 'no smoking' sign: NO EXTERNALISATION.

> Ultimately, thanks in large part of shareholder action, big tobacco has come to comply with law, disclose the impact of its products on the health of consumers, and exercise restraint in dealing with government. This strategy has provided the greatest long-term value for its owners.
>
> ★ 'Big tobacco did not hesitate to dig into its deep pockets to resist the social tide through the purchase and manipulation of the political process … Just how much money the industry spent in this connection can only be guessed at based on clues provided by the few disclosure rules imposed on the lobbying game.' Richard Kluger, *Ashes to Ashes* (New York: Knopf 1996), p. 683.

THE ROLE OF INDEPENDENT AUDITORS

In establishing a New Language of ownership, it is very important to consider the precise relationship between an independent auditing firm and the corporation it serves. To whom do a company's independent accountants owe ultimate loyalty?

This has always been an uncomfortable question. In theory, the auditors work for the owners, but in practice their employment is in the gift of management.

Independent accountants are selected by the officers of client companies and (in many companies) ratified by shareholder vote. Even though the actual importance of shareholder ratification is open to question, shareholders do and should value it. Mellon Bank took special pains to note in its 1997 proxy statement, 'Although the appointment of independent public accountants is not required to be approved by shareholders, the board of directors believes shareholders should participate in such selection through ratification.'[19]

Commercial Union provoked wrath when it broke with this practice. The *Financial Times* had a tone of indignation when it reported that 'Commercial Union, the insurance group, has broken with normal practice, and removed the right of shareholders to vote on its report and accounts.' Commercial Union at first tried to bluff it through but then quickly backed down.[20]

The New Owners should ensure that their role in the appointment of auditors is meaningful. This requires among other things that the New Owners organise themselves with respect to a particular company so as to have a competency to receive reports, give instructions, exact loyalty from *their* auditors. The New Owners will be free to ask the auditors to certify that management has complied with the owners' directions set forth above. No legal change is required to carry out this arrangement, but having corporation money available to pay the costs of shareholders' monitoring will go far to ameliorate the 'free rider' problems we have mentioned in the previous chapter.[21]

A CONTINUING PROCESS

The New Language of ownership will be in the *continuing process* of definition, change, and redefinition. This process is based on the interaction between owners and managers with owners being rationally informed and managements being effectively accountable. One way of eliminating the financial disadvantage for a monitoring shareholder is to have the corporation pay the auditor's expenses directly. Another technique is to provide (in each company's enabling documents) for qualified owners to be authorised to spend company funds for monitoring.

Corporate functioning must be continually compatible with the needs of the citizenry, which necessitates a government role in defining what is and is not desirable conduct. (Note the observations of Carl Kaysen, Chapter 4, note 9.) The Department of Labor, which sets the standards for fiduciary responsibility for the ERISA trustees, who are responsible for 30% of the total outstanding capital stock of publicly traded companies, has left very plain clues that it expects 'activism' to extend beyond the conventional bottom line: 'Active monitoring and communication activities ... may include such matters as consideration of ... the corporation's investment in training to develop its work force, other workplace practices and *financial and non-financial measures of corporate performance*' (emphasis added).[22]

These guidelines for trustee consideration comprise the 'legitimacy link' whereby corporate power is ultimately *directed by and based in popular sovereignty*.

Unless the private sector is sensitive to the need for accommodating corporate power to the concerns of society, there is always the threat that government will intervene directly. There could even be a swing of the pendulum back to nationalisation and away from the current trend of privatisation. The Democratic administration in Washington served notice that the public has a transcending interest in corporate score keeping. As former Labor Secretary Robert Reich said: 'Corporate success is maximized only when every worker at every level is enlisted as a partner in the all-out effort to achieve top performance.'

The current Democratic administration (or some future one) may well attempt to provide incentives for what it considers to be 'good' corporations and thereby penalise the rest. Perhaps the most thoughtful articulation is a Full Report dated 28 February 1996 entitled *A Set of Comprehensive, Specific Democratic Proposals to Address Wage and Income Stagnation – to Produce Long-term, Higher Rates of Economic Growth, Shared with Working Families, in the United States,* by Senator Jeff Bingaman. This would take the form of a tax advantage for those who meet quantitative standards of corporate 'goodness'. It is proposed that businesses would become eligible (on their own nomination and with the certification of their accountants and lawyers) for 'extremely favourable tax, regulatory, and government contract treatment' if they:

- contribute an amount equal to 3% of payroll to pension plans
- devote an amount equal to 2% of payroll for training or education
- offer to all employees and pay half the cost of a minimum health care plan
- provide profit sharing or an ESOP
- limit the highest-paid employee to a salary 50 times that of the lowest paid
- show that in the previous three years, 50% of R&D and 90 percent of capital investment was made within the United States
- maintain an above average safety record, and
- belong to a Department of Commerce-certified association for the general promotion of 'good' objectives.

Senator Edward Kennedy introduced the 96-page American Workers Economic Security Act on 15 April 1996, containing many of these same recommendations, and more.

Communism is barely cold in its grave, and government is already contemplating new central control over business energies. 'There they go again!'

There is no need for government intervention. The present success of American corporate enterprise is a function of a shared belief that corporate purpose and legitimacy are congruent with marketplace value. The market can and will respond appropriately if it has the right information. This is where the New Language comes in. Assuming appropriate laws and proper disclosure, a corporation's 'social responsibility' – to other constituencies, employees, customers, suppliers, and to host communities – will be reflected in the value accorded to corporations by the market. In other words, if a corporation treats its employees poorly or has a sub-optimal relationship with the communities in which its operations are located, the market will (in theory) respond adversely, reducing the value of the company's stock.

The marketplace is no more or less than ratification by millions of beneficial owners, who accurately, appropriately, and promptly reflect the most important aspects of corporate functioning. But this will only work if owners have the right information. If they do, the system will be self-correcting (including owners as part of the system). As new information comes to the market, the market will adjust values – and this adjustment in turn will inspire improved behaviour by corporations.

Contemplating a self-correcting system composed of fully informed investors making decisions for the long term naturally raises the question of risk aversion. Classical economic theory, according to George G. Szpiro of the Israeli Centre for Academic Studies in Kiriat Ono, Israel, suggests that the degree of risk aversion of rational agents diminishes when the time horizon increases. If classical economics is right, this would cast a shadow over our proposal, which is not intended to encourage reckless choices. Fortunately, Szpiro's work with cellular automata contradicts classical economics with respect to risk aversion in long-term investing. His recent research shows that 'the automata produced by genetic algorithms adapt to the new situation and behave in a rational manner' consistent with prudent risk aversion.[23]

This notion of a self-correcting system that can maximise shareholder wealth over the long term has enormous appeal. It appeals to corporate managers because it legitimates their use of investment funds from outside sources, while leaving them maximum flexibility to direct the corporation as they wish. And it has appeal to everyone else because it requires no additional attention or energy beyond investor activism to make it 'work'. We can and must relay on a sort of invisible perpetual motion of market correction. But we must periodically and carefully evaluate to see whether it is still moving – and in what direction.

SUMMARY AND CONCLUSION

There are cracks in the foundation. Clearly, compliance with law, disclosure of material information, and restraint in dealing with government are essential elements for a healthy ongoing corporate existence within a democratic society. The shareholder is in the best position of any of the corporate stakeholders to be informed and to be effective in monitoring management's adaptation of the New Language.

Government will always have the critical role in defining society's interest in the limits of corporate power. The corporate constituencies have a choice: take a chance at being able to contain the static and bureaucratic restraints of government or participate in a process of accountability that is sensitive to society's needs. The New Language comprises a process between newly empowered owners and effectively responsible managers that liberates the energies of the capitalist system within a framework of legitimacy.

In some situations, the best course of action involves loss in the short term and only uncertainty as to gain in the long term. Owners are the only constituent in the corporate structure who can authorise such action. After all, it is their money at risk. The corporate journey involves so many uncertainties that we need a language of ownership spacious enough to accommodate the public interest while retaining the productive and competitive advantages of 'profit optimisation' under the traditional corporate mode.

Conclusion

Listening to the beautiful truth of the nightingale, we are 'tolled back' to our true selves. We can wind up the golden bird of short-term profit maximisation, or welcome back the nightingale of long-term economic value rooted in the social good. Which will it be?

Conclusion: The Restored Corporation in the New Millennium

> *The servants entered the room to look at their dead master. There they stood gaping when the emperor said: 'Good morning!'*[1]

At the end of Hans Christian Andersen's 'The Nightingale', the shock is palpable when the emperor's servants see that their dying ruler is alive after all – and well enough to bid them good morning. We readers, however, are not surprised. The emperor has regained his health, we know, because he has reconciled two very important aspects of the human universe – the mechanical and the natural.

We understand that the golden bird that entertained the court with its logical and predictable songs will continue to have a place of honour, but from a high perch far removed from daily life. It is the natural bird, the spontaneous nightingale, who will enjoy a regular audience with the emperor, thus connecting him to his people.

In a similar fashion, this book has painted an optimistic picture of the future of humanity in reconciling two aspects of the corporation: the mechanistic and the dynamic. As previous chapters of this book have asserted, corporate life has two distinct aspects. One aspect is the corporation's basic drive toward limitless life, size, power, and license; this is the corporation's basic programming, its systemic reality. But corporations are not only 'systems', they are complex adaptive systems open to renewal – and this is their saving grace.

The basic program of corporations as self-seeking entities wars against the interests of human beings. Yet the living 'complexity' of corporations – their tendency toward multiplicity, spontaneity, accommodation, adaptability, transformation, and metamorphosis – links corporations to us humans. It makes them capable of serving our purposes, and it makes them more akin to us – for we, too, are alive, complex adaptive systems, and superior ones at that! Through our human ingenuity we can see what is missing in the corporate system today. And that missing element is accountability. By restoring accountability in each and every corporation, one corporation at a time if need be, we can ensure that the corporations in our lives adapt not only to the environment in general, but to us humans as well.

It is a fearsome thing to behold the corporation as a leviathan – a vast system with a lifelike force. But we cannot wish the beast away through panaceas such as philosopher-kings or councils of expert advisors. Our best hope is to recognise the corporation for what it is, both in its mechanistic aspect as a profit machine and in its larger nature as a living entity, and to learn what we must do to live with it – and through it – accordingly.

CHOICE

This book has brought the reader on a long and sometimes winding journey. In Chapter 1 we met Andersen's nightingale and contemplated the paradox of the mechanical versus the natural. In Chapters 2, 3, and 4 we saw how the fundamental drives of the corporate form can threaten human welfare. Then, in Chapter 5, we saw that corporations are not only systems, but complex *adaptive* systems capable of creativity and change.

In Chapter 6 we continued to describe corporations as complex adaptive systems, rejecting common notions of corporate philosophy and offering a new model in their stead. This model, the centrepiece of our work, represents a real advance in corporate theory and potentially practice. In Chapter 7 we ventured into the realm of simile, comparing the corporation to the 'Class IV' of the cellular automata so popular among scientists who study complex systems. In Chapter 8 we used these insights to profile a company in the throes of change. The key to change, we found in Chapters 9 and 10, is a New Owner and a New Language. In particular, we saw the importance of compliance, disclosure, and last, but not least, political restraint.

Compliance, disclosure, and political restraint. These values bear repeating day in and day out. They should be inscribed on every corridor of corporate power – or better yet, in every conscience. Are these values achievable? It is up to you. As a corporate director, employee, or owner, which path do you see in your future? Will you stand by and let the corporation in your life seek unlimited life, size, power, and license, or will you do what it takes to enable your corporation to fulfil its broader, better nature? To help you visualise the difference, consider these two diagrams: the Existing Corporation (Fig. A) and the Restored Corporation (Fig. B).

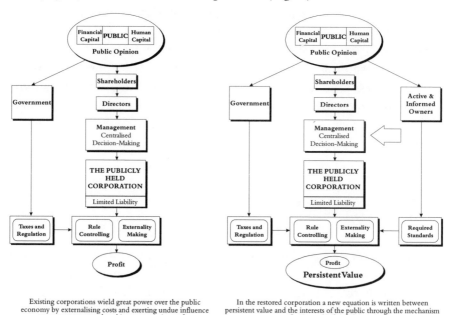

Existing corporations wield great power over the public economy by externalising costs and exerting undue influence over government rulemaking to maximise profit.

In the restored corporation a new equation is written between persistent value and the interests of the public through the mechanism of active and informed owners.

Fig. A   The Existing Corporation.

Fig. B   The Restored Corporation.

GRAVEN IMAGES

Throughout this book, we have put forth certain values. Chief among these are legal compliance, disclosure, and restraint in politics. These by definition will foster greater accountability and, eventually, economic wealth for corporations and for society.

Resistance to these values is understandable. They are not neat and pretty. It is not always easy to predict them or make them add up. And as a race, we humans like things to be orderly. We are driven to construct artificial entities in order to minimise our sense of being alone in a world where neither origin, nor purpose, nor end can be known. This need also expresses itself in quantification – our arrangement of reality into category, language, and number. The 'artificial' in this sense provides a framework for the human drama; for the expression of beauty and the fulfillment of personal relevance. But it can also protect us from the vagaries of consciousness and intuition – depriving us of precious gifts.

As human beings, we must live with the artificial; it is a part of our life. It takes courage to accept a quality that one does not like about oneself or ones own creations, but as psychologist Maria von Franz has noted (writing about fairy tales), 'If one does not accept the quality, then it functions behind one's back.'[2] We cannot ignore the mechanistic nature of corporations. As the same time, we cannot let the mechanical take over our lives. While the motive to reduce anxiety by providing an appearance of beauty is understandable, the reduction of human essence to a mechanical process seems akin to the conduct proscribed in sacred texts banning the worship of 'graven images'.

CONCLUSION

Humankind must never allow itself to lose sight of the real conditions under which we live – uncertainty at best. We must never tolerate domination from a system that is based on demonstrably false mechanical premises. We need to insist on human-scale accountability.

The beautiful jewelled bird need not be smashed into a thousand pieces or banished from the empire. After all, it 'did the best it could'. But its time is up. Never again should its wheels turn; never again should its voice inspire imitation. It is a kind of static in the continuing effort to develop the ability to listen. It does not deserve a central place in the world of people, for it has no respect for the individual human being and the human condition.

Human beings must accustom themselves to the coming and going of the nightingale, the cycle of its life, the genius of its song ... its mystery and its infinitely beautiful insistence on raising the real and eternal questions of human existence.

In the words of John Keats, writing over a century ago,

> *Thou wast not born for death, immortal Bird!*
> *No hungry generations tread thee down;*
> *The voice I hear this passing night was heard*
> *In ancient days by emperor and clown.*
> *Perhaps the self-same song that found a path*
> *Through the sad heart of Ruth when, sick for home,*
> *She stood in tears amid the alien corn;*
> *The same that oft-times hath*
> *Charm'd magic casements, opening on the foam*
> *Of perilous seas, in faery lands forlorn.*
> *Forlorn! The very word is like a bell*
> *To toll me back from thee to my sole self!*

The poem says so much, but above all it urges us to live our human condition. Cleanth Brooks, commenting on 'Ode to a Nightingale', makes this crucial point: 'The nightingale symbolizes the immortality of nature, which, harmonious with itself, remains through all its myriad changes unwearied and beautiful.' Keats does not see 'the particular biological mechanism of flesh and bone and feathers as deathless ... Keats has clearly specified the sense in which the bird is immortal; it is in harmony with its world – not, as man is, in competition with his.'[3]

We may protest that we are not 'in competition' with our world. Yet we continue to work for and invest in corporations that operate according to these dynamics. It is time to change; it is time to listen, to be tolled back to our true selves.

★★★

In this book, we have relied on the language of story and poem to make fundamental statements about our lives with corporations. I hope that our lyrical medium has not obscured our simple message. If I had to summarise this book in once sentence, it would be this: *Corporations are living systems that can either oppress or foster human life – the choice is ours.* We can wind up the 'golden bird' of short-term profit maximisation, or welcome back the 'nightingale' of long-term economic value rooted in the social good. Which will it be?

In my view as both observer and participant, there is no contest. We can and must always choose the future. Only that far horizon can guide us as we collectively strive to understand and improve our tenure on this planet.

Epilogue

A parable: an optimistic future.

Epilogue: The Nightingale Sings – 2010

> *Suddenly, through the window, came the sound of an exquisite song.*
> *It was the little, living Nightingale perched on a branch outside.*[1]

The history of effective shareholder involvement in corporate governance worldwide can be seen most vividly through the career of a single individual, Ruth, chief executive of New Fiduciary Trust Company, one of a new kind of enterprise organised at the turn of the century to discharge the growing ownership responsibilities of institutional investors. These new ventures – institutional investors themselves but also working on behalf of other institutions – had sprung into being to fill a growing need for shareholder competency and independence in the world's largest multinational companies in the new millennium. Although they took a full decade to become fully accepted, the so-called 'special purpose trust companies' would eventually change the face of large-scale enterprise around the world.

The following chapter looks back on the decades of transition from the so-called 'corporate governance' movement of the 1980s and 1990s to the 'corporate accountability movement' at the turn of the 21st century and beyond – years that coincided with a profound shift in the outlook of Ruth and other investors like her. During this era, as corporate power expanded beyond the scope of traditional national states, many corporate owners began to recognise their new importance as the only party able to require accountability in this increasingly critical domain.

ACCOUNTABILITY

Accountability was indeed the key term – the vital element that had been missing in the preceding corporate governance movement. That movement, a collection of diverse concerns from internal controls to chief executive succession, brought many meaningful reforms, but never succeeded in galvanising the profound change necessary to restore systemic integrity to large corporations. One sign of continued lassitude was the persistence of corporate welfare – direct grants, subsidies, and tax favours to large businesses from out of the public coffers. This outflow continued despite the collective revulsion of political observers across party lines and ideological spectrums, unstaunchable by both 'government' and 'governance' efforts at reform. And corporate welfare was only a symptom of a larger problem: the corporation's insatiable quest for unlimited life, size, power, and license.

The 'g' words – governance and government – failed to curb the corporate leviathan because they were attacking in from the outside. The catalyst for change would be internal: active involvement by the institutions – public pension funds, private pension funds, money managers, banks, insurance companies, and foundations. Spurred, inspired, and eventually helped by activists like Ruth, they began to change their habit of convenient neglect and assume the responsibilities of ownership. The world had truly changed from the centuries James Hurst described so well in *The Legitimacy of the Business Corporation in the Law of the United States, 1780–1970*, and from the following three unchanged decades. Only shareholder action at the turn of the 21st century brought an end to 'general failure of shareholding to supply the steady surveillance by which stockholders were supposed to legitimate the power wielded in business corporations'. In its place was dynamic vigilance and its natural result – increased corporate 'competitiveness' and value.

TURNING POINT

One of many turning points for Ruth as a pioneer in the Corporate Accountability movement was reading an *Atlantic Monthly* article by George Soros, 'The Capitalist Threat'. Soros, writing in February 1997, said what Ruth had long believed: that 'free market' capitalism posed as much of a threat to a free society as did communism and fascism in earlier times. Soros concluded his essay with a call for humility – a sense confirmed by science of the fallibility of human beings and their structures.

Soros had posed a problem; Ruth believed she knew the answer. She and several other shareholder activists were growing ever bolder in their belief that fiduciary owners could and would assume responsibility for the functioning of corporate enterprises. This was not a certainty; rather, it was the beginning of hope that a new faith would emerge.

That change took a full score of years to emerge and even in the year 2010, when Ruth retired, it was only beginning to take full shape. True, for the past half-century, there had been a movement some called 'shareholder activism'. During those years, several major public and private pension funds, followed by mutual funds, bank trusts (and even some insurance companies and money managers) began to take full advantage of their rights and responsibilities under the law. But in all that time – the entire lifetime of Ruth – owner activism was the exception, never the rule.

The vast majority of investors continued to carry an unshakeable albatross – conflicts of interests inherent in the diversity of services that they provided to corporations. (Ruth, in observing this, was often reminded of Samuel Taylor Coleridge's 'Rime of the Ancient Mariner': *Day after day, day after day, / We stuck, nor breath nor motion; As idle as a painted ship / Upon a painted ocean. / Water, water, every where, / And all the boards did shrink; Water, water, every where, / Nor any drop to drink.*) The dead weight of conflicts did not drop until a US Supreme Court decision triggered the declaration of a *federal standard of ownership* – and so triggered a new and vital player in the field of fiduciary capitalism: the *special purpose trust company* (SPTC).

REICH VERSUS HAWLEY: PROGENITOR OF THE SPECIAL PURPOSE TRUST COMPANY

No one had to invent SPTCs; they arose from existing law. No mandate of Congress forced them on the economy; no presidential decree called them from the void. SPTCs were not even mentioned in any juridical decisions. But the US Supreme Court left the industry little choice when it ruled in *Reich* versus *Hawley*[2] in the year 2000 that the 'exclusive benefit' rule under ERISA literally meant what it said.

> *'Under the section 404(a) duty of loyalty, the central question is whether the fiduciaries acted solely in the interests of the beneficiaries and for the*

exclusive purpose of providing them with benefits ... Where the potential for conflicts is substantial, it may be virtually impossible for fiduciaries to discharge their duties with the single focus that must animate all their actions: the interests of the beneficiaries. Lacking such a focus, the fiduciaries may need to step aside, at least temporarily, for the management of assets where they face potentially conflicting interests.'

As counsel for the beneficiaries of the Carter Hawley Hale (CHH) employee benefit plans (*Reich* versus *Hawley* – 2000) Ruth had acquired the widespread favourable recognition in legal and financial circles that made her the virtually inevitable leader of the new arrangements for fiduciary owners. When The Limited, the fast-growing clothing chain, made an unsolicited bid for the shares of CHH, the old-line retailer easily repelled it. The trustees of the employee benefit plans, all chosen by management, simply refused to tender their indispensable shares. Tight interlocking ruled out rebellion: the Bank of America was the trustee of all of the company's employee benefit plans, and the CEO of CHH served as chairman of the bank's compensation committee, while the CEO of the bank was a director of CHH.

By successfully defending itself against a 'hostile' takeover, the CHH board drove the company to the brink of a demise that could have been avoided. CHH declared bankruptcy, the plans lost virtually all of their value, and the savings and pensions of tens of thousands of past and present employees vanished without a trace.

Ruth took on the case, taking almost a decade to guide the *Hawley* case through the procedural obstacles and delays allowed well-lawyered defendants. Like a detective who carries the picture of a crime victim to inspire his search for an assailant, Ruth kept in mind the picture of a pensioner impoverished by lack of corporate accountability. Optimising long–term value to pensioners had to be the sole priority for fund trustees. Anything else was a breach of trust. The only way out of this legal maze was to insist that employee benefit plan fiduciaries have no class of customers other than plan participants. Only by requiring such exclusive focus could would employees' interests be served.

In the end, Ruth prevailed. The Supreme Court's opinion in *Reich* versus *Hawley* held that in the many instances where banks, insurance companies, and other trustees had relationships other than as fiduciaries of its employee benefit assets with a particular company, they would have to prove that these relationships did not work to the detriment of the plan participants. The ERISA statute, said the Court, provided that those who violated their fiduciary duties under the statute would be prohibited subsequently from exercising *any* other fiduciary roles under the statute. None of the financial conglomerates wanted to take the risk of exposing all of their lucrative ERISA relationships to possible forfeiture.

The opinion also called critical attention to the long term – almost permanent – nature of the traditional relationships between plan sponsors and trustees. Indefinite tenure, said the Court, suggested the absence of a continuing fiduciary concern. The safest course, the Court opined, would be to change trustees at least every five years, if not more frequently.

The choice was clear: the traditional multi-service fiduciary institutions had to give up either fiduciary work or all the rest. They took the easier course, and a new institution was born. At first in the United States and later in the United Kingdom and Canada there emerged the SPTC, whose sole function was to act as owner with respect to the securities it held in portfolio companies.

These companies marked a seismic change in the corporate governance landscape, where they ushered in a truly 'new governance' – a new mode of corporate accountability that was continually defining and redefining itself. The SPTCs brought to an abrupt end the old world of comfortable, unchallenged, and circuitous power in which managements traded their bestowal of business for owner acquiescence. Under this old order, 'co-operative' financial institutions received lucrative contracts, exacting mute compliance in return. Those days were gone forever.

Now, as a result of *Reich* versus *Hawley*, there was a clear standard for ownership – one so forceful that it was often referred to as the federal *law* of ownership. This was a declaration by the US government that 'the existence of independent and informed owners in the governance of public companies is in the public interest'. The US government, in response to a presidential directive, issued a summary of existing standards concerning the fiduciary duties of owners, and formed an inter-agency group to ensure enforcement of existing law in a consistent manner. This environment naturally created a market for the SPTCs, which provided a channel for this new current in fiduciary capitalism.

RUTH: AN ENERGIZING FORCE

The SPTCs emanated from many complex forces, but one of these was Ruth herself. Indeed – it could be said that the evolution of the post-Communist development of corporate accountability owed as much to Ruth as to any other individual. Innovator and catalyst, Ruth had helped engineer many of the underpinnings of the new structures, and imbued them with life through her boundless energy. She was perfect for the job.

Born and raised in New England, Ruth possessed a pilgrim-like commitment to personal improvement and a thirst for reform slaked only through constant involvement in public service. Born just after the end of World War II, her generation spanned some of America's most troubled waters. Ruth was barely a teenager when the 'best and the brightest' in her parents' generation were struggling to move beyond the mistakes and crimes of Vietnam. Years later, the fall of the Berlin Wall left her own generation, then fully adult, with a search for meaning. Communism lost, but who won? Certainly not the system of 'free enterprise', which seemed in her day to be neither free nor enterprising.

By the turn of the century, Ruth had succeeded in raising her young family and was fully engaged in running a money management business called PRISM. The mission of PRISM was to invest in underperforming companies and, through activism, help bring about improvements in governance. Ruth ran PRISM based on one proposition – a company having informed and effectively involved owners is worth more than one without. Over a relatively brief period (brief in hindsight!) of five years, several companies changed their entire direction thanks to PRISM's involvement.

PRISM provided not only personal wealth but the indispensable proof that companies having informed and involved shareholders were worth more in the marketplace than those without. PRISM's healthy financial performance disproved a common assumption – never spoken, but often implied – that shareholder activism was merely a gathering of malcontents. (Ruth detested the term 'gadfly'.) As long as shareholder involvements could be trivialised as representing the diverse opinions and piques of a variety of individuals, ownership could not serve as the base of a new system of accountability.

During the early years of the SPTCs, Ruth's reality unfolded in a seemingly perpetual frenzy of deadlines and drama. Through the tireless exercise of her legal skills, writing several books, and appearing at schools, forums, and television programs across the North American continent, she had carried as single message: *In a free society, you cannot have power without accountability.* Her parents' generation had brought a message like this to the halls of government; she was bringing it to the private sector.

A CODE OF CONDUCT

Proxy season after proxy season and door behind closed door Ruth and others like her worked for change both publicly and privately. This train of events became the Long March on which this particular revolution was built. And the first major battle in this march was annual meeting season in the spring of 2001. In wave after wave, the practice of including shareholder-originated resolutions had spread to every one of the 500 largest companies.

In describing the new activists, people always referred to the so-called Standard & Poor's (S&P) companies while in fact the 500 companies included in this representative index performed relatively well and companies in the top decile were not particularly likely to be targeted by the new activists. Ruth and others reserved shareholder involvement for companies not conspicuous for magnificent management. During the 2001 annual meeting season, they proposed resolutions at several companies asking that directors put in place standards and structures so as to assure that the enterprises (1) comply with the law and avoid criminal activity (2) disclose as fully as possible the corporation's likely impact of their functioning on society, and (3) minimise their involvement in politics. These three resolutions, originally known as the Engel Triad after their originator, David Engel, became known collectively as the Corporate Civility Code (CCC).

Managements of these companies argued that they were not required by law to include these resolutions in the company proxy statements, claiming the resolutions were part of 'ordinary business' that should be left to management discretion. The Securities and Exchange Commission (SEC) disagreed, finding that these resolutions were in advisory form ('precatory' was the Commission's legalistic phrase) and therefore permissible.

No one was prepared for what followed. *Every single one of the resolutions was supported by a majority of the votes cast at the meetings.* Over the next months, managements of the chosen companies caucused and met at length with worthy counsel to develop appropriate response that would be perceived as responsive but not diminishing of their status or prerogatives.

VOX POPULI

Meanwhile, public opinion coalesced in a rare consensus. If the people had been a Greek chorus on a stage, they would have spoken as one, intoning: *Why should corporations commit crimes? Why shouldn't they reveal all they know about how their functioning affects us? Why should they be able to 'buy' elections?*

Information, the people knew instinctively, would be key. Neither corporations nor societies can become great unless effort is made to identify the real costs of various corporate alternatives, including all of the costs that traditionally had been borne by society. The more people talked about it, the more enthusiastic they became.

In times past, this would have been irresistible grist for ambitious politicians. In this unique instance, however, public opinion was as persuaded of the inappropriateness of government involvement as it was of the merits of the propositions themselves. No doubt the catalyst was the absolute futility of government action to curb the amounts that corporate chief executives were paying themselves, largely via stock options – culminating in the US Senate's craven vote (88–9 in 1995) to direct that the cost of such options not even be reflected in the financial statements!

CRITICAL YEARS: 2001–2003

By late fall of 2001, precatory shareholder CCC proposals had been received at *all* of the nation's 500 largest companies – and several companies also received resolutions in the form of by-law amendments mandating management action. Managements protested, saying that shareholders had no right to 'tell them what to do', and successfully persuaded the SEC not to require inclusion of the mandatory resolutions. Nonetheless, the deluge had begun.

There ensued a proxy season that would come to be known in the economic history of the United States as the corporate equivalent of the Lincoln-Douglass debates. In all the newspapers, on television, and across the Internet, shareholders sought each others' support. A landslide followed: the proposals won a majority of votes in two-thirds of the companies. Because they were phrased in precatory language, however, no management action followed.

Activist shareholders took the next logical step in 2002 and required that candidates for election to the board of directors of S&P 500 companies in the annual meeting season of 2003 publicly and explicitly agree to adopt the CCC policies in the manner of Parliamentary candidates in the United Kingdom binding themselves to the party platform. They took the further precaution of proposing a slate of alternative directors who supported the CCC resolutions to take the place of any unwilling to commit themselves. Those who supported CCC were resoundingly elected in the annual meetings of the year 2003; those who failed to do so were defeated.

A GRUELLING PROCESS

The preceding brief history gives the impression of an ineluctable process inclining towards an inevitable result. A more accurate view is suggested by Otto von Bismarck's caution that the squeamish should not witness the making of sausages or laws.

By the year 2005, activist shareholders, emboldened by long overdue court judgments prohibiting the 'conflict of interest' of many trustees, had created very serious problems for the financial conglomerates who controlled the fiduciary 'industry'. No longer could the great banks, the highly paid money managers, or the 'independent' directors of investment companies simply and discreetly do the bidding of company managements. There was literally no place to hide from the necessity of voting on the activists' proposal and, in the absence of management initiatives, there was no way to avoid supporting them.

Again and again, the principal executives of the financial conglomerates were embarrassed by their inability to reciprocate their customers' trust (the valued relationship being in the purview of management). Slowly but surely, the true meaning of independence began to dawn on everyone in Corporate America: the trustee function should – and someday would – be exercised by institutions who had *no other commercial relationship with portfolio companies*.

Owner independence: Of all the myriad themes woven into the corporate governance movement of the late 20th century, this was primary – and Ruth was one of the first to realise it. Without owner independence, all the good corporate governance practices in the world could come to naught; with it, a new and improved corporate world could be constructed. Yet few organisations recognised the importance of this element. The Paris-based Organisation for Economic Cooperation and Development was a rare exception. Its 1997 conference on Corporate Governance was one of the first of many to usher in a new era of Corporate Accountability.

Neither ideologue nor crusader, Ruth delighted in the human condition and its necessary commitments. Active involvement in the world around her was both a joy and a responsibility. Thoughtfulness, articulation, and perseverance may seem like commonplace virtues, but in Ruth they converted to brilliance. She was truly a 'star', knowing always the right word – 'le mot just'. Her gift for analogy from the everyday world communicated as effectively as famous talk show hosts. A lawyer by education and a government official by vocation, she did not pretend to be a businesswoman. Rather than great commercial expertise she was informed by a profound sense of what was right.

Ruth brought this sense of rightness to her observation of the inner and outer workings of her country's largest corporations. Ruth and shareholders like her held up a mirror to corporations, asking them to face their problems. Too often corporations saw only a face – the face of the CEO – and fired these individuals, paying them a king's ransom to go. Although the press credited Ruth and other activists with this result, Ruth called it the off-with-their-heads fallacy. In her view, CEO dismissal provided only a superficial answer to the continuing problems of the corporation. Independent owners, she knew, were the key; and the only way to encourage owner independence would be to build a place for it. That place was the special purpose trust company.

EARLY MODELS

One of the models for the new SPTCs was the Investors' Responsibility Research Center (IRRC) of Washington, DC, established in the early 1970s by the Ford Foundation, Harvard University, and others anxious to pool their resources in a search for the most ethically satisfactory and economically effective way of dealing with the social ramifications of their funds' investments – especially investments in apartheid South Africa. Although it never explicitly endorsed shareholder-led protest over investments in that nation, IRRC's patient record-keeping of such protests became an information clearing house for that cause, proving that shareholder resolutions can change the world. Nelson Mandela, after his release from prison, generously applauded the concern of Western businesses as a significant contributor to the establishment of South African democracy.

But the IRRC was also a model of what *not* to do when facilitating shareholder activism. As a non-profit organisation, it could not pay its top executives a competitive salary; the legal restrictions governing non-profits combined with a trend toward private sector generosity, created an inevitable gap in this respect. Also, as a non-profit, it had few competitors, and thus little urge to change with the times. The rise of Institutional Shareholder Services (ISS), a private-sector company, did lead to some IRRC innovations such as a proxy voting advisory service, but this was more the exception than the rule.

No, the SPTCs needed to attract the best and most competition-minded talent – especially given the fact that some might represent the full authority of ownership in a large enterprise. Compensation had to be tied to performance, and could not be artificially depressed (as it would be in a non-profit). Moreover, the compensation paid to the head of an SPTC had to be substantial because of the limited tenure of the job – which might be the incumbent's last: to avoid conflicts of interests, individuals becoming SPTC principals would pledge to decline work in the private sector following their self selected tenure in the ITC. For these reasons – and because these companies needed to have a competitive nature in order to mirror the objects of their attention – the model for the SPTC was the private professional partnership along the lines of a management consulting firm like McKinsey & Company, or an investment banking firm like Goldman Sachs.

LEGAL UNDERPINNINGS

Ruth knew trust law, which at the turn of the century had gained urgent importance. By the year 2010, pension funds and other trusts owned nearly two-thirds of the equity of American companies. Bank regulation was in a semi-permanent state of upheaval, but the Controller of the Currency, the Federal Deposit Insurance Corporation, and the Federal Reserve System had all recognised that the fiduciary responsibility of their banks was a matter of concern. The SEC liberalised proxy rules in the corporate domain, but basically ignored the question of owner activism in investment companies – despite requests from shareholder activists to clarify what level of ownership involvement was required under the Investment Company Act of 1940.

The only place where careful instruction had been developed over many years was the Pension and Welfare Benefits Agency (PWBA) of the Department of Labor, which has authority over the pension funds in corporations

– by then some 40% of the total equity in the country. In the late 1990s PWBA, under the superb leadership of assistant secretary Olena Berg, had issued a release that provided substantial guidance for the exercise of owner-ship responsibility by ERISA fiduciaries.

> *'An investment policy that contemplates activities intended to monitor or influence the management of corporations in which the plan owns stock is consistent with a fiduciary's obligations under ERISA where the respon-sible fiduciary concludes that there is a reasonable expectation that such monitoring or communication with management, by the plan alone or together with other shareholders, is likely to enhance the value of the plan's investment in the corporation, after taking into account the costs involved.'*
>
> (*Department of Labor, Interpretative Bulletin* 94–2 29 CFR Part 2509; 59 Federal Register no. 145, p. 38664)

Under ERISA, trustees and investment managers may delegate their own-ership responsibilities to an appropriate third party. The statute makes it clear that there are *two separate aspects* of the function of 'managing money':

- the choice of asset, its purchase, its supervision, and its sale; and
- the exercise of ownership authority and responsibility during the time that the asset is held by the trust.

From this two-part paradigm flowed the logic and – Ruth's generation saw – necessity of special purpose institutions. Traditional institutions such as corporate pension funds made the decision to invest in particular assets – but were they the best qualified parties to act as owners? Not if they had con-flicts of interest, the post-*Hawley* world saw. And so it was that in a mere decade – from 2000 to 2010 – the ownership functions of much of the 60% institutional equity holdings in the 1,000 largest American public compa-nies were being exercised by SPTCs.

ACTIVE VERSUS PASSIVE SERVICES

One impact of the Supreme Court decision in *Hawley* was to force a critical eye on the fees paid for money management services – approximately 1% of

$4 trillion, appropriated almost entirely by the proprietors of these service firms – and the value received from 'active' versus 'passive' managers.

Active managers in areas such as 'venture capital' certainly earned their keep. The success of their investments depended on a substantial investment of a managers' time and personal expertise, and so deserved fees at the upper end of the scale. Passive managers could not claim the same merit. The preponderance of 'managed' accounts usually did worse than index funds, and so could not justify fees higher than the few basis points customary in bond management – especially in light of the low costs of a money management operation.

This inclination to think of fee entitlement in terms of the actual commitment of personal attention and expertise led to a rough rule of thumb: half of the fiduciary fees paid – both to trustees and to managers – were for the traditional jobs of selection, buying and selling; the other half were for the various 'active' tasks required. Thus, investment management was available at roughly half the cost of full management.

The marketplace offered surprisingly little resistance to the allocation of so much money to a new and unproved industry. Many people were finally beginning to feel that the competitiveness of American industry was in large measure a function of the effective involvement of shareholders. PRISM's well known success in this regard helped to turn the tide. So did the 1996 publication of a survey in the influential *McKinsey Quarterly* showing that respondent CEOs and institutions valued good governance as being worth a whopping 11% premium on the stock price. Previous studies had shown the value of shareholder involvement (research by Wilshire Associates and by Lilli Gordon, for example) but they did little to dispel general mistrust of activism. The McKinsey article, although it appeared nearly a decade before the Hawley decision, imprinted a kind of *nihil obstat* on active ownership, giving it legitimacy and so preparing a climate of acceptance for the Hawley decision and its aftermath, the creation of SPTCs.

SPTC START-UP DAYS

The legendary American entrepreneurial spirit responded to the SPTC opportunity with vigour and brilliance. In one respect, Ruth's early days were easy. The SPTC industry had a ready-made clientele: thousands of employee benefit plans that not only could but *had to* secure its services immediately. So there was always enough business, and no need for a sales department.

The trouble was just the opposite: too *much* business, and all of it new and unprecedented. Every question had to be dealt with as a matter of first impression. On all sides – government, corporate management, customers, and suppliers – there was expectation that the SPTCs could immediately meet whatever needs arose. Everything had to be done immediately and in full public view. Moreover, not everyone wished the new ventures well. Because the SPTCs had acquired power, others had to have lost it; history is silent on those who lose power pleasantly.

A first chore was to develop a professional training program. The nucleus would be the few individuals who, like Ruth, had a background in corporate governance and the emerging field of corporate accountability. The early SPTCs needed to expand beyond this group to bring in new talent.

These SPTC pioneers knew they would not be managing businesses. Instead, they were concerned with creating standards to guide the managers and by which managers could be judged. Their function was more legislative and judicial than executive. And so the principals SPTCs sought were neither business managers nor specialists. Instead, the key people would be generalists by temperament – individuals capable of adjudicating in *all* of the traditional professions – law, management, public administration, and ethics, to name the most pertinent.

The excitement of a new field and the unprecedented amounts of potential fees brought forth a stellar array of candidates – many of them from traditional money management and consulting firms. Equal opportunity laws needed no enforcement: both women and minorities – and particularly women – flocked to the field. This fortuity contributed to the availability of a cadre of professionals with a more holistic predisposition than traditionally educated men.

SPTCs generally organised themselves as professional service firms, with a cadre of 'principals' having ultimate authority and ownership. The fiduciary nature of the ownership responsibilities was so personal that Ruth organised New Fiduciary Trust Company as a partnership in which each of the partners would have personal liability for the firm's debts. Ruth understood the narcotic of power and realised that it could be the ultimate breakdown of the ownership system.

Ruth wrote the simple article of partnership that was copied virtually universally and became the essential genius of the SPTCs: 'At the time each person accepts selection as a principal, he must simultaneously execute a letter of resignation as of a date of his choice and a letter offering to sell back his interest to the partnership at its value on the firm's books.'

This reminder of the oft-cited *Hawley* term-limit principle needed such clear reiteration. 'If men were angels' are the starting words of many otherwise plausible books about human salvation; men are not angels, nor are women; any system that ignores this fact is failure-bound, and the SPTC was not exempt from this imperative. The principals of the SPTCs simply exercised too much power to permit the whole system to be jeopardised by conflicts of interest. Individuals serving SPTCs simply had to be freed from present or future commercial needs in order to make decisions with an eye to their own financial future.

FUNDAMENTAL PRINCIPLES

The pioneers of SPTCs reached a quick and firm consensus on underlying principles. Corporations are the source of great potential wealth for all human beings. As a structure that enables owners to share and limit the risk of investment, the corporate form gives unique protections and impetus for the expression of individual genius. The SPTC's role would be to bring an essential balance to corporate life, accommodating society's interests without unduly inhibiting human genius.

The SPTCs were in business to make money, and make it they did. As planned, the SPTCs generated enough funds to permit generous pensions for retiring partners, thus making up for the opportunity cost of term limits. The money came not only by doing things right, but by doing the right thing. The SPTCs set forth policies that not only affirmed the basic value of ownership involvement, but also affirmed the basic *values* recognised by owners and the equity marketplace: compliance with the law, full disclosure of social costs, and restraint in political involvement – the so-called Engel Triad.

Since institutional investors were already dominant in the marketplace, these values automatically became marketplace values. Meanwhile, individual investors also came to recognise the superior value of companies that met the basic standards of the Engel Triad, further boosting the market values of companies that conformed to the triad's values.

Each SPTC took on the responsibility for several hundred portfolio companies when it entered into relationships with the larger pension funds or investment companies. Obviously, this was a challenge way beyond the competency of any single SPTC, so the largest SPTCs gradually developed a pattern of working together based on comparable experiences with shared investments – for example, investments in venture capital or in developing large new mineral reserves.

Flexibility was the rule of the day and all manner of relationships existed in order the better to demonstrate a value added to the customer. There was no limit to the number of companies with which an SPTC might establish an activist relationship; nor was there a limit to the number of SPTCs that could function as agents of a single trustee or investment manager. The industry strove to maintain an open market for providers and consumers.

In some companies, a single SPTC acted as a kind of 'lead monitor'. In others, several SPTCs would meet periodically with other shareholders to develop an agreed upon agenda, sometimes failing to do so, but always operating from the conviction that the best answer would emerge from a dialogue between independent parties having different perspectives.

Over a relatively brief time, it became clear that the SPTCs would function in two sharply different roles. The first was as a monitor of the management of the company. If the company persisted in underperforming, the SPTCs were prepared to take whatever remedial steps were most appropriate, including changing the board of directors and senior managers, but never involving the principal of an SPTC serving in such capacity. The second role was to provide guidance to management of the long-term needs of owners and to articulate the *new language of accountability*.

GLOBAL REACH

SPTCs operated in a truly global market. Countries having well-funded pension systems like Japan and Holland had liberalised their investment practices with the result that their percentage of equity holdings approximated those in the United States (70%). At the same time, other countries like France moved away from government toward privately funded systems.

It was somewhat of a surprise to find that the American, British, Canadian, and Australian SPTCs exercised ownership rights with respect to over 50% of the equity securities in domestically domiciled companies, and 25% of total capital of public companies in other countries. The existence of the aggressive and efficient anglophone SPTCs – particularly American ones – presented a huge challenge to other countries. In most countries outside the

United States, ownership involvement in corporate governance was only nominal, so the presence of an articulate American stake constituted practical control in many cases.

Trustees all over the world were confronted with the *de facto* control of all companies by the anglophones. Over a relatively brief time, an international association of ownership institutions developed and the trustees began the tasks of defining their work programs, objectives, and mode of operations in a global context.

Perhaps the greatest ingenuity and effort went into the process of informing trust beneficiaries of the issues and alternatives facing owners of portfolio companies. Fortunately, SPTCs were twinned at birth with the Internet and the growth of that new medium provided the basis for rapid, comprehensive, and responsive communication and action between SPTCs and their beneficial owners.

Few countries had traditions of trusteeship and none had developed the practice of involving millions of participants in any way beyond receiving notices and money. The SPTCs could align all participants' interests for the first time in history. The *hundreds of millions* of pensioners *all* had an interest that business be conducted so as to permit 'sustainable development'. *All* of the trusts had holdings in multinational companies doing business in *every* country in the world; they controlled virtually *every* significant industry – and, in those where they did not have actual control, they had a strong marketplace presence.

Ruth articulated well the paradox of the new entities. 'We will have power only if we appear not to have it. We can keep power only if we do not overextend it.'[3] This was the basis of SPTC policies of restraint – both with respect to individual careers as SPTC principals and with respect to their mode of operating. The SPTCs insisted only on their right to be informed. As long as they owned a controlling block of the stock, they already had the power to control. Management continued to have the full authority to run the business, and government was undiminished in its authority to set standards, issue regulations and levy taxes.

Eventually, the focus of the SPTC movement extended beyond underperformance to performance itself. Instead of saying, 'You can't quarrel with success', the new motto of the SPTCs was, 'The good is often the enemy of the best'. Increasingly, the activists realised that virtually every company – even the star performers – can benefit from the energy of independent, informed, motivated, and empowered owners.

PARTING WORDS

Early in the development of SPTCs, principals began the practice of publicly authoring a careful explanation of decisions made in particularly challenging situations of ownership initiatives. Over time, these 'opinions' became a resource available to the whole industry. This practice, akin to that of judges in the legal system, provided experience and predictability to the managers and owners of American business. It also provided a record by which the experience of fiduciary ownership could be evaluated by the public and its elected representatives.

Ruth, on the last day of her career, entered the annals of corporate history with such an opinion. As principal of the SPTC that provided fiduciary service for the many institutional owners of General Electric, she wrote the 'opinion' that announced the decision by a majority of GE shareholders to replace a majority of members of GE's board of directors.

This decision came after considerable deliberation over the many crimes GE employees had committed from 1985, when it pleaded guilty to fraud charges for overcharging the US Air Force on its Minuteman missile contract, to 2009, when the so-called 'GE Discounts Scandal' emerged.[4] These crimes, although 'white collar', had begun to give shareholders the sense that (to quote a September 1995 Fortune article) 'somewhere in the highly successful and celebrated GE culture, something is not right'.

Before delivering the opinion, she paused to reflect on the enormity of the occasion. After all, this was GE – the company with the largest market capitalisation in the world, the cynosure of many capitalist eyes. GE was only one of the two Dow Jones companies on its original list before the turn of the century still on the list at its end. GE had been led by several of the authentic geniuses of the American political establishment – from Owen Young, to 'Electric Charlie' Wilson, to Ralph Cordiner, to Jack Welch. To be asked to be a director of GE was the nearest American equivalent to British nobility. GE, year in and out, was one of the outstanding performers among the very best American companies. Not only was it in the top 100 in performance rankings by Fortune, Forbes, and other publications; it was invariably one of the top ten. Indeed, it had even been the #1 performer.

Ruth's opinion was awaited with more than usual interest. It did not disappoint, going directly to the heart of the matter:

> 'We are now engaged in a great experiment: whether a society can long
> endure the existence of vast power in organizations whose functioning is

not subject to control by the citizens. The critical premise underlying this experiment is the assumption of responsibility by the owners of the enterprises — trustees for hundreds of millions of beneficial owners — for the impact of corporations on society.

'*The owners have signaled over the last decade an unmistakable determination that their corporations should obey the law, disclose facts known to them about their impact on society, and exercise restraint in their involvement in the political process — a normative agenda commonly referred to as a corporate code of conduct, or CCC. In a democratic society, we know that only government — in full possession of the facts and in the absence of undue influence from affected parties — can appropriately set limits on the actions of corporations.*

'*Only governments can determine what actions are inappropriate, and where lines should be drawn. Only government can determine which costs should be born by corporations, and which by the society at large. By classifying certain activities as criminal, government makes its clearest determination that such conduct is not acceptable within a free society. It is therefore critical that corporations should obey the law, that they should avoid criminal acts, and that they should act as citizens of their communities, their nations, and the world. Such an attitude of compliance and respect — modelling forth in large scale the values of our human flesh and blood — is clearly necessary for a civil and a fair society.*

'*Today we are taking the unusual step of changing a majority of the board of directors of a great company in order to provide a solid basis for the development of fiduciary capitalism — the life source of corporate accountability. It is a fact as old as myth and as true as science: living systems have special properties that we suppress at our peril. Just as in a nation the people should be sovereign, so in a corporation the owners should reign. It is up to owners to determine permissible ranges of conduct by corporate managers and directors in matters both large and small. GE's leaders have spoken of being "responsible", but they have never answered the burning question to whom? In this new world of heightened corporate accountability, a sense of the public interest must run deep, and legal compliance must be unstinting and full. These qualities must be inextricably imbedded in the equally important task of value maximization over the long term.*

'*Society has benefited greatly from the riveting energies of the corporate system and that system's demonstrated capacity to create wealth. Yet society has also suffered from lack of corporate accountability. A free people rejoice when corporations spin new technologies out of dreams or reward ingenuity with millions, but the people mourn when thousands lose work in a single firing, or when nationwide chains drive out corner stores without a second thought.*

'Corporations must be responsive to the clearest societal signal that certain conduct is unacceptable. We cannot live in a world with two kinds of people – those with flesh and blood and mortality and those creations of law with perpetual life. The corporate form of organization has enabled lives to be extended, pain to be alleviated, living standards to be raised and burdens to be mitigated. All of this and the creation of jobs, products, and wealth can be preserved only so long as we recognize that the corporate system is analogous to many of the complex systems invented by humankind to improve the conditions of life – dangerous if not suitably monitored.

'At the very least, corporations must be held to comply with criminal laws. These are the most solemn and clear message from society as to conduct which is incompatible with a free society. As has long been noted, corporations have no soul to save and no body to incarcerate. There is no effective way of enforcing criminal laws against corporations. A measure of respect and restraint is needed. When one encounters a pattern of sustained and repeated abuse of these laws, someone must be held responsible.

'As corporations have frequently demonstrated, when the standard for performance is to achieve a given quantified standard – be it sales, earnings, cash flow, or stock market price level – incentive mechanism can be devised to reward the managers for success. This same ingenuity can be used to ensure that the responsible corporation officials ensure compliance with criminal statutes.

'This stricture applies to the greatest of corporations as well as the meanest; it applies to the grandest of boards of directors and to the humblest. It applies to us today, and to our children tomorrow, and to the next generation, if such there be.

'Our noble effort to align the interests of ownership and management helps to ensure that there will be future generations – endlessly creating wealth for all to share in accordance with their efforts and ideas in a free and civil society.'

In the years to come, historians looked back on that day and called it in awe the beginning of the 'GE Market'. GE's stock opened weakly the morning after the decision, with the losses recouped by lunch time. Then, in an afternoon surge that lasted for the better part of a week, GE's stock gained an incredible 30% in value. The market as a whole took off and did not stop until almost 12% gains had been recorded. Money that had been stuffed in mattresses, invested in 'collectibles', and frozen in gold expressed its belief that fiduciary capitalism not only could work – but was already working.

Appendices

Appendix to Chapter 2
Early Business Structures
(Adam Smith)

Appendix to Chapter 3
The Line-Up: Corporate Crime
(Robert A.G. Monks)

Appendix to Chapter 6
The Corporation as a Complex Adaptive System: Notes
on the Brightline Model
(Robert A.G. Monks)

Appendix to Chapter 8
Can an Old Guard of Directors Effectively Govern a 21st-
Century Corporation?
(Joann S. Lublin)

Appendix to Chapter 2

Early Business Structures: Excerpts from *The Wealth of Nations*[1]

Adam Smith

Adam Smith's description of 'joint stock companies' in the Inquiry into the Nature and Causes of the Wealth of Nations *provides the earliest known eye-witness description of the risk-transferring, profit-maximising entity we now call the corporation. The following text quotes Smith at some length on the peculiar alchemy of this form of enterprise.*

The protection of trade in general has always been considered as essential to the defense of the commonwealth, and, upon that account, a necessary part of the duty of the executive power ... But in this respect, as well as in many others, nations have not always acted consistently; and in the greater part of the commercial states of Europe, particular companies of merchants have had the address to persuade the legislature to entrust to them the performance of this part of the duty of the sovereign ...

When those companies do not trade upon a joint stock, but are obliged to admit any person, properly qualified, upon paying a certain fine, and agreeing to submit to the regulations of the company, each member trading upon his own stock, and at his own risk, they are called *regulated companies*. When they trade upon a joint stock, each member sharing in the common profit or loss in proportion to his share in this stock, they are called *joint stock companies*. Such companies, whether regulated or joint stock, sometimes have, and sometimes have not, exclusive privileges.

Regulated companies resemble, in every respect, the corporations of trades [guilds] so common in the cities and towns of all the different countries of Europe; and are a sort of enlarged monopolies of the same kind ... The monopoly is more or less strict according as the terms of admission are more or less difficult; and according as the directors of the company have more or less authority, or have it more or less in their power to manage in such a manner as to confine the greater part of the trade to themselves and their particular friends. In the most ancient regulated companies the privileges of apprenticeship were the same as in other corporations [and] the usual corporation spirit, wherever the law does not restrain it, prevails in all regulated companies ... When they have been allowed to act according to their natural genius, they have always, in order to confine the competition to as small a number of persons as possible, endeavored to subject the trade to many burdensome regulations. When the law has restrained them from doing this, they have become altogether useless and insignificant ...

Joint stock companies, established either by royal charter or by act of parliament, differ in several respects not only from regulated companies, but from private copartneries.

First, in a private copartnery, no partner, without the consent of the company, can transfer his share to another person, or introduce a new member into the company. Each member, however, may upon proper warning, withdraw from the copartnery, and demand payment from them of his share of the common stock. In a joint stock company, on the contrary, no member can demand payment of his share from the company; but each member can, without their consent, transfer his share to another person, and thereby introduce a new member. The value of a share in a joint stock is always the price which it will bring in the market; and this may be either greater or less, in any proportion, than the sum which its owner stands credited for in the stock of the company.

Secondly, in a private copartnery, each partner is bound for the debts contracted by the company to the whole extent of his fortune. In a joint stock company, on the contrary, each partner is bound only to the extent of his share.

Appendix to Chapter 3

The Line-Up: Corporate Crime

Robert A. G. Monks

This appendix was originally written as part of Chapter 3 (under Danger Number 4), but it grew too long! The sheer volume of examples contained herein provides ample proof of the persistence of corporate crime.

Large household-name corporations live down crime as easily as photogenic people. The only difference is that in most cases top corporate managers almost never have to have to serve jail time.[2] When senior executives are caught red-handed on videotape (remember Archer Daniels Midland?), all is forgiven and forgotten after the fines are paid.

Even when it comes to the national defense, the public seems impervious to company wrongdoing. Consider Boeing Corporation.

- A sting called Operation Undercover exposed the seedy side of Boeing in 1980, but less than three years later, reports Louis Paztor in *When the Pentagon Was for Sale*, "Boeing made the list of the ten 'most admired' companies, alongside popular consumer-goods marketers such as Procter & Gamble, Wal-Mart Stores, and Coca-Cola."[3]
- In the four years from 1990 to February 1994, Boeing had paid nearly $20 million dollars to settle four lawsuits against it for fraud, waste, and/ or abuse, yet by mid-1997, the company was the darling of the nation.[4] The Clinton Administration threatened a trade war against Europe if the European Commission would not approve the giant's merger with McDonnell Douglas (completed midnight, 1 August 1997).

The financial rewards of most corporate wrongdoing are so high and the costs so low (as discussed in Chapter 3) that criminal activity is all too common. One of the few tools that US corporate crime fighters have at their disposal is the False Claims Act, which punishes corporations that try to defraud the government. Not surprisingly, many of the major government contractors have tried to weaken this law, especially those that had paid fines under the law in previous years. After all, in 1994, the US government had already recovered $588 million in fines from these companies over a period of four years. Fortunately, this lobbying effort failed. From 1994 to 1996, the government collected an additional $2 billion in fines under the Act.[5]

Here is a list of the companies that signed the lobbying paper, followed by the number of settled fraud cases from 1990 to 1994 involving these companies: The Boeing Company (4); Eaton Corporation (2); FMC Corporation (0), General Electric (16); Grumman Corporation (5); GTE Government Systems (0); Honeywell Inc. (3); Hughes Aircraft Company (9); Litton Industries (4); Magnavox Electronics (3); Martin Marietta Corp. (5); McDonnell Douglas (4); Newport News Shipbuilding (11); Northrup Corporation (4); Raytheon Company (4); Rockwell International (4); Sunstrand Corporation (1); Teledyne Corporation (5); Texas Instruments (3); TRW Inc. (1); Unisys Corporation (2); United Technologies (3).[6] It is obvious from this list that fraud is a common practice at defense contractors, especially General Electric.

The marketplace seems indifferent to the sources of corporate gain, even when it is ill-gotten. And the press is quick to forget yesterday's dirt in the search for today's gold. In a February 1994 cover story, *Fortune* looked at 'Jack Welch's Nightmare on Elm Street' (the nightmare being scandal-plagued Kidder Peabody) and concluded that 'misdeeds ... are not an isolated case at GE'. Yet just two years later, in its January 1996 issue, *Fortune* crowned GE's charismatic leader Jack Welch as America's most successful generator of shareholder value.

A LITANY OF SINS

Here is an incomplete list of GE's wrongdoings over the past decade, based in part on the *Fortune* list, and in part on a February 1997 report by the Project on Government Oversight in Washington, DC[7] Only major settled incidents are listed.

1985   GE pleads guilty to fraud charges for overcharging the Air Force on its Minuteman missile contract; GE agrees to pay $2 million in criminal and civil penalties.

1989   GE settles four civil suits brought by whistleblowers who alleged that GE cheated the government out of millions of dollars by issuing faulty time cards. GE pays some $3.5 million.

1990   GE is convicted of defrauding the Defense Department by overcharging the Army for a battlefield computer system. GE pays $30 million in penalties for that and other defense contracting overcharges.

1992   GE pleads guilty to defrauding the Pentagon of more than $30 million in the sale of military jet engines to Israel after an employee received bribes. GE pays $69 million in fines.

1993   GE's NBC News unit issues an on-air apology to General Motors for staging a misleading simulated crash test. NBC agrees to pay GM's estimated $1 million legal and investigation expenses.

1995   GE pays $7.1 million to settle a lawsuit alleging that the company failed to satisfy electrical bonding requirements for its jet engine contracts, thereby creating a safety risk. Also, in a separate development, GE and Martin Marietta together paid $5.87 million to settle a lawsuit associated with improper sales of radar systems to Egypt.

1997   GE loses a lawsuit filed in the Federal court of Canada in Toronto. Justice Bud Cullen ruled in favor of the plaintiff, Whirlpool, which alleged that GE violated its patent on dual-action agitators with flexible fins. GE plans to appeal.[8]

Considering these crimes, one must ask: how can a company that breaks the law so often do so well in equity markets? High shareholder value and high corporate crime go together quite well, the answer may come, so if it ain't broke, don't fix it. The problem is that the current system for assessing shareholder value is about to break, and there will be no fixing. Instead, there will be a major change in how we value corporations.

Appendix to Chapter 6

The Corporation as a Complex Adaptive System: Notes on the Brightline Model

Robert A.G. Monks

When we at LENS first began our work developing a dynamic, interactive model of the corporation as a CAS, we had visions of a computer game that could closely 'simulate' the reality of corporate life. Yes, corporation are complex, but we had no fears. Computers today have vast amounts of memory and can handle extremely complex problems. Surely our computers could handle a full-scale corporation!

We were naïve. An agent-based model, we have come to realise, is not quite the same thing as a simulation, although the term 'simulation' is often used to describe agent-based models. As David Lane has written, 'The Santa Fe Institute modeling efforts described here all share one feature: they are not "simulations" … The very entities and relationships that appear in SFI models are highly abstracted from any world of direct experience. The abstractions, in turn, are based on presuppositions about what "worlds of experience" are like.' These presuppositions, says Lane, are 'far from the "common sense" views of Western European/American cultural tradition that most of us have inherited', but they allow us to 'construct interpretation of our own worlds of experience that open up new possibilities for effective action'.[9]

This language certainly reflects the process we went through in creating our model – especially the part about new possibilities for effective action.

We also received helpful guidance from the writings of John Holland of the Santa Fe Institute, particularly his book *Hidden Order: How Adaptation Builds Complexity*. Holland defines seven basic concepts (some 'properties', some 'mechanisms') necessary to modelling the complex adaptive system. In order of importance, these are:

- *Aggregation* (property). This means putting similar things together and treating them as equivalent.
- *Tagging* (mechanism). This is a function that makes aggregation possible – like a banner or flag.
- *Nonlinearity* (property). Linearity means that we get a value for the whole by adding up the sum of its parts. Nonlinearity means that we may get less, the same, or more, depending on circumstances.
- *Flow* (property). Flows are movements over a network made up of nodes (processors such as agents) and connectors.
- *Diversity* (property). This concept says there are many niches, and if the inhabitant of a niche fails to adapt to change, some other inhabitant will fill that niche, ensuring diversity.
- *Internal models* (mechanism). This is a means of anticipation, bringing the Cartesian *res cognitans* (the inside world) in contact with the Cartesian *res externa* (the outside world), so to speak.[10] (Another term is 'schema', but that has a different meaning in math so we will not use it here.)
- *Building blocks* (mechanism). This is the ability to break complexity down into parts and then recreate or create using the parts.

While substantially less ambitious in scope than originally intended, the final model we implemented does in fact exhibit all of these general characteristics.

VARIABILITY AND DEPLOYMENT

The Brightline model is intended for continual reuse in a number of settings. It was written in Java, and in such a way that all agent attribute variables can be changed at run-time by the user.

The model has also been successfully deployed on a Web-based server, and thus made available via the Internet. Run-time users make a series of attribute variable settings and then run the model accordingly, with the results of each run presented both graphically, via behavioural pattern trendlines for each variable, and statistically, showing the relative changes in the corporation agents' market shares and corresponding shareholder responses.

Appendix to Chapter 8

Can an Old Guard of Directors Effectively Govern a 21st-Century Corporation?

Joann S. Lublin

This report questions how vigorously a counsel of elders can serve corporations in a fast-changing world.

No, they can't, assert increasing numbers of investors at underperforming businesses overloaded with older directors. Blaming the old guard for being entrenched or stale, these shareholders are doing what they can to rejuvenate boards.

Most major companies require directors to retire at a certain age, typically 70, surveys show. Directors usually lack protection under the federal age-bias law, which exempts outside board members because they aren't employees and inside members if they are top-level executives. Still, people past the age of 70 hold at least 10% of the board seats at 296 of the nation's 860 biggest public companies, concludes a proxy analysis by Directorship, a research firm in Greenwich, Connecticut. Board members over 70 hold between 33% and 56% of the seats for 39 of those concerns.

At the top of that list is Digital Equipment Corp. Five of Digital's nine board members are over 70 years old, including two who joined during the

1950s. In 1993, the computer maker adopted a policy that new board members must retire at age 72. Those appointed before 1993 may stay until they turn 75.

Until last week, investor activist Herbert A. Denton, unhappy with Digital's sagging performance, had been pushing for the replacement of some of the older board members with younger people. However, Mr. Denton, who is president of Provident Capital Inc., a small New York brokerage house, gave up his campaign this week because Digital now says it is looking for new directors. (Digital denies that news reports about a candidate search are related to Mr. Denton's prodding, however.)

Shareholder dissatisfaction over too many older directors recently spurred shakeups at W.R. Grace & Co., Occidental Petroleum Corp., and Stone & Webster Inc. Twelve of Grace's 25 directors were aged 72 or older in 1993. A cadre of big institutional shareholders led by the College Retirement Equities Fund persuaded directors of the Boca Raton, Florida, packaging and specialty-chemicals company to alter the by-laws weeks after the investors approached them in spring 1995. The change triggered the immediate departure of eight board members over 70 years old.

Occidental Petroleum acted less swiftly. Directors of the Los Angeles oil and gas concern embraced a mandatory retirement age of 72 in 1995 – following eight years of failed shareholder resolutions seeking such a policy. And its shift to a more youthful board won't be completed for three more years. The oldest of Oxy Pete's four octogenarian directors: Retired Tennessee Sen. Albert Gore Sr., the 88-year-old father of the nation's vice president.

At Stone & Webster, older directors became a bone of contention soon after dissident investors began to attack the Boston engineering and construction company three years ago. Those critics claimed the company's share price had suffered because it was slow to move beyond the nuclear-power business.

'Why are the companies doing poorly the ones with the old, old board members?' one large Stone & Webster shareholder asks, and then answers: 'Because they never upset the apple cart'.

In such situations, 'all the board members should be looking for their replacements – and the way should be led by those over 70', says Robert A.G. Monks, a principal of LENS, a Washington activist investment fund that owned about 3% of Stone & Webster's shares in 1995.

Under intense pressure from such holders in the spring of 1995, Stone &

Webster directors decided that they would begin to require retirement at age 70 the following year. They also agreed to exempt three older members until 1999.

Nevertheless, that trio quit in May 1996 when they were 71, 73, and 74 years old, respectively. The men felt 'it would create difficulties for the company if they stayed another term', explains Kent F. Hansen, the board's lead outside director. The departing board members were 'all very sharp individuals' even though dissident investors saw them as 'too much part of the old school of thought', adds H. Kerner Smith, named president and CEO of Stone & Webster in February 1996.

H.J. Heinz Co., whose board has been criticized for having too many insiders, raised its retirement-age guidelines for outside board members to 72 years old from 70 in June 1996. Five non-employee directors were over 70 as of last August, according to Heinz's latest proxy statement. 'Ageism is not something we want to engage in', says a spokeswoman for the Pittsburgh food giant. Directors 'felt that people remain very active and vital' beyond age 70, she says.

Activist investors may be misdirecting their dissatisfaction by focusing on directors' ages rather than their tenure or performance, some observers suggest. 'The longer you stay [on a board], the more the you become part of the problem', says Charles Elson, a Stetson University law professor in St Petersburg, Florida. He favors ten-year term limits for directors.

Mandatory retirement at age 70 means 'you don't have to judge whether a director is asleep or alive', says Donald Frey, retired CEO of Bell & Howell Co. But he wasn't happy that he had to give up seats at three major corporations – Springs Industries Inc., Cincinnati Milacron Inc., and Clark Equipment Co. – when he turned 70 four years ago.

'I would have liked to have stayed on – I felt like I was contributing and I could have contributed more', says Mr. Frey, now a Northwestern University professor of industrial engineering and management science.

'I've known board members useless at 60 – or sharp as hell at age 80', Mr. Frey observes. It makes more sense, he adds, 'to apply judgment whether this guy still has his marbles'.

Reprinted (with minor changes for stylistic uniformity) by permission of *The Wall Street Journal* © 1997. This article appeared on 3 July 1997, p. B-1.

Complexity Resources

Complexity: A Glossary of Terms

Complexity Bibliography
  Articles
  Books

Who's Who in Complexity: Pioneers in Complexity

Complexity: A Glossary of Terms

This glossary features concise definitions of key terms in the science of complexity – including the term 'complexity' itself. Some of the terms in this glossary are not used in this book, but we are including them anyway so that the reader can get a feel for complexity fundamentals. Some definitions are in my own words based on multiple sources. When a single source is used verbatim, it is credited accordingly.

Agent. From the Greek *agein,* meaning action: something or someone that produces an effect on matter. In complexity science, the main player in a ***complex*** adaptive system. In corporate terminology, this term means something or someone that takes action on behalf of something or someone else.

Algorithm. A method of solving a problem, involving a finite series of steps (Oxford 1996). A set of rules for getting a specific output from a specific input. Each step must be so precisely defined it can be translated into computer language and executed by machine (Knuth 1977). A heuristic algorithm (also called 'greedy', 'fast', and 'quick and dirty') is a solution to a problem that is expedient – based on a best choice in the present moment – but not necessarily optimal (COMAP 1988).

Automaton. From the Greek *automatos,* acting of itself. A being whose actions derive from its internal workings. Computer scientists use very simple or cellular automata in models that test decision-making behavior. These automata are essentially stimulus-response machines that trade (Szpiro 1997).

Bifurcation. A phenomenon whereby the number of solutions of a dynamical system changes suddenly, as one of the parameters of a system crosses a critical value (Tsonis 1996).

Bond. In chemistry, a strong force of attraction holding atoms together in a *molecule* or crystal (Oxford 1996).

Cellular automata. See *automaton.*

Complex. As an adjective, this term means having the attributes of *complexity*. As a noun in the physical sciences, the term signifies a compound formed by particles (*molecules* or ions) (Oxford 1996).

Chaos. A pattern of behaviour that is unpredictable. High-dimension chaos is a pattern generated by so many rules that it displays very little structure, and appears to be random. Low-dimension chaos is a pattern generated by only a few, simple mathematical rules. It is unpredictable over the long term, but it does have a recognisable structure, indicated by a positive Lyapunov coefficient – a mathematical property discovered by Russian mathematician Alexandr M. Lyapunov a century ago (Gullberg 1997).

Complexity. The levels of self-organisation of a *system*. In physical systems, complexity is associated with broken *symmetry* and the ability of a system to have different states between which it can make phase *transitions*. It is also associated with having coherence in space over a long range. Examples of complexity include ordered phases that arise when a system is driven far from thermal *equilibrium*. It is not necessary for a system to have a large number of degrees of freedom in order for complexity to occur. The study of complexity is greatly aided by computers in systems that cannot be described analytically (Oxford 1996).

Compound. A substance formed by the combination of elements in fixed proportions. The formation of a compound involves a chemical reaction:, i.e. there is a change in the configuration of the valence electrons of the atoms. Compounds, unlike mixtures, cannot be separated by physical means (Oxford 1996).

Emergence. A property of a system or subsystem that cannot be possessed by its component parts, but usually depends on those component parts and on how they are connected together (Johnson 1995).

Energy. A measure of a system's ability to do work. Like work itself, it is measured in joules. Energy is conveniently classified into two forms: potential energy is the energy stored in a body or system as a consequence of its position, shape, or state (this includes gravitational energy, electrical energy, nuclear energy, and chemical energy); kinetic energy is energy of motion and is usually defined as the work that will be done by the body possessing the energy when it is brought to rest (Oxford 1996). In the corporate world, we tend to use the term 'energy' in the kinetic sense.

Entropy. A thermodynamic property of a system that corresponds intuitively to the degree of disorder (Tsonis 1996). Also, energy in a state that cannot perform further work, hence, stasis, disorder, and waste. (Shannon Clyne, in correspondence dated 4 September 1997).

Equilibrium. A state in which a system has its energy distributed in the statistically most probable manner; a state of a system in which forces, influences, reactions, etc., balance each other out so that there is no net change (Oxford 1996).

Field. A region in which a body experiences a force as the result of the presence of some other body or bodies. A field is thus a method of representing the way in which bodies are able to influence each other. The four fundamental **interactions** occur in fields.

Gödel's incompleteness theorem. A theorem published by Czech–Austrian mathematician Kurt Gödel in 1931. The theorem stated that any consistent formal system adequate to describe arithmetic must contain statements that can neither be proved nor disproved (Gullberg 1997).

Interaction. An effect involving a number of bodies, particles, or systems as a result of which some physical or chemical change takes place to one or more of them. A fundamental interaction is a type of interaction that can occur between bodies. There are four fundamental types of interactions. These interactions can take place even when the bodies are not in physical contact, and together they account for all the observed forces that occur in the universe (Kaku and Thompson 1995). The unified *field* theory is a search for the unification of these four types of interaction into one model, theory, or set of equations (Oxford 1996).

Lever points. A property of a **complex** adaptive system, namely the ability of a small input to produce major, predictable, directed changes (Holland 1995).

Life. The condition, quality, or fact of being a living organism; the condition that characterises animals and plants (when alive) and distinguishes them from inanimate matter, being marked by a capacity for growth and development and by continued functional activity; the activities and phenomena by which this is manifested. The concept of life is intertwine with the concept of death. Life can mean animate existence continued or prolonged (as opposed to death), and it can mean the possession of which one is deprived in death. In a general biological sense, it can also mean animate life dependent on sustenance or favourable physical conditions. Most deeply, it can mean the cause or source of living; the animating principle (Oxford 1993).

Link. In mathematics, a collection of elastic circles that are mutually entangled and cannot be separated spatially into subcollections; in chemistry, a catanae, or collection of circular molecules held together by *topological* bonds, not chemical bonds (Oxford 1996).

Molecule. One of the fundamental units forming a chemical compound; the smallest part of a chemical compound that can take part in a chemical reaction. In most covalent compounds, molecules consist of groups of atoms held together by covalent or co-ordinate *bonds.*

Multiagent. A term used in the modelling of complex adaptive systems to signify a cluster of related *agents.*

Phase transition. See *transition.*

Self-organisation. The spontaneous order arising in a system when certain parameters of the system reach critical values. Self-organisation occurs in many systems in physics, chemistry, and biology. Self-organisation can occur when a system is driven far from thermal *equilibrium.*

String. A one-dimensional object used in theories of elementary particles and in cosmology (cosmic string). String theory replaces the idea of a point like elementary particle (used in quantum field theory) by a line or loop (a closed string). States of a particle may be produced by sending waves along this string. The combination of string theory with supersymmetry leads to superstring theory.

Symmetry. In physics, the set of invariances of a system. In biology, regularity in the arrangement of the parts of an organism. Scientists have observed symmetry and its variant, broken symmetry, a situation in which the ground state of a many-body system (or, in quantum physics, vacuum state) has a lower symmetry than the measure defining it. They have theorised but have not yet observed supersymmetry, a situation in which elementary particles are paired. In physics, *strings* with supersymmetry, called superstrings, may be the best approach to unifying the four fundamental *interactions.*

System. A group of interacting, interrelated or interdependent elements forming a complex whole. A *complex* adaptive system (CAS) consists of a number of agents interacting with other according to schemas, that is, rules of behaviour, that require them to inspect each other's behaviour and adjust their own in light of the behaviour of others. In other words, complex adaptive systems learn and evolve, and they usually interact with other complex adaptive systems. They survive because they learn or evolve in an adaptive way: they compute information in order to extract regularities, building them into schemas that are continually changed in the light of experience (Stacey 1996).

Topology. The branch of geometry concerned with the properties of geometrical objects that are unchanged by continuous deformations, such as twisting or stretching. Topology is of great importance in modern theories of the fundamental *interactions* (Oxford 1996).

The Türing machine. A model of the computational process created by English mathematician Alan Mathison Turing, a **Gödel** contemporary (see Gödel) who showed that even very simple computer programs can be undecidable (Waldrop 1993).

Transition. The process or an instance of changing from one form, state, activity, or place to another. A transition element is any one in a series of elements in which an inner electron shell (rather than an outer shell) is only partially filled (Oxford 1996).

SOURCES FOR GLOSSARY

Concise Science Dictionary. Oxford: Oxford University Press, 1996. Cited as Oxford 1996.

Consortium for Mathematics and Its Application. *For All Practical Purposes: An Introduction to Contemporary Mathematics.* Project Director, Solomon Garfunkel. New York: W.H. Freeman and Company, 1988.

Gullberg, Jan. *Mathematics from the Birth of Numbers.* New York: W.W. Norton & Company, 1997.

Kaku, Michio, and Thompson, Jennifer. *Beyond Einstein: The Cosmic Quest for the Theory of the Universe.* New York: Anchor Books, 1995.

Knuth, Donald. 'Algorithms', *Scientific American.* April 1977, pp. 63 ff.

The New Shorter Oxford English Dictionary. Oxford: Oxford University Press, 1993. Cited as Oxford 1993.

For additional sources, including sources used in this glossary, see the Complexity Bibliography immediately following.

Complexity Bibliography

The following annotated list of articles and books is really not a 'bibliography' in the purest sense. Rather, it is acknowledgement of the materials on complexity science that have been most useful to me in writing this book. Many important materials are not included – simply because as a newcomer to the field I have not yet had the pleasure of reading them! For a comprehensive bibliography in complexity (and one that I plan to use in guiding further study), see Francis Heylighen, 'Publications on Complex, Evolving Systems', *Complexity*, Vol. 2, No. 5, pp. 31–6, described below.

ARTICLES

Readers are referred to two excellent periodicals in this field. One is the *Bulletin of the Santa Fe Institute*, published regularly since 1987. (See also the SFI Web site at http://www.santafe.edu.) The other is the relatively new journal called *Complexity*, published by John Wiley & Sons, Inc., New York, in affiliation with the Santa Fe Institute. In my enthusiasm for this publication, I have taken the liberty of summarising my favourite articles from *Complexity*, with annotations. Whenever possible, I cite (with quote marks) the authors' own language.

Volume 1, no. 1 (1995)

Murray Gel-Mann, 'What is Complexity?', pp. 16–19.

The complexity of an entity is the 'length of a concise description of the entity's regularities'. In our era (since life began on earth), the complexity of the natural world has been increasing. However, it is conceivable in the future that 'the era characterized by fairly well defined objects may draw to an end, while self-organization becomes rare and the envelope of complexity begins to shrink'.

Brian Arthur, 'Complexity in Economic and Financial Markets', pp. 20–25.

The economy is a 'collection of activities, technologies, and needs, all interacting through a market system peopled by decision-making agents such as firms, banks, consumers, and investors'. But it can also be seen as 'a collection of beliefs, anticipations, expectations, and interpretations, with decision-making and strategizing and action-taking predicated upon these beliefs and expectations'.

Melanie Mitchell, 'Genetic Algorithms: An Overview', pp. 31–39.

Genetic algorithms work by 'discovering, emphasizing, and recombining good building blocks of solutions in a highly parallel fashion'. Applications include problems of optimisation, automatic programming, machine learning, economic models, immune system models, ecological models, population genetics models, and the interaction of evolution and learning.

Volume 1, no. 2 (1995)

David A. Lane, 'Models and Aphorisms' pp. 9–13.

'The Santa Fe Institute modeling efforts described here all share one feature: they are not "simulations" ... The very entities and relationships that appear in SFI models are highly abstracted from any world of direct experience. The abstractions, in turn, are based on presuppositions about what "worlds of experience" are like [presuppositions] far from the "common sense" views of Western European/American cultural tradition that most of us have inherited.' Yet, if the intuitions of the SFI modellers are right, the presuppositions allow us to construct interpretations of our own 'worlds of experience' that open up new possibilities for effective action.

E. Atlee Jackson, 'No Provable Limits to "Scientific Knowledge"', pp. 14–17.

In the physical or natural sciences, 'knowledge' requires 'understanding', a process that includes three steps: (1) to gather information through physical observation, a mathematical model, or computer experiments; (2) to discover correlations within these sets of observables; and (3) to apply an accepted scientific method involving formal reasoning to these discoveries. Because the types of observables in step one are separate and apart from one another, they are 'not susceptible to any logical proof concerning limitations' of their internal correlations with one another. Rather, it is the human mind that has limitations.

Lee A. Segel, 'Grappling with Complexity', pp. 18–25.

A complex system is 'typically composed of a large number of elements whose interaction is nonlinear'. The system seems 'hierarchically organized with disparate space and time scales and a variety of intercommunication functional layers. The interaction of the system components gives rise to higher-level emergent properties that are often not apparent in the lower levels.' Complex systems are described through models (mathematical equations) or simulations (computer programs). 'But models need not be mathematical. The can be verbal as well as formal. Examples of useful verbal models include the "invisible hand" in economics.' Complexity science determines degrees of complexity, examines consequences of hierarchy, and studies artificial life (AL). The AL field could be called 'artificial biology'. Should there be 'artificial physics' and 'artificial chemistry' as well? There may even be a place for 'artificial everything' – in pure mathematics.

Volume 1, no. 3 (1995)

Harald Atmaspacher, Gerda Widenmann, and Anton Amann, 'Descartes Revisited', pp. 15–21.

The dualism of Rene Descartes involves a distinction or 'cut' between *res cogitans* (thinking substance) and *res extensa* (extended substance). That is, it contrasts ideas, models, or concepts versus material facts, events, or data. The dualism of Werner Heisenberg starts in *res extensa* and goes further: it separates the facts, events, or date observed from the observer. These two cuts make possible another: 'exo' versus 'endo'. An exo-perspective requires an external observer. From an endo-perspective, there is no observer. The behaviour of the system is experienced by an internal participant whose viewpoint does not include a distinction between system and environment. Complexity and meaning both fall in the 'endo' realm, where they make a 'bridge across the Cartesian cut'.

Jeffrey Johnson, 'A Language of Structure in the Science of Complexity', pp. 22–9.

'How can we understand complex systems? In general, we represent systems in an eclectic and pragmatic mixture of natural language such as English, pictorial languages such as drawings, numerical languages such as arithmetic, and symbolic languages such as mathematics ... This paper presents the basics of what has been called a "language of structure," which adds new linguistic, pictorial, numerical, and symbolic vocabulary to the representation repertoire. The central idea is that relational structure constrains the behavior of systems.' (Includes glossary.)

Volume 1, no. 4 (1996)

Ricard V. Sole, Susanna C. Manrubia, Bartolo Luque, Jordi Delgado, and Jordi Bascompte, 'Phase Transitions and Complex Systems', pp. 13–26.

'It is well known, from the theory of phase transitions, that a given system (possibly made of many subsystems) can undergo strong qualitative changes in its macroscopic properties ... At critical points, fractal structures, complex dynamical patterns, and optimal information transfer appear in a spontaneous way. Observing such properties in those systems which we call "complex," we can conjecture that complexity tends to appear close to instability points.'

Murray Gell-Mann, 'Nature Conformable to Herself', pp. 9–12.

Scientific activity often involves 'peeling the onion' to discover simple laws, but we can also 'start with the heart of the onion – the simple unified quantum field theory of all the elementary particles and their interactions'. We need not look for more. 'Life can perfectly well emerge from the laws of physics plus accidents, and mind, from neurobiology. It is not necessary to assume additional mechanisms or hidden causes. Once emergence is considered, a huge burden is lifted from the inquiring mind. We don't need something more in order to get something more ... At each new level new laws emerge that should be studied for themselves; new phenomena appear that should be appreciated and valued at their own level.'

Volume 1, no. 5 (1996)

Brian Goodwin, 'Emergent Form: Evolving Beyond Darwinism', pp. 11–15.

The developing organism is a 'nonlinear system that generates patterns in space and in time (technically, a field). Such systems are no infinitely plastic. To understand the dynamics of these morphogenic fields it is necessary to construct models that depend on more than a knowledge of genes and their products. What is required is an integration of relevant molecular and cellular properties into nonlinear dynamic processes whose bifurcations simulate the discontinuous transitions of form that developing organisms undergo during morphogenesis.'

Harold Gutowitz, 'Cellular Automata and the Sciences of Complexity' (Part I), pp. 16–22.

The models called 'cellular automata' describe the 'interaction of a multitude of simple individuals...such as when ants interact to form a colony or water molecules interact to form a fluid'. This type of model 'chooses an initial state of the system and observes the resulting sequence of states'. This approach 'permits descriptions of natural processes in computational terms (computational biology, computational physics) but also of computation in biological and physical terms (artificial life, physics of computation).

A.A. Tsonis, 'Dynamical Systems as Models for Physical Processes', pp. 23–33.

Consideration of fractal sets in geometry, chaos, and cellular automata provides evidence linking randomness and its interplay with dynamical systems ('rules') to physical processes. (Fractal geometry describes 'irregular and fragmented patterns that have a noninteger fractal dimension'. Chaos is 'random-looking behavior occurring in deterministic nonlinear dynamical systems'. Cellular automata are 'mathematical realizations of physical systems in which space and time are discrete, and physical quantities take on a finite set of discrete values. They are constructed from many identical components, each simple, but together capable of complex behavior.') Conclusion: if rules and randomness coexist, then approaches used to model and predict the outcome of physical systems should combine both! (Includes glossary.)

Volume 1, no. 6 (1996)

Harold Gutowitz, 'Cellular Automata and the Sciences of Complexity' (Part II), pp. 29–35.

One can base a cryptosystem on cellular automata. 'Let the secret key of a cryptosystem be the initial state of a publicly known dynamical system.... The longer a cryptosystem is in wide use ... without being broken, the better it is. Is it the same for complex systems? The suggest is that unpredictability and complexity are concepts meaningful only in relation with a specification of the set of prediction tools at ones disposal, and of how much force one is willing to apply to use them.'

Daniel C. Dennett, 'Hofstadter's Quest', pp. 9–12.

The Hofstadterian school of phenomenology stresses the need to ask how cognition works. In a recent anthology of his writings, *Fluid Concepts and Creative Analogies*, he lists eight discoveries, including the fact that 'making analogies is a central component in high-level cognition'.

Volume 2, no. 1 (1996)

Douglas S. Robertson and Michael C. Grant, 'Feedback and Chaos in Darwinian Evolution' (Part I), pp. 10–14.

'The conventional list of fundamental elements of Darwinian evolutionary mechanisms contains two essential components: (1) reproduction with heritable variation, and (2) natural selection. We contend that feedback is a third essential component, which will be the dominant, controlling factor in nearly all cases ... It shows, most fundamentally, that Darwinian natural selection is a mathematically unstable and chaotic process. As a result of the chaotic instabilities introduced by feedback, natural selection will commonly cause fitness to decrease, in sharp contrast to the conventional view that selection only increases fitness.'

Martin Shubik, 'Simulations, Models, and Simplicity', p. 60 ('Endpage').

'Frequently even very simple models manifest complex properties. A safe rule of thumb is: do not reject the simplest models because they are a priori too simple. Reject them when a quick investigation shows that the phenomenon of interest to you cannot appear at this level of simplicity ... I evolved a simple rule in economic modeling: "Do not believe in any economic model which cannot be played as an experimental game". General equilibrium theory has many virtues, but it 'made it more difficult to appreciate the role of process and institutions as the carriers of process. The emphasis on equilibrium killed the role of time.'

Volume 2, no. 2 (1996)

'Turbulent Landscapes', a dialogue between Jim Crutchfield and Ned Kahn, pp. 3–7.

Here is an excerpt of the dialogue between Crutchfield, a scientist, and Kahn, an artist and curator.

NK: 'What's intriguing to me is that very diverse systems display similar movements, similar kinds of flow patterns. The mathematician Ralph Abraham used a phrase – the geometry of behavior – to describe how there can be an underlying geometry of movement, of flow patterns, the same way there's an underlying geometry of status objects, such as crystals ... JC: 'There are several different kinds of commonality: Dynamical similarity where two different systems share the same shape of behavior in their state spaces. Commonality also arises from constraints in those shapes and in how behavior can change as you vary a control perimeter ...'

Douglas S. Robertson and Michael C. Grant, 'Feedback and Chaos in Darwinian Evolution' (Part II), pp. 18–30.

'We demonstrate the operation of a numerical model that incorporates three fundamental elements of neo-Darwinian theory plus one crucial extension: feedback. The resulting conceptually simple simulation produces some striking results, some of which are counter intuitive and even contradict current evolutionary thinking. In particular, we: (1) show how pure natural selection can lead to reduced fitness, (2) show that reduced fitness leads naturally to regular or periodic extinction, (3) exhibit population dynamics that range from static to both regular and chaotic fluctuations, (4) provide an explanation for Cope's rule (the observation that organisms within a lineage tend to evolve toward larger size).'

Volume 2, no. 3 (1997)

John L. Casti, 'Computing the Uncomputable', pp. 7–12.

Of all the models used for computation, the Turing machine still appears to be the best. 'It remains true to this day that no one has yet produced a knockdown argument to show that any model of computation computes a larger class of objects than the Turing-machine model.' But we may go beyond the TM if we could use a 'rapidly accelerating computer' to calculate problems that are presently incalculable.

Steen N. Durlauf, 'Limits to Science or Limits to Epistemology?', pp. 31–7.

Science in general and social science in particular have no limits. There may, however, be limits to human (and thus scientific) epistemology. 'It is more plausible to believe that our ability is limited in identifying generic limits to scientific breakthroughs than it is to believe that such generic limits have been reached ... I therefore conclude that reports of the end of science, natural or social, have been greatly exaggerated.'

Volume 2, no. 4 (1997)

Harold Morowitz, 'Teilhard, Complexity, and Complexification', pp. 7–8.

'Putting together evolution and the emergence of consciousness, Teilhard referred to the Law of Complexity and Consciousness. He never states the law, but I take it to mean that evolution proceeds to complexity, and complexity leads to the potential of consciousness becoming manifest.'

George G. Szpiro, 'The Emergence of Risk Aversion', pp. 31–9.

'In this paper I present automata, i.e. stimulus-response machines that trade. The stimulus is the price of a share on the stock market; the automaton responds by buying or selling. This happens once in each period during the automaton's lifetime. I show that genetic algorithms can "breed" automata which evolve into wealth maximizing traders. Furthermore – and quite surprisingly – we find that if uncertainty prevails, risk aversion develops among these automata.' Risk aversion 'enhances fitness, which in turn enhances the rate of survival'. In contrast to classical economic theory, which suggests that the degree of risk aversion of rational agents diminishes when the time horizon increases, 'the automata produced by the genetic algorithm adapt to the new situation and learn to behave in a rational manner' consistent with prudent risk aversion.

George Markowsky, 'An Introduction to Algorithmic Information Theory', pp. 14–22.

Algorithmic information theory, the use of algorithms to measure amounts of information, grew out of three key concepts: the algorithm ('a well-defined procedure for computing something'), entropy ('a measure of the randomness of a collection of entities such as molecules'), and information theory (a science that measures the 'information content of messages' and studies 'how to transmit messages correctly in the presence of noise'). AIT shows that 'logic does not produce more than you put in'. That is, an axiom system cannot prove consequences that are significantly more complicated than the axiom system itself. Legal systems and economic systems can be thought of as axiomatic systems. 'If one believes that there is no a priori limit on the complexity of possible behavior in a legal or economic system it would appear that no system of laws or economic doctrines are likely to capture and control the behavior of the systems.'

Volume 2, no. 5 (1997)

John L. Casti, 'Can You Trust It?', pp. 8–11.

'Evaluating a computer model requires checking it operational, empirical, and theoretical validity. The model should not contain any logical contradictions, and should produce believable results. Finally, the model should be capable of testing in the real world. The utility of computer models comes down to two principal issues: what question we want the model to answer, and how accurate that answer must be.' Different models serve different purposes. 'Moreover, once the job is completed, we have to turn to expert opinion about the system under study to ultimately decide whether the answers provided by the model are satisfactory. So the final resolution of both these issues ultimately rests on expert human judgment.'

Francis Heylighen, 'Publications on Complex, Evolving Systems: A Citation-Based Survey', pp. 31–6.

'The field of complex, evolving systems studies the processes by which these systems – consisting of many interacting components – change their structure in response to external or internal pressures … Despite being new and not yet very well established, this subject has been studied by some of the greatest scientific minds of the 20th century … Fortunately, I had an opportunity to collect relevant material when I organized a symposium on the subject of complexity…in 1995 at the Free University of Brussels as part of the large interdisciplinary congress entitled "Einstein meets Magritte."' Heylighen's research produced 1,500 citations, which he then narrowed down according to a number of criteria, including citation-based rankings. That is, the more often a work was cited in other works, the more likely it was to be included in Heylighen's final bibliography, which had 66 citations.

Volume 2, no. 6 (1997)

Michael Shermer, 'The Crooked Timber of History', pp. 23–9.

This article sets forth a theory of history called *contingent necessity*. 'History is contingently cyclical … The reason is that while there are an infinite number of combinations of historical contingencies (undesigned conjuncture of events), there are a limited number of historical necessities (economic forces, social trends, population changes, laws of nature) to channel those contingencies into a handful of necessities that resemble one another and thus repeat themselves in the main. Every historical event is unique, but not randomly so.' Shermer's article presents six corollaries that encompass various aspects of the model of contingent-necessity. The sixth and most important corollary states that 'Between origin and bifurcation, sequences self-organize through the interaction of contingencies and necessities in a feedback loop driven by the rate of informative exchange.'

Christa Sommerer and Laurent Mignonneau, 'Interacting with Artificial Life: A-Value', pp. 13–21.

'When we look at how nature has been perceived throughout the centuries, we observe that the 18th century was marked by Newton's mechanistic conception of the world.' In the 19th century, the view of nature was largely based on materialism and brought about the technical revolution. A more diverse and abstract concept of nature was reached in the 20th century, described by Warner Heisenberg: 'The natural sciences are not any more spectators of nature, but recognize themselves as part of the interplay between mankind and nature. Synthesis, interdisciplinarity, and interacting will be the key words in the 21st century, and a closer connection between the sciences, humanities, and arts [is] making a revival.'

Volume 3, no. 1 (1997)

Murray Gell-Mann, 'Fundamental Sources of Unpredictability', pp. 9–13.

Two basic laws govern the behaviour of all matter: the initial condition of the universe and the dynamical theory of all matter (superstring theory). But knowing these laws does not eliminate uncertainty. 'Suppose we know the two basic laws that govern the behaviour of all matter. What then? Can we predict, in principle, the history of the universe? Of course not. Because the laws of physics are quantum-mechanical, prediction is limited to probabilities for alternative histories of the universe. The limitations go far beyond the famous, but rather trivial, uncertainty principle of Heisenberg.' Yes, we can make certain assumptions: quantum mechanics is correct, the elementary particles and their interactions obey a definite dynamical law, and the density matrix of the universe near the beginning of its expansion is knowable. These assumptions, however, do not eliminate unpredictability. Drawing on the decoherent histories approach to quantum mechanics (developed by Gell-Mann with James B. Hartle), one can conclude that the fundamental sources of unpredictability are coarse graining (relating to the dynamics of summarisation), branching (relating to the dynamics of accident and probability), human ignorance (limitations on an information gathering and utilisation system), and computational limits (approximations and limitations on accuracy imposed by computational tools).

Philip W. Anderson, 'Is Measurement Itself an Emergent Property?', pp. 14–16.

There are four fundamental sources of unpredictability in physics: the measurement process, emergence of measurable quantities (space, time, field strength, etc.), sensitivity to boundary conditions of variables, and emergence of categories and concepts. As to the first point, 'decoherence' (a concept developed by James Hartle and Murray Gell-Mann, as mentioned above) implies unpredictability: measurement itself is an emergent process. Second, the quantities we measure are defined not by the system we measure (for example the quantum system) but by the apparatus with which we do the measurement: orientation, position, velocity. 'It was not by accident that Einstein's writings were full of clocks and meter sticks.' As for the third point – sensitivity to boundary condition – Anderson refers us to the works of David Ruelle (see below). In concluding, Anderson stresses the important of the fourth source of unpredictability – categories and concepts. 'The structure of Nature is so completely hierarchical, built up from emergence upon emergence upon emergence, that the very concepts and categories on which the next stage can take place are themselves arbitrary.' Thus predictability is an 'illusion', and futurology a 'mug's game'.

Martin J. Rees, 'Anthropic Reasoning', pp. 17–21.

Some surprising aspects of our universe appear to be prerequisites for our existence. Furthermore, the universe seems to harbour an 'interesting degree of complexity'. This complexity 'might lead to consciousness', and may suggest 'requirements for the physical laws and parameters governing our universe'. One can 'use anthropic arguments to actually suggest, far in advance of our having such a theory, what that theory's nature might be'. That is, 'anthropic reasoning should not be completely dismissed, and may actually offer clues to which of the fundamental constants are actually predictable by a fundamental theory, and which are merely secondary accidents that are not even in principle predictable by theoretical physicists'.

James B. Hartle, 'Sources of Predictability', pp. 22–5.

'It is a logical possibility that every feature of our experience – the shape of each galaxy, the number of planets circumnavigating each star, the character of each biological specie, the course of human history, and the result of every experiment – is the output of some short computer program with no input. However, there is no evidence that our universe is so regular … To ask about the fundamental sources of predictability is to ask for the regularities implied by the basic laws that apply universally to all physical systems – without exception, qualification, or approximation.' Two laws are basic to quantum cosmology: the basic theory of dynamics (string theory), and the theory of the initial condition of the universe (the 'no boundary' wave function). 'Predictable regularities in this specific quantum universe arise from particular features of its fundamental laws of dynamics and the initial condition.' Our ability to observe these features is consistent with the nature of the features themselves. There is a reason for this. 'Individually and collectively, we are complex adaptive systems within the universe that evolved to exploit the emergent regularities that the universe presents.' Hence 'our adaptation to the regularities of our specific universe is another source of predictability in physics'.

David Ruelle, 'Chaos, Predictability, and Idealization in Physics', pp. 26–8.

We speak of the world in terms of theories, which 'differ not only in being more or less accurate, but also in proposing concepts that are more or less useful'. Theories are fundamental to prediction: 'speaking of the predictability of the behavior of a system is possible only after choosing a description of the system'. There are limits to predictability. 'For systems where the dynamics is not well understood one may hope for (possibly great) improvements in predictability, but when the dynamics is well understood and chaotic, there is no such hope for improvement: we face a real wall of predictability … My view is that science has great power in making the world understandable, but has its limitations, and that the impossibility to predict the long-term future of chaotic systems is one of those limitations.'

BOOKS

Anderson, Philip W., Arrow, Kenneth J., and Pines, David, eds. *The Economy as an Evolving Complex System*. Reading, MA: Addison-Wesley Publishing Company, 1996.

Arthur, Brian. *Increasing Returns and Path Dependence in the Economy*. Ann Arbor, MI: The University of Michigan Press, 1997.

Brockman, John. *The Third Culture: Beyond the Scientific Revolution*. New York: Simon & Schuster, 1995.

Gleick, James. *Chaos: Making a New Science*. New York: Penguin Books, 1988.

Holland, John H. *Hidden Order: How Adaptation Builds Complexity*. Reading, MA: Addison-Wesley Publishing Company, 1995.

Stacey, Ralph D. *Complexity and Creativity in Organizations*. San Francisco: Berrett Koehler Publishers, 1996.

Waldrop, M. Mitchell. *Complexity: The Emerging Science at the Edge of Order and Chaos*. New York: Touchstone/Simon and Schuster, 1993.

Who's Who in Complexity:
Pioneers in Complexity

Among the scores of prominent adherents to the complexity movement, these pioneers deserve special recognition. Not surprisingly, they all figure prominently in M. Mitchell Waldrop's story of *Complexity: The Emerging Science at the Edge of Order and Chaos*, which tells the story of the Santa Fe Institute (SFI) – the undisputed nucleus of the complexity movement in science.

Philip Anderson. A Princeton physicist specializing in condensed matter, Anderson studies emergent properties and behaviors in matter. He co-chaired the first economics workshop at the SFI.

Kenneth J. Arrow. This economist from Stanford University co-chaired the first economics workshop at the SFI and served as an editor of its oft-cited proceedings.

Brian Arthur. An Irish-born economist who taught at Stanford University before joining the SFI as an early director. His most well-known works concern the implications of positive feedbacks in the economy.

Robert Axelrod. A political scientist from the University of Michigan, author of *The Evolution of Cooperation*, he joined with Anotol Rapoport of the University of Toronto and others to develop the TIT FOR TAT model, important for understanding complex adaptive systems.

Per Bak. This Danish-born physicist studies 'self-organized criticality', asking why and how organisms have become more complex since life began.

Arthur Burks. A combination philosopher-programmer at Michigan University, he found new ways to use the computer to solve problems. An intergenerational figure, Burks was a mentor to John Holland at the University of Michigan and a disciple of the famous mathematician John Von Neumann.

George A. Cowan. Particle physicist, former head of research at Los Alamos, and a member of White House Science Council, Cowan saw a connection between physics and microbiology in the form of computer simulation, a type of adaptive computation. He cofounded the SFI, serving as its first president.

Doyne Farmer. Physicist. Worked with Arthur and Langton. Developed node-and-connection structure in computer simulations and the new 'second law' of cooperation/competition, and progress/feedback loops. (Power is in the connections, not the nodes.)

Murray Gell-Mann. A particle physicist, Gell-Mann pioneered in the grand unified theory of interparticle forces (known as quarks). He cofounded the SFI, where he served as founding chairman. Today he chairs SFI's board of directors.

John Holland. A computer programmer (with expertise in economics and genetics) from University of Michigan, he originated the classifier system in 1977, and wrote the first genetic algorithm.

Stuart Kauffman. This cellular/molecular biologist, affiliated with SFI from the earliest days, was one of the first to apply computer programming to biology. He used simplified polymer chemistry to simulate 'genetic networks' of reactions through math.

Christopher Langton. A self-described 'mechanic', Langton was a primary inventor-discoverer of artificial life. Building on the work of English mathematician John Conway, he developed the Game of Life as a computer model.

David Pines. This theoretical physicist from the University of Illinois was founding director for that school's Center for Advanced Study, and cofounded the first economics workshops at SFI.

Warren McCulloch. A neurophysiologist from the Massachusetts Institute of Technology, McCollough pioneered the neural network.

Stanislas Ulam. This Polish mathematician, who is affiliated with the Los Alamos laboratory in New Mexico, suggested the formula that became known as the cellular automaton. The SFI's publication on *The Economy as an Evolving Complex System* is dedicated to him.

Stephen Wolfram. An English physicist affiliated with the Institute for Advanced Study at Princeton, Wolfram pioneered in cellular automata.

Endnotes

CHAPTER 1
THE EMPEROR'S NIGHTINGALE: HARBINGER OF CORPORATE RESTORATION

1   Hans Christian Andersen, *The Nightingale*, illustrated by Beni Montresor, adapted by Alan Benjamin (New York: Crown Publishers, 1985).

CHAPTER 2
THE DISCONSOLATE DAWN OF THE MODERN CORPORATION

1   Hans Christian Andersen, *The Nightingale*, translated by Erik Haugaard in *Hans Christian Andersen: His Classic Fairy Tales* (New York: Doubleday, 1978), p. 19.

2   Adam Smith, *An Inquiry into The Nature and Causes of the Wealth of Nations*, original text as published 9 March 1776. Edited by Edwin Cannon (New York: The Modern Library/Random House, 1994), Book V, Chapter 1, Part 3, Article 1, pp. 791–2 and 799. (For Smith's verbatim language in comparing these two forms of business to the joint stock company, see Appendix to Chapter 2.)

3   The number 55 came from 'an eminent French author, of great knowledge in matters of political economy, the Abbe Morellet', said Smith, who confirms the number. *Ibid.*, p. 815.

4   *Ibid.*, p. 791.

5   *Ibid.*, p. 814. The word 'terminate' replaces the word 'determine', which meant 'terminate' in Smith's day. Emphasis added.

6   *Ibid.*, p. 800. Emphasis added.

7   *Ibid.*, p. 805.

8   *Ibid.*, p. 811. Emphasis added.

9   *Ibid.,* Emphasis added.

10   *Ibid.*, p. 812. Emphasis added.

11   *Liggett v. Lee*, 288 U.S. 517 (1932). Emphasis added. For a discussion of *mortmain*, see p. 30 in this book.

12   *Liggett*, 487 ff. Emphasis added.

13   *Ibid.*

14   Randall P. White, Philip Hodgson and Stuart Crainer, *The Future of Leadership* (London: Pitman Publishing, 1996), p. 63.

15   John Archibald Wheeler, *At Home in the Universe* (Woodbury, NY: The American Institute of Physics, 1994), p.188.

CHAPTER 3
FOUR CORPORATE DANGERS

1   Hans Christian Andersen, 'The Nightingale', translated by Pat Shaw Iversen, a Penguin Books translation obtained from *Machine* magazine, an Internet publication at url: http://www.word.com:80/textword/machine/andersen.html.

2   Elizabeth MacDonald, 'Auditing Standards Board is Named Amid Concerns by Business Executives', *The Wall Street Journal*, 18 June 1997, p. A-6.

3   Charles Handy, *The Age of Unreason* (London: London Books: Random House, 1989). The quote is from the cover of the 1990 Arrow paperback edition.

4   George Soros, 'The Capitalist Threat', *The Atlantic Monthly*, February 1997, p. 55.

5   'Alfred Marshal explained the free enterprise system more or less this way: under a free enterprise system, anyone has a right to enrich himself, provided he enriches others more.' Charles Berg, in correspondence dated 4 September 1997. Alfred Marshall was a Yale economist who wrote at the turn of the century.

6   Thanks to Charles Berg for contributing to this discussion (in corre-
     spondence dated 4 September 1997).
7   Douglas S. Robertson and Michael C. Grant, 'Feedback and Chaos in
     Darwinian Evolution' (Part II), *Complexity*, Vol. 2, No. 2, pp. 18-30.
     Complexity is published by John Wiley & Sons in affiliation with the
     Santa Fe Institute.
8   'The ideal capitalist firm is relentlessly engaged in profit maximization.'
     Oliver E. Williamson, *The Mechanisms of Governance* (Oxford Univer-
     sity Press, 1996), p. 167.
9   If there is one subject on which there is world-wide agreement, it is
     respect for the quality of financial disclosure in the United States.
10   Steven M.H. Wallman, 'Updating Disclosure for a New Century',
     New York Times, 24 September 1995, p. F14.
11   Jack Ciesielski, 'A Call to Arms – Make Restructuring a Routine Cost
     of Doing Business', *CFO*, November 1996, p. 10.
12   Thomas A. Stewart, 'Trying to Grasp the Intangible', *Fortune*, 2 Octo-
     ber 1995, p. 157. In 1997, hard assets made up only about one-quarter
     of a company's value.
13   Robert A.G. Monks and Neil Minow, *Power and Accountability* (New
     York: HarperCollins, 1992), p. 24.
14   W. Brian Arthur, *Increasing Returns and Path Dependence in the Economy*,
     with a foreword by Kenneth J. Arrow (Ann Arbor, MI: University of
     Michigan Press, 1997).
15   *Concise Science Dictionary* (Oxford: Oxford Paperback Reference, 1996).
16   See, for example, Douglas S. Robertson and Michael C. Grant, 'Feed-
     back and Chaos in Darwinian Evolution' (Part I), *Complexity*, Vol. 2,
     No. 1, p. 11.
17   Ruth Marcus and Charles R. Babcock, 'The System Cracks Under the
     Weight of Cash: Candidates, Parties, and Outside Interests Dropped a
     Record $2.7 Billion', *The Washington Post*, 9 February 1997, pp. A-1 ff.
18   Leslie Wayne, 'Two Parties Raised Total of $15 Million in "Soft
     Money"', *The New York Times*, 13 June 1997 (via Internet).
19   Peter H. Stone, 'Labyrinth of Loopholes', *National Journal*, 25 No-
     vember 1995, pp. 2912, 2914.
20   'Lobbyists Spent $400 Million to Influence Government', *The Wall
     Street Journal*, 23 September 1996 (interactive edition).
21   Dick Armey, Press Release, US House of Representatives, 19 June
     1996.

22   Kevin Sack, 'Gambling Industry Spends Lavishly to Make Itself Heard', *New York Times*, 18 December 1995, p. B12.

23   'New Study Shows Enormous Influence of Big Tobacco and Effect of McCain–Feingold Legislation', Press Release from Public Citizen dated 9 May 1997.

24   Doug Bandow, 'Corporate Welfare Remains Unchecked', *Business and Society Review*, Number 97, pp. 10, 11.

25   Robert J. Shapiro, *Cut-and-Invest: A Budget Strategy for the New Economy*, Progressive Policy Institute Policy Report No. 23, March 1995, p. 17.

26   Linda Grant and Robert F. Black, 'Getting Business off the Dole', *U.S. News & World Report*, 10 April 1995, p. 38.

27   Soros, *op. cit.* (note 4), p. 52.

28   Derek Bok, *The Cost of Talent: How Executives and Professionals Are Paid and How It Affects America* (New York: The Free Press, 1996), p. 89.

29   William W. Horne, 'GE Crushes the Trustbusters', *The American Lawyer*, January 1995, p. 57.

30   *Ibid.*

31   On 20 June 1997, America OnLine's Reuters Hourly News Summary reported the following: 'Historic Tobacco Deal is Reached: Tobacco companies agreed today to pay $368.5 billion, admit that tobacco is addictive and accept extensive federal regulation over their products and their advertising as part of a landmark agreement. In return, the companies, which have never before been forced to pay for tobacco-related illnesses, would be given immunity from any further punitive liability for deception, fraud or conspiracy that might have occurred in the past. The agreement is by far the largest ever involving an industry and concludes two months of negotiations that grew from an innovative lawsuit filed by Mississippi's attorney general. The deal was hailed by President Clinton, who said he would appoint a task force to review its terms.'

32   Jeffrey Johnson, 'A Language of Structure in the Science of Complexity', *Complexity*, Vol. 1, No. 3, p. 22.

33   Melissa S. Baucus and David A. Baucus, 'Paying the Piper: An Empirical Examination of Longer-Term Financial Consequences of Illegal Corporate Behavior', *Academy of Management Journal*, February 1997, p. 149.

34   'A Washington, D.C.-based public interest group, The Project on Government Oversight, studied the histories of these companies and found

that they had been engaged in adjudicated fraudulent activities, some of them criminal, many of them having been convicted three or more times. The study found that General Electric engaged in fraudulent activities 16 times since 1990.' Russell Mokhiber, 'Soft on Crime', Internet. Note also 'General Electric Continues Its Reign as the Top U.S. Company in Market Value', *Business Week,* 15 January 1996, p. 6.

CHAPTER 4
THE LIMITS OF CONVENTIONAL CORPORATE
WISDOM – AND HOW TO SURPASS THEM

1   Hans Christian Andersen, 'The Nightingale', translated by Pat Shaw Iversen, cited in Chapter 3, note 1.
2   Ralph Nader and Mark Green, Op-Ed, *New York Times*, 28 December 1979.
3   James Willard Hurst, *The Legitimacy of the Business Corporation in the Law of the United States 1780–1970* (Charlottesville, VA: The University of Virginia, 1970), pp. 107–8.
4   Sir Adrian Cadbury in correspondence dated 3 September 1997.
5   Morton Mintz and Jerry S. Cohen, *Power, Inc.* (New York: Viking, 1976), p. 348.
6   Frank Rich, 'Fear and Favor', *The New York Times*, 15 November 1995.
7   Ira M. Millstein and Salem M. Karsh, *The Limits of Corporate Power* (New York: Macmillan, 1981).
8   *Ibid.*, p. xviii.
9   Carl Kaysen, ed., *The American Corporation Today: Examining the Questions of Power and Efficiency at the Century's End* (Oxford: Oxford University Press, 1996).
10 *Ibid.*, pp. 19, 20.
11 Kim McQuaid, *Big Business and Presidential Power: From FDR to Reagan,* (New York: William Morrow, 1982), p. 308.
12 Tim Smart, 'Knights of the Roundtable: Tracking Big Business' Agenda in Washington', *Business Week*, 21 October 1988, p. 39.
13 Charles Wilson, former chairman of General Motors, told the Senate Armed Forces Committee in 1952, 'What is good for the country is good for General Motors, and what is good for General Motors is good for the country'.

14   Letter from John S. Reed on the letterhead of The Business
      Roundtable, dated 23 June 1992. Emphasis added twice to the word
      'education'.

15   Alison Leigh Cowan, 'Executives are Fuming over Data on Their Pay',
      The New York Times, 25 August 1993, p. D1.

16   *Ibid.*

17   Walter P. Schuetze, *A Mountain or a Molehill*, Twenty-First Annual
      National Conference of the AICPA, 11 January 1994, p. 8.

18   'In 1984 and 1985, in response to the Invitation to Comment that
      began the FASB's reconsideration of the existing accounting rules for
      stock options granted to employees, all of the then Big Eight account-
      ing firms except one wrote to the FASB supporting (a) reconsideration
      of the accounting rules and (b) a charge to compensation cost/expense
      for all options granted to employees. But in February 1993, even be-
      fore the FASB issued its exposure draft on the subject on June 30,
      1993, all of the Big Six accounting firms joined forces with certain
      members of industry and a group of users to recommend to the FASB
      that there be no formal recognition for the cost of stock options. (I
      understand that the AICPA's Accounting Standards Executive Com-
      mittee recently changed its mind and now will recommend to the
      FASB that there be no recognition for the cost of fixed stock options.)
      The Big Six accounting firms did not, in February 1993, offer an ex-
      planation for their change of mind. I would be the first to say that
      anyone could change his or her mind. I have changed my mind on
      several accounting issues over the years. But, I think that the public
      deserves an acknowledgment of that change of mind by the firms and
      the reason why. Such a change in position, without a corresponding
      change in the underlying concepts and issues that led the firms and the
      AICPA initially to support the FASB's project, has left some members
      of the public with the impression that the switch was in response to
      the fear of losing clients or other forms of retaliation. I do not know if
      this is true.' *Ibid.*

19   'Recognizing that the public might see free trade as a special-interest
      issue if touted by an exclusive club of the country's 200 largest
      transnationals, the Roundtable created a front organization,
      USA★NAFTA, that enrolls some 2,300 U.S. corporations and asso-
      ciations as members. Although USA★NAFTA claimed to represent a

broader constituency, every one of its state captains was a corporate member of the Business Roundtable.' David C. Korten, *When Corporations Rule the World* (New York: Kumarian Press and Berrett-Koehler Publishers, 1995).

20 Warren Buffet, in correspondence dated 18 November 1993. At least one company has begun to make voluntary, full disclosure of the impact of options: Microsoft has volunteered alternative income statements showing the impact of charging the current value of options on current quarterly earnings down from 50 cents to a loss of 5 cents, and for the year to date down from $2.65 to $2.05. See Floyd Norris, 'Microsoft: A Pioneer in Quality Accounting', *The New York Times*, 16 November 1997, p. C1.

21 *Business Week*, 24 April 1995, p. 93.

22 The struggle continues to this day with SEC Chairman Arthur Levitt trying to preserve a measure of independence for FASB over the continuing objections of big business.

23 Roger Lowenstein, 'Coming Clean on Company Stock Options', *The Wall Street Journal*, 26 June 1997, p. C1.

24 Because of the difficulty of proving causality, the Pension and Welfare Benefits Administration of the Department of Labor has never brought an enforcement action against a fiduciary on account of conflict. Thus, the situation has been permitted to continue. Everyone is making too much money to contemplate change – even if it is legally and logically required. Over a ten-year period my partners and I have been trying without success to get the SEC to issue guidance on how pension fund trustees should act in the situations of conflict of interest that are inevitable in our complex economy. (I will return to this important subject in Chapter 9.)

25 Charles Gasparino, 'SEC Studying Public-Retirement Funds: "Pay-to-Play" Issue Is Under Scrutiny', *The Wall Street Journal*, 27 June 1997, p. C1.

26 Carolyn Kay Brancato, *Institutional Investment Report,* Vol. 1, No. 1 (New York: The Conference Board, January 1997).

27 For example, Institutional Shareholder Services, a proxy advisory firm based in Bethesda, Maryland, reported in 1993 that UK institutional shareholders owned 67 percent of the equity of UK public companies.

CHAPTER 5
THE CORPORATION AND THE ECONOMY AS
COMPLEX ADAPTIVE SYSTEMS

1   Hans Christian Andersen, 'The Nightingale', retold by Sheila Black, in *A Treasury of Children's Literature* (Boston: Ariel Books, 1992).

2   'Law and economics are activities which have been carried on sufficiently long and thoroughly, and to a sufficiently high level of self-consciousness, as to have a deep underlying logic which permeates the threads of each and draws them together. By contrast, complexity has not achieved the status of a mode in this sense. It has not yet moved from the ambitious to the conditional phase of its existence. It is not, in short, settled.' Jesse Norman, in correspondence dated 31 August 1997.

3   John Holland, *Hidden Order: How Adaptation Builds Complexity* (Reading, MA: Addison-Wesley Publishing Co., 1995), p. 4.

4   Murray Gell-Mann, 'What is Complexity?' *Complexity*, Vol. 1, No. 1, p. 18.

5   Santa Fe Institute cofounder Murray Gell-Mann extols the 'unified field theory of the elementary particles and their interaction' as the 'heart of the onion' in scientific inquiry ('Nature Conformable to Herself', *Complexity*, Vol. 1, No. 4), but he does not elaborate on it. Rather, he seeks to encourage research beyond this basic level. 'At each new level new laws emerge that should be studied for themselves; new phenomena appear that should be appreciated and valued at their own level' (p. 12).

6   The term 'model' is used in two different ways by complexologists. Some use it to mean a mathematical formula. Others use it to mean a computer program that is similar to (yet different from) a simulation. For the first definition, see Lee A. Segel, 'Grappling with Complexity', *Complexity*, Vol. 1, No. 2, p. 18. For the second, see David Lane, 'Models and Aphorisms', in the same issue, p. 9.

7   Lane, *op. cit.*, pp. 9–13.

8   This is not the same thing as the famous 'winner's curse', but it is compatible with it. The 'winner's curse' hypothesis, first advanced by E. Capen, R. Clapp, and W. Campbell in 'Competitive Bidding in High Risk Situations', *Journal of Petroleum Technology*, June 1971, pp. 641–53, notes that the highest bid is most likely to win in an auction, but if the bidder overpays, it is cursed by its success.

9 Robertson and Grant, *op. cit.* (Chapter 3, note 16), p. 11.

10 Holland's four properties are aggregation, nonlinearity, flows, and diversity. His three mechanisms are tagging, internal models, and building blocks. We will return to this list in Chapter 6 when discussing models of complex systems. See Holland, *op. cit.* (note 3), pp. 10–37.

11 In the vivid opening of Mitchell Waldrop's *Complexity: The Emerging Science at the Edge of Order and Chaos* (New York: Touchstone/Simon and Schuster, 1993), pp. 11–12, we read of complexity, spontaneity, self-organisation, unconsciousness, accommodation, adaptation, intricacy, coherence, cohesion, disorderliness, dynamism, unpredictability, transcendence, transformation, and 'the ability to bring order and chaos into a special kind of balance'.

12 Segel, *op. cit.* (note 6).

13 It also has the secondary agent of a board of directors, representing owners and/or other primary agents.

14 Arthur, *op. cit.* (Chapter 3, note 14), p. 5.

15 Gell-Mann, *op. cit.* (note 4), p. 16.

16 Karl Sigmund, 'What is Life without Schroedinger's Cat' (book review), *Complexity*, Vol. 2, No. 2, pp. 43–4.

17 Arthur, *op. cit.* (Chapter 3, note 14), pp. ix–x.

18 Harold Gutowitz, 'Cellular Automata and the Sciences of Complexity' (Part I), *Complexity*, Vol. 1, No. 5, pp. 16–22.

19 Martin Shubik, 'Simulations, Models, and Simplicity', *Complexity,* Vol. 2, No. 1, p. 60.

20 Holland, *op. cit.* (note 5), p. 13. Emphasis added.

21 Cited in Alexandra Reed Lajoux, *The Art of M&A Integration: A Guide to Merging Resources, Processes, and Responsibilities* (New York: McGraw-Hill, 1998), p. 20. For description of this and 17 other post-merger studies indicating the importance of accommodation, see Lajoux, pp. 13–21.

22 Waldrop, *op. cit.* (note 11), p. 11.

23 Soros, *op. cit.* (Chapter 3, note 4), p. 50.

24 *Ibid.*

25 'The "invisible hand" was in effect a negative feedback mechanism inducing equilibrium – a kind of divine (or at least Newtonian) necessity, like a single answer to a linear equation. This belief has facilitated the dangers of the corporate form.' Shannon Clyne, in correspondence dated 2 September 1997.

26   Arthur Kleiner, in correspondence dated 22 August 1997. Many thanks to Art Kleiner for his astute observations on General Electric.

CHAPTER 6
MODELLING CORPORATE ACCOUNTABILITY

1   Hans Christian Andersen, 'The Nightingale', translated by Pat Shaw Iversen, cited in Chapter 3, note 1.
2   SWARM is a specialised modelling environment created by programmers at the SFI to provide a broad-based tool for exploring complexity theory.
3   Taken from a speech by Robert A.G. Monks, 'The American Corporation at the End of the Twenty First Century', at Cambridge University, July 1996. 'Institutional investors need a government drawn "bright line" delineating the obligations of institutions to act as owner and the limits of permissible conflict of interest in acting as a fiduciary.'
4   Larry J. Stockmeyer and Ashok K. Chandra, 'Intrinsically Difficult Problems', *Scientific American*, May 1979, pp. 140 ff.
5   Holland, *op. cit.* (Chapter 5, note 5), p. 3.
6   *Ibid.*, p. 4.
7   The McKinsey Institute completed in the summer of 1996 a major study of the relative competitiveness of industry in the United States, Germany, and Japan. One of the principal factors explaining superior rates of return in the United States has been the existence of owner activism. The most well-known study linking shareholder activism to improvements in share price was Wilshire Associates, *Rewards from Corporate Governance*, January 1992. This study, which was sponsored by the California Public Employees Retirement System, showed that companies targeted by CalPERS had returns superior to comparable companies over the same period. More generally Lilli Gordon and John Pound showed that companies that implemented governance reforms championed by shareholder activists (whether in response to activism or not) yield better returns to shareholders than companies that do not. *Governance Matters: An Empirical Study of the Relationship Between Corporate Governance and Corporate Governance,* June 1991.
8   Brancato, *op. cit.* (Chapter 4, note 26). See also http://www.mceo.org/library/control_eq.html.

CHAPTER 7
INTERMEZZO: THE 'FOUR PHASES' OF
CORPORATE LIFE

1   Hans Christian Andersen, 'The Nightingale', translated by Mrs. E.V.
     Lucas and Mrs. H. B. Pauli, in *Andersen's Fairy Tales* (New York:
     Grosset & Dunlap, 1955).

2   R.H. Dicke, 'Dirac's Cosmology and Mach's principle', *Nature* 192,
     pp. 440–41 (1961), and B. Carter, 'Large Number Coincidences and
     the Anthropic Principle in Cosmology', in M.S. Longair, ed., *Con-
     frontation of Cosmological Theories with Observational Data* (Dordrecht:
     Reidel, 1974), pp. 291-298, cited in Wheeler, *op. cit.* (Chapter 2, note
     15), p. 316.

3   Searching   the   World   Wide   Web   with   the   terms
     'artificial+life+definition' recently, the 'Net Find' program of America
     On Line found 192,880 documents! One site, http://
     www.umcs.maine.edu/~obelix/ar/ar.html, notes that 'emergent struc-
     tures … usually get branded as "a-life forms", and the systems producing
     these forms as "a-life systems". In an attempt to lessen the confusion,
     the term "artificial reality" (AR) could be used to describe a system at
     its most fundamental level … while "A-Life" could be used to de-
     scribe the instances of "life" that crawl out of AR systems.' In this
     book, using 'A-life' to describe corporations, I mean 'artificial reality'
     in this sense. Because this term is extremely new, however, I choose
     conventional usage and will call the corporation an 'artificial life sys-
     tem'.

4   Segel, *op. cit.* (Chapter 5, note6), pp. 18–25.

5   From http://www.brunel.ac.uk:8080/depts/AI/alife/a-life.htm,
     searched on AOL NetFind 23/4/97.

6   A.A. Tsonis, 'Dynamical Systems as Models for Physical Processes',
     Complexity, Vol. 1, No. 5, p. 33. In more concrete terms (quoting
     Waldrop, *op. cit.* [Chapter 5, note 11], p. 87), these are essentially 'pro-
     grams for generating patterns on a computer screen according to rules
     generated by the programmer'. This definition shows a great deal of
     humility but underplays the meaningfulness of this type of model. It is
     more than a computer game; it is a representation of reality. A pithier
     definition of cellular automata comes from George G. Szpiro in 'The
     Emergence of Risk Aversion', *Complexity*, Vol. 2, No. 4, pp. 31–9.
     He calls automata 'stimulus–response machines that trade' (p. 31).

7   For a description of the Game of Life, see Waldrop, *op. cit.* (Chapter 5, note 11), p. 201.

8   Carol J. Loomis, 'Dinosaurs?' *Fortune*, 3 May 1993, p. 36.

9   Arie de Geus, 'The Living Company', *Harvard Business Review*, March–April 1997, p. 51, based on de Geus' book, *The Living Company* (Boston: Harvard Business School Press, 1997).

10 *Ibid.*, pp. 53–4.

11 James C. Collins and Jerry I. Porras, *Built to Last: The Successful Habits of Visionary Companies* (New York: HarperBusiness, 1997), pp. xv–xvi.

12 *Ibid.*, p. 227.

13 *Ibid.*, p. 235.

14 Shubik, *op. cit.* (Chapter 5, note 19), p. 60.

15 E. Atlee Jackson, 'No Provable Limits to Scientific Knowledge', *Complexity*, Vol. 1, No. 2, pp. 14–17.

16 Segel, *op. cit.* (Chapter 5, note 6).

17 Ralph D. Stacey, *COmplexity and Creativity in Organizations* (San Francisco, CA: Berret Koehler Publishers, 1996), p. 106.

18 William Greider, *one World, Ready or Not: The Manic Logic of Global Capitalism* (New York: Simon and Schuster, 1997).

19 Ricard V. Sole, Susanna C. Manrubia, Bartolo Luque, Jordi Delgado, and Jordi Bascompte, 'Phase Transitions and Complex Systems', *Complexity*, Vol. 1., No. 4, pp. 13–26.

CHAPTER 8
STONE & WEBSTER: A JOURNEY TO THE EDGE OF CHAOS

1   Hans Christian Andersen, 'The Nightingale', translated by Eva Le Gallienne, illustrated by Nancy Eckholm Burker (New York: Harper & Row, 1965).

2   For a discussion of directors' ages, see Appendix to Chapter 8: Joann S. Lublin, 'Can an Old Guard of Directors Effectively Govern a 21st-Century Corporation?', which mentions Stone & Webster.

3   That is, 41,000 shares at $27 in July 1993 and 50,400 shares at $27½ in August 1993.

CHAPTER 9
THE NEW OWNERS

1   Hans Christian Andersen, 'The Nightingale', retold by Sheila Black, cited in Chapter 5, note 1.

2   This phrase was coined by Dwight D. Eisenhower in his farewell radio and television address to the American people, 17 January 1961.

3   Brancato, *op. cit.* (Chapter 4, note 26).

4   A.A. Sommer, Jr, 'Corporate Governance in the 1990s: Management vs. Institutions', *University of Cincinnati Law Review*, Vol. 59, No. 2, 1990.

5   On the nomination of then Senate Majority Leader Robert Dole, I was appointed to serve President Ronald Reagan as one of the original trustees of FERSA in 1986.

6   'CalPERS's board members typically drive over to the fund's Ikea-like offices – 8 of the 13 are from the Sacramento area – for a week of meetings every month for little or no pay. Even Crist [the president since 1992] gets only his professor's salary, with CalPERS reimbursing Cal State for his time.' Barry Rehfeld, 'Low-cal CalPERS', *Institutional Investor*, March 1997, p. 44.

7   *Ibid.*, p. 49.

8   Sheryl Pressler, chief investment officer of CalPERS, has reported a cost of over half a billion dollars from the fund's South African investments ($529,177,918, to be exact). Many thanks to Jim McRitchie, publisher of the Web site corpgov.net, for providing much of the CalPERS information here.

9   Brancato, *op. cit.* (Chapter 4, note 26).

10 For example, Alliance Capital is owned by Donaldson, Lufkin & Jenrette, which in turn is owned by Equitable, which in turn is owned by AXA.

11 Mellon Bank Corporation, 1996 Annual Report, pp. 26–7.

12 This makes sense. Whenever statisticians and/or computers compare the total rates of return from various classes of investment, stocks always win.

13 Brancato, *op. cit.* (Chapter 4, note 26).

14 'On the plus side, the insidious problem of institutional conflicts of interest is to a certain extent diminished by the increasingly international spread of pension fund investments ... It will probably be some

time before a U.S. pension fund employs a 'foreign' fund manager, although in the end, the management of funds will become as international as the spread of institutional investment.' Sir Adrian Cadbury, in correspondence dated 3 September 1997.

15   Robert C. Pozen, 'Institutional Investors: the Reluctant Activists', *Harvard Business Review,* January-February 1994, pp. 140–49. Pozen estimates that if mutual fund managers became more actively involved with their portfolio companies, this would necessitate a 1% or 2% base fee plus 10% or 20% of all profits – clearly an alternative that would be unacceptable to Fidelity's clients. I have to say that with all due respect to Robert Pozen and his free rider insights, there is no justification for higher fees. The mutual fund industry is already hugely profitable. Through a dozen visits over the past several years, I have been actively involved in getting the SEC to require more activism of investment company trustees and the managers to whom they entrust mutual fund assets.

16   See, for example, Chapter 6, note 7, for studies by McKinsey, Wilshire, and Gordon.

17   The quote in full is as follows: 'It is only under the shelter of the civil magistrate that the owner of that valuable property, which is acquired under the labour of many years, or perhaps of many successive generations, can sleep a single night in security.' Adam Smith, *An Inquiry into the Nature and Causes of the Wealth of Nations, op. cit.* (Chapter 2, note 2), pp. 766–7.

18   Some historical background may be of interest here. The Senate Banking Committee was concerned over the voting of the shares in the FERSA trust. After several proposals for voting by a combination of federal agents, the statute was passed with an absolute prohibition against any instrumentality or individual associated with the federal government being involved in the vote. The scriveners limited the discretion of pension beneficiaries to choosing an 'index' for equity investment – rather than making industry or company choices – and so no government 'energy' made buy/sell or hold decisions with respect to the securities of a particular company, and voting power ultimately was conferred on Wells Fargo bank, the winning bidder for the trusteeship of the federal plan.

19   McKinsey Institute, *Capital Productivity* (July 1996), Chapter 6, pp. 5–6.

20   Again, see studies by McKinsey, Wilshire, and Gordon, cited in Chapter 6, note 7.

21 Michael Useem, *Investor Capitalism: How Money Managers are Changing the Face of Corporate America* (New York: Basic Books, 1996) p. 36.

CHAPTER 10
THE NEW LANGUAGE

1 Hans Christian Andersen, 'The Nightingale', translated by Pat Shaw Iversen, cited in Chapter 3, note 1.

2 F.A. Hayek, *Law, Legislation, Liberty, Volume 3: The Political Order of a Free People* (Chicago, IL: University of Chicago Press, 1979), p. 82.

3 David Engel, 'An Approach to Corporate Social Responsibility', 32 *Stanford Law Review* 1 (1979).

4 Kew Gardens is a reference to the apartment complex in Queens, New York, where the teenaged Kitty Genovese was repeatedly stabbed in a courtyard and *no one* made an effort to help her.

5 Under the current system, investors are nowhere near as hungry for information on social issues as they are on financial ones. Social issues simply do not drive share prices to the extent that financial issues do – neither in the short nor in the long term. So, for example, under the current system, few if any insiders (or people they might 'tip' with such information) would trade because they knew in advance of the general public that a company plans to adopt a comprehensive environmental policy. If, however, such information were mandatory, and if equity investors considered this information relevant to shareholder value, then the problem of 'insider trading' would broaden. In my view, however, this is a small price to pay for improving corporate valuation and disclosure.

6 *In Re Caremark International Inc. Derivative Litigation*, Del. Chancery C.A. 13760 (15 September 1996).

7 Paul Blustein, 'Major Nations Agree to Ban Trade Bribery', *Los Angles Times*, 24 May 1997, p. D-1.

8 John Byrne, *Informed Consent*, (New York: McGraw-Hill, 1995).

9 Sir Adrian Cadbury, *The Company Chairman* (London: Director Publications, 1995), p. 154.

10 The Business Roundtable, *The Role and Composition of the Board of Directors of the Large Publicly Owned Corporation* (1978).

11 In his foreword to Brian Arthur's *Increasing Returns and Path Dependence in the Economy*, Kenneth J. Arrow traces the notion of externalities

back to Alfred Marshall. See also Chapter 3, note 5.

12   John Plender, *A Stake in the Future: The Stakeholding Solution*, (London: Nicholas Brealey, 1997), p.72.

13   Lee J. Seidler and Lynn Seidler, *Social Accounting: Theory, Issues, and Cases – The Social Audit Concept Applied* (Cambridge, MA: Abt Associates, 1971), pp. 205 ff.

14   James E. Heard, et al., *Corporate Social Reporting in the United States and Western Europe,* US Department of Commerce (1978).

15   Thanks to William Dean Howells for this observation (in correspondence dated 26 August 1997).

16   *First National Bank of Boston v. Bellotti,* 436 U.S. 765, 822, 824 (1977).

17   'The Backlash Against Soft Money', *Business Week,* 31 March 1997, pp. 34–6.

18   'The Real Party of Big Business', *The Weekly Standard,* Vol. 2, No. 19, 27 January 1997, p. 2.

19   Mellon Bank, 1997 Proxy Statement, p. 27.

20   'CU Backs Down on Voting Proposal', *Financial Times,* 4 April 1997, p. 20.

21   Many thanks to Dwight Allison, Sir Adrian Cadbury, and Richard Koch for their comments on the role of board audit committees and the role of outside auditors. Also helpful to this chapter was correspondence from Allen Sykes to the UK's Hampel Committee.

22   Pension and Welfare Benefits Administration, Department of Labor, Interpretive Bulletin 94-2, p. 26.

23   George G. Szpiro, 'The Emergence of Risk Aversion', *Complexity,* Volume 2, No. 4 (March–April 1997), pp. 31–9.

CONCLUSION

1   Hans Christian Andersen, 'The Nightingale', translated by Erik Haugaard, in *Hans Christian Andersen: His Classic Fairy Tales,* cited in Chapter 2, note 1.

2   Maria von Franz, *Shadow and Evil in Fairy Tales* (Boston: Shambalah, 1995), p. 5.

3   Cleanth Brooks, 'Keats: Ode to a Nightingale', in *Master Poems of the English Language,* edited by Oscar Williams (New York: Simon & Schuster, 1966), pp. 620–21.

EPILOGUE

1 Hans Christian Andersen, *The Nightingale*, Translated by Eva Le Gallienne, illustrated by Nancy Eckhol Burker, cited in Chapter 8, note 1.

2 This chapter combines history (events up to 1997) and fiction (events from 1998 on). The 'case' of *Reich versus Hawley* (2000), 'initiated' by former Secretary of Labor Robert Reich, is a fiction based in part on the history of the real Carter Hawley Hale, a company that in the mid-1980s experienced takeover threats, financial difficulties, and the ruin of its employee benefit plans.

3 'Institutional forms that concentrate rather than distribute power are themselves a problem and a barrier to the next step in human evolution.' David Korten, in correspondence dated 22 August 1997.

4 See box in Chapter 4 for further background on criminal activity by GE and other major corporations.

APPENDICES

1 Adam Smith, *op. cit.* (Chapter 2, note 2), pp. 691–2, 699.

2 Rare exceptions proving this rule are two 1995 fraud cases – Gary Singer, co-chairman of Cooper Companies, sentenced to 18 months in US prison, and Didier Pineau-Valencienne, chairman of Schneider, sentenced to 12 days in Belgian prison for alleged crimes against Belgian shareholders.

3 Louis Pasztor, *When the Pentagon Was for Sale: Inside America's Biggest Defense Scandal* (New York: Charles Scribners & Sons, 1995), p. 264.

4 *Survey of Defense Contractor Signatories of the 'Position Paper: Reform of the Federal Civil False Claims Act'* (Washington, DC: Project on Government Oversight, January 1994).

5 Terence P. Parre, 'Jack Welch's Nightmare on Wall Street', *Fortune*, September 5, 1994; *Defense and Health Care Industries: Rather than Clean up their Act, They Attack the Act* (Washington, DC: Project on Government Oversight, February 1997).

6 Only 11 of the cases cited against the 20 companies were False Claims Act cases, but those cases recovered over $125 million for the government. Source: 'Defense Companies that Lobby for Weaker False Claims

Act Have Defrauded Government, Study Finds', *Corporate Crime Reporter*, Vol. 8, No. 9 (28 February 1994), pp. 2–3.

7   *Defense and Health Care Industries, op. cit.* (note 5).

8   William M. Carley, 'A Load Off Its Mind: Whirlpool Beats Foe in Washer Action', *The Wall Street Journal*, 15 September 1997, pp. A1, A6.

9   David A. Lane, *op. cit.* (Chapter 5, note 6), pp. 9–13. Lane follows with the four aphorisms cited in Chapter 4 and worthy of repetition here: chance as cause, winning as losing, organisation as structure and process, and rationality as limitation.

10   See Harald Atmaspacher, Gerda Widenmann, and Anton Amann, 'Descartes Revisited', *Complexity*, Vol. 1, No. 3, pp. 15–21.

Index